'For God's sake . . . let us remain as
Nature made us, Englishmen, Irish-
men and Scotchmen, with something
like the impress of our several countries upon each.'

Sir Walter Scott.

[Frontispiece] Whitehall c.1810 showing the pillared
portico to Melbourne House—later Dover House.
(Courtesy of the Guildhall Library.)

THE THISTLE

AND THE

CROWN

A History of the Scottish Office

JOHN S GIBSON

Foreword by
The Rt. Hon. George Younger MP
Secretary of State for Scotland

EDINBURGH
HER MAJESTY'S STATIONERY OFFICE

Designed by HMSO/R Burnett

ISBN 0 11 492396 5

CONTENTS

✳

ACKNOWLEDGEMENTS

CKNOWLEDGEMENT first to the historians: in enabling me to pick my way through recent research and to follow the curiously winding road which led from the Scottish Secretaries of State of the earlier eighteenth century to the creation of the Scottish Office in 1885. I owe much to Professor Emeritus Gordon Donaldson, Historiographer in Scotland to Her Majesty the Queen; to Professor Rosalind Mitchison of Edinburgh University; to Mr Bruce Lenman of St Andrew's University; to Dr Athol Murray, now Keeper of the Records of Scotland; and to Dr John Shaw also of that department. My thanks are also due to the staff of the Scottish Record Office in bringing to attention many important papers from the earlier years of the Scottish Office. Mr James Mitchell, in undertaking post-graduate research on the Scottish Office of between the wars, collaborated freely and generously (I hope that in years to come Mr Mitchell will be able to take his research into Scottish government still further). So, for more recent educational history, did Mr Charles Raab of Edinburgh University.

The Earl of Wemyss and March gave me access to the unpublished memoirs of his ancestor who was a 'Scotch Lord of the Treasury' and so a power in the handling of Scottish parliamentary business in early Victorian times.

For more recent times, I was privileged to be able to draw on the recollections of Viscount Muirshiel and Mr Bruce Millan, both former Secretaries of State for Scotland; also on those of other friends of the Scottish Office. These were: Baroness Elliot of Harwood; Lady Mitchison; Lord Cameron; Mr Alastair Dunnett, whose own recent autobiography 'Among Friends' touched on the development of the Scottish Office, particularly during the years of the Second World War; Dr William S Robertson, late of the Scottish Council (Development and Industry); Dr Wilfred Taylor; and Mr R W Munro.

For these more recent times the main substance of the book was also widely drawn from the recollections by so many retired colleagues. So I gratefully record the generous help given by Sir Matthew Campbell, Sir Charles Cunningham, Mr Jack Fleming, Mr Ronald Fraser, Mr William Gauld, Sir Norman Graham, Sir Robert Grieve, Sir Douglas Haddow, Miss Isobel Haddow, Mr Forsyth Hardy, Mr James Hogarth, Sir Alan Hume, Sir Ronald Johnson, Miss Mary Macdonald, Mr James McGuinness, Sir William Murnie, Mr George Pottinger, Mr Peter Rendle, Mr Ian Robertson and Mr Matthew Wilson (now a veteran of 92 with memories which go back to Whitehall before August 1914). I must also make special mention of the considerable help which had been given me by the late Mr John Aglen.

Unstinted and invaluable help was also given by so many colleagues still in service. Let my mention of Sir William Fraser, our Permanent Under Secretary of State stand for individual acknowledgement to them all; appropriately so when I recall that the constant impetus he gave was matched by the encouragement (not untinged by curiosity) from so many friends throughout the Office to the writing of this book.

A word of special thanks is also due to those ladies of our secretarial and typing staffs who to help the book on its way typed and typed and typed again (or so it must have seemed to them). The Library staff, too, showed great forbearance.

I am indebted to the Earl of Rosebery for permission to reproduce the famous Millais portrait of his grandfather, the 5th Earl. My thanks also go to the Trustees of the National Portrait Gallery for permission to reproduce works from their collection; and to the photographic libraries of the *Glasgow Herald* and the *Scotsman*. Dr Rosalind Marshall of the National Portrait Gallery of Scotland gave much help and valuable advice over the illustrations.

In conclusion I must pick up the point made by the Secretary of State in the foreword he has written. This is not the 'Official History' of the Scottish Office, but rather the views of one who had the honour of serving in it; and it concentrates on what seems to him were the significant stages in its growth and development down the years. So while this book is firmly based on academic research and on the recollections of so many, its author takes entire responsibility for the opinions it voices.

J S GIBSON

April 1985

FOREWORD

by

The Rt Hon George Younger TD MP
Secretary of State for Scotland

NINETEEN EIGHTY-FIVE is the Centenary Year of the Scottish Office, and since this provides an occasion to pause and reflect on how the Office has developed, I decided that there should be a book about its first hundred years. I asked John Gibson, who retired recently from a senior post in the Scottish Office, to take on this task because, parallel to his Scottish Office career, he had made a reputation for himself as an historian and writer. He was asked to write for the general public a history of the Scottish Office, right up to the present, and to do it from his own viewpoint. It is not—and was not intended to be—an official history.

I think the outcome amply justifies my conviction that there is a story here which Scots would want to know. Decade after decade the story intertwines with Scotland's chequered social past and with political movement both north of the Border and at Westminster. The last of my eighteenth-century predecessors is sacked on failing to stop Bonnie Prince Charlie's southward march in 1745. A hundred and thirty years later the Office is revived in curious and fascinating circumstances. The First World War brings national resolve to tackle Scotland's huge housing problem. The Second World War is made the opportunity for industrial renaissance. And so on.

As he says, John Gibson has sought to distil a great deal of valuable work by leading historians. He has added significantly to this by research in various archives—personal and official—and by putting on record the recollections of many colleagues, some of whose memories go back half a century or more. At the same time he draws attention to the clamant need for more attention by the academics to some crucially important stretches of Scottish history of the past hundred years. We do need a better understanding of our own 'case history'—social, political and administrative—since

Dover House in Whitehall opened its doors as 'The Scottish Office' a hundred years ago.

I suppose that politicians and civil servants must expect to be jabbed from time to time by the media. 'Yes, Minister' will no doubt have its equally enjoyable successors. Heaven forbid that the day should ever come when we cannot take it all in good part! However, in taking the reader within St Andrew's House and its (to me) much less attractive neighbour, New St Andrew's House, John Gibson has shown the other side of the coin—that the debates, discussions, tussles and turrivees which go on in politics and administration are about real issues, and that they *matter*.

I am sure that Scots will find much in this book that is new and of absorbing interest. But anyone concerned with the government of Great Britain will also detect a great deal of importance. For the Office over which I have had the honour to preside for six years, grouping so much as it does under the one Cabinet Minister, represents a significantly different way of ordering things in our United Kingdom; and it is one which has proved itself over the years.

GEORGE YOUNGER

April 1985

I

THE ROAD TO
DOVER HOUSE

A HUNDRED YEARS ago, the Duke of Richmond and Gordon, experienced Tory politician, owner of the two best salmon rivers in Scotland, held a reception in the Advocates' Library in Edinburgh to mark his appointment as Secretary for Scotland. The Lord Provost and bailies attended along with bench and bar, and other dignitaries national and local down to the Governor of the mock-mediaeval prison on the side of the Calton Hill. 'It was rather an affair—and not much in my line' reported the diffident Duke to Lord Salisbury, the Prime Minister, a diffidence in line with his initial reluctance to take the job. 'You know my opinion of the office and that it is quite unnecessary', he had written to Salisbury only two months past.

Nor did the following day's 'Scotsman' make a big story of the events in Parliament House, though His Grace had spoken suitably enough to the assembled crush about the high honour conferred on him. That newspaper's headlines were about the Servo-Bulgarian war, inviting its readers to feel concern at the Serbian defeat before Slovnitza; and of its two leading articles one was about imperial annexation ('What shall be done with Upper Burmah at our feet, or with King Theebaw when we catch him?'); the other about the Church of Scotland having recorded 'its devout thankfulness for the success that had been given them in contending against their enemies over the way'—the foe being the Free Church of Scotland in its Assembly Hall on the other side of Edinburgh's Lawnmarket. As to Mr Gladstone, leader of the Liberal Opposition, we can guess what he felt about this new ministerial post in government. That day he was at Dalmeny, the charming country house of his young colleague, the Earl of Rosebery. That there should be a new post of Secretary for Scotland had been Rosebery's achievement while Gladstone was in power; but rigorous economy in government

Old Parliament House, Edinburgh where the
Scottish Privy Council met.
(Courtesy of Edinburgh Central Library.)

expenditure was ever the watchword of the 'Grand Old Man'; and
the re-creation of a Scottish Office had for long been against his
wishes.

Though the modest celebrations of November 1885 were in
Edinburgh, the Scottish Office which the Duke of Richmond and
Gordon would have as his headquarters was in London. On this its
centenary, we also recognise that while Dover House in Whitehall is
still the Office's dignified London presence, that is about all that has
not changed. Moreover, there are many in the five departments
of the present day Scottish Office who look back to beginnings
earlier than 1885. Some in the Department of Agriculture and
Fisheries recently affected disappointment that the centenary of the
Fishery Board for Scotland had not been better marked. The
Scottish Education Department has always been acutely aware that
there was a *Scotch* Education Department before there was a
Scottish Office. The Chief Medical Officer finds his origins in the
sorely needed public health legislation of the 1860s; and the prison
administrators of the Scottish Home and Health Department find
theirs in still earlier decades of the nineteenth century. Some of the
younger blades on the industrial development side have been
known to take pride in their lack of departmental ancestry, and
would have it that they are in the business of breaking new frontiers
in government: in a way they are wrong, the Treaty of Union with
England in 1707 itself envisaging a modest annual expenditure on
the promotion of Scottish manufacture and industry.

Yet, despite the uncertainty felt by the Duke of Richmond and Gordon and the apparent preference of the 'Scotsman' of a hundred years ago for weighty issues international or theological, despite Mr Gladstone's misgivings, despite the many diverse sources of the present day Scottish Office, 1885 *is* a date to commemorate. The ministerial presence Scotland then secured for herself in Whitehall and Westminster, was, in time, to be her means of meeting sharply accelerating change in social and economic need.

Half a century ago John Buchan spoke of what a unified and coherent Scottish Office could do for Scotland; and he said

'We do not want to be like the Greeks, powerful and prosperous wherever we settle, but with a dead Greece behind us. We do not want to be like the Jews of the Dispersion—a potent force everywhere on the globe, but with no Jerusalem.'

This book is an historical review down to the present day of the domain of the Secretary of State for Scotland as seen by one member of the Scottish Office. It has involved a great deal of discussion and help from historians and from colleagues past and present, though its views are his own. And John Buchan's thoughts are somewhere on its horizon.

A word about the historical perspective. When one is asked about any current Scottish problem there is an abiding temptation to give its genealogy rather than a straight answer. But the present relationship between Scotland and England *is* the child of history. Down the years it has been in constant change as the economic and social fortunes of the two countries oscillate in rather different tempi from each other. Some of the story has only recently been uncovered. It will surprise many to learn that the Union of 1707 envisaged a continuing presence of central government in Scotland; and that when at long last the post of Scottish Secretary was restored in 1885, restoration owed as much to chance and individual ambition as to Scotland's sense of nationhood.

King James I of England, VI of Scotland, as unsentimental about his motherland as he had been about his mother, gleefully announced soon after 1603 that henceforth Scotland would become as Northumberland and Cumberland. A century later the Union of the Parliaments did not fulfil his prophecy. In the years between, Stair had given Scotland a sound system of civil law based on moral principles which was not lightly to be surrendered; Sir George MacKenzie had constructed the outlines of a fair and durable criminal law; and, in the reign of William of Orange, Principal Carstares had reconciled the Church of Scotland and the monarch to each other. Despite the tribulations of civil war, Scottish nationhood had also grown since 1603: contrast the great Marquis of Montrose, or his equally great adversary Argyll, with the craven nobility of Queen Mary's Scotland. Thanks to all this and to the bargaining power given the Scots by England's war with France, the Union settlement of 1707 safeguarded both the Scottish legal system and the Church of Scotland and so precluded any complete administrative Union.

'There's naethin sae gude on this side o' time but it might hae been better, and that may be said o' the Union', reflected Bailie Nicol Jarvie as he jogged towards Rob Roy's highlands. The Bailie was right: the Union should have provided continuing government *in* Scotland—something which might well have evolved into a Scottish Office a century or so before the Lion Rampant was hoisted at Dover House. For the post of Secretary of State, its roots deep in the middle ages, survived the Union. So did the Scottish Privy Council meeting regularly in the Parliament House, its historic role the maintenance of law and order. However, with the Union, the ministerial heart of the old Privy Council had vanished; no longer was there a Lord Chancellor to take the chair, a Lord Privy Seal or a Lord Treasurer. Only the Lord Justice Clerk, the link with the judiciary, survived, and this was not enough. In an atmosphere of division and dismay, party considerations in Scotland now joined with those of opposition members at Westminster to bring about the reckless abolition of the Scottish Privy Council; in factious Edinburgh the overriding consideration was that Queen Anne's Ministers in London should not be able to use its mechanism to influence Scottish elections to the new Parliament of Great Britain.

There was, indeed, at this time, more effective thought given at Westminster to the adequacy for Scotland of the Union settlement. It was recalled by one who saw these years that 'the English were content there should be somewhat of a form of government in Scotland, in room of the Scots Council; and that the Lord Godolphine [Queen Anne's Chief Minister] was particularly for this. That several projects were formed in order to do this; a Council for Trade and Manufactures was spoken to have some standing power, and after that the Commission of Police and a Committy of the British Council to sit at Edinburgh.' But nothing came of this.

Within months the doing down of the historic Scottish Privy Council almost led to disaster, when the menacing sail of an invasion fleet from France, the Jacobite King on board, was clearly seen from Edinburgh Castle to lie in the jaws of the Firth. The Castle's governor was in no small panic at the lack of any body of government in Scotland to organise resistance. Only the luck of the winds now saved Scotland from civil war.

The 2nd Duke of Queensberry, architect of Union;
by Kneller.

From the now fragmented government of old Scotland there
still remained the Scottish Secretary of State, now at Westminster
not Edinburgh. In 1709 the persuasive Duke of Queensberry, the
architect of Union, was appointed to the post: and had he lived
events might have taken a different turn. But Queensberry died
within two years, and by now there was the malign influence of
Daniel Defoe, confidant of Harley, the Queen's first minister. The
author to be of 'Robinson Crusoe' put himself forward as an expert

on Scotland on the strength of his clandestine activities in Edinburgh on Harley's behalf while the Act of Union debates were at their height in the Parliament House. In his eager and confiding way he wrote to Harley in July 1711, deprecating the need for a Scottish Secretary, gnawing away at the reasoned basis of the Union settlement. The post, wrote Defoe, had become

> 'the centre of the hungry sollicitations naturell to that country, and mightilly increased and encouraged them, by which Her Majtie would in time be under a constant painfull opperation from a poor, craving and importunate people' . . .

The office, he went on, kept up

> 'a kind of a form of separate Management, which being destroy'd by Union, all vestiges of the seperate state of things ought to dye with it, and the very remembrance if possible be Taken away; Scotland No More Requires a Secretary Than Yorkshire or Wales. Nor (the clamour of petitions excepted) can it supply bussiness for an office with two clarks.'

Now well into his stride, Defoe could not stop

> 'The very appointing a Scots Secretary has severall inconveniences in it. It keeps up a faction in Scotland, and forms a Party to Support the intrest of that person, as also another to Supplant him . . . He constitutes himself a kind of a Governour of Scotland.'

Last of all was the clinching argument

> 'It layes the Crown under a constant and needless expence'.

The Scots being unable to agree among themselves about the running of Scotland, Defoe's poisonous advice had its effect. Harley appointed no successor to Queensberry, keeping patronage and power in 'North Britain' in his own hands. Then he fell from office, and clever, vacillating Mar★ was Scottish Secretary. The post, however, continued to be a political football. Mar, too, was soon out of favour and turned Jacobite. His successors were recent ducal creations of not much standing; and the Duke of Argyll, he who as Queen's Commissioner had pushed the essential preliminaries to Union through the Edinburgh Parliament, was now determined that the House of Argyll should be the major influence in Scottish affairs.

The Jacobite rebellion of 1715 had given Argyll the opportunity to shine. He defeated the bigger Jacobite army, and neither the lack of a Scottish Privy Council nor that of a strong Scottish Secretary

---

★This was 'Bobbing John'—his portrait hangs in Dover House—who found decisive action so difficult in the Jacobite rebellion of 1715, and led it to disaster.

of State was felt.* After the collapse of the 'Fifteen, Argyll used his success to bolster his position. Even though he fell out of favour at George I's court the following year, his influence continued to obstruct the Duke of Roxburghe, nominal Secretary of State for Scotland. The Scottish Secretary had become a cipher, as indeed was inevitable with the abolition of the Scots Privy Council as his means of influence in Edinburgh. Now there was in Edinburgh only the continuing financial administration of the Court of Exchequer in which the 'Barons of Exchequer', some English, some Scottish, acted as a Treasury and Revenue Board for 'North Britain'. But with many sinecures to dispense—salaries for the Clerks of the Wardrobe at now deserted Holyrood, for the King's Falconer who did not hawk, for the Auditors of the Exchequer who never audited, and for the King's Limner who did not paint, and so on—there was patronage to reward the friends of government.

Nevertheless, Scotland was still in need of a recognised centre of internal power, albeit power delegated from London, all of a week's journey or more from Edinburgh as it was. The serious riots in Glasgow in 1725 against the proposed Malt Tax—itself an indirect consequence of Union—bore this out. For several days the mob ruled in Glasgow, the Lord Provost's town house was sacked, and order was not restored until the Earl of Ilay, Argyll's brother, was sent up from London to cool tempers. Duncan Forbes as Lord Advocate and so the chief Law Officer of Scotland took it on himself to call out the military. But the Scottish Secretary of State, fearing unpopularity by enforcement on Scotland of unwelcome taxation, had not stirred himself; and so he was dismissed from office. Nor was his post filled. The management of Scotland now rested exclusively with the House of Argyll.† At Court Argyll was Scottish grandee-in-chief, but Ilay his brother who 'loved power too well to hazard it with ostentation' was the real Minister for Scotland. At Edinburgh the Lord Justice Clerk—an Argyll appointee—handled the Scottish end of government business. Duncan Forbes, now on the way to becoming Lord President, regarded the new arrangements with satisfaction. There was, he wrote, no need for 'that nuisance which we have so long complained of, a Scots Secretary either at full length or in miniature'.

*There were, briefly, during the rebellion *two* Secretaries of State for Scotland, when the old Pretender, holding Court at Scone during his brief sojourn in Scotland, appointed Viscount Stormont's Jacobite heir to the post. We recalled this when the latter's descendant, the present day Earl of Mansfield, became our Minister of State in 1979.
†So it was that Sir Walter Scott had Jeanie Deans walk to London to seek a reprieve for the hapless Effie through the Duke of Argyll, rather than at the hands of either of King George's English Secretaries of State.

In the intrigues of Westminster, Argyll fell from power in 1741; and since there had to be *someone* to manage Scotland the post of third, in effect Scottish, Secretary of State was now recreated. The need for soundly based government of Scotland was seen clearly enough. On taking up office, the new incumbent, the Marquis of Tweeddale said that he wished to devise 'some general plan or scheme for the Government of Scotland . . . as may tend to create a confidence in and give a more universal content to the people'. But nothing had taken the place of the Scottish Privy Council. 'By taking away the Privy Council', complained the Lothian laird, Sir John Clerk, as he surveyed the Scottish scene from his fine new house at Cammo, 'there is very little of government to be seen amongst us'. In 1745 a Highland army descended on Edinburgh from the hills, and there was in the lowlands no civil authority to concert vigorous counter-measures. A Scottish Privy Council *might* have dissuaded Jacobite-minded lairds of Aberdeenshire, Angus or Perthshire from their ruinous adventure. The Marquis of Tweeddale's uselessness as Secretary of State for Scotland having been so demonstrated, the post was again abolished even before the Battle of Culloden put paid to Jacobite hopes.

In the aftermath of the 'Forty-five, the Lord Justice Clerk in the person of the ambitious Lord Milton—as it were a one-man Privy Council—assumed the national security role. It was to Milton at Edinburgh that the commodore of the Royal Navy, cruising in the Minch with his frigates and sloops, reported on 'the summer's hunting' for Prince Charles Edward Stuart. At Westminster, legislation quickly swept away the enclaves of local power of Scottish magnates, and covered the whole country with efficient, modernised and durable sheriffdoms. There was a fairly enlightened approach in the administration of the Forfeited Estates by commissioners appointed for the purpose, in this even adumbrating some of the development plans for the highlands and islands of the twentieth century. In the officers of the Scottish Excise and Customs Boards there were also recognisable civil servants. But day in, day out, the House of Argyll and Milton ran Scotland, the latter working to the former's bidding. 'It was', a contemporary wrote, 'always deemed prudent to obtain Lord Milton's goodwill before making any application, even for places of the most inconsiderable emolument and importance'. Burgh administration remained in the hands of self-perpetuating town councils, their fingers in every burghal pie. In the counties, the landward gentry sat together as Commissioners of Supply. Justices of the Peace played their part, particularly in revenue cases. There was, unevenly, improving education in the burgh and parish schools with some progression for 'lads o' pairts' to the Scottish universities. The Church saw to poor relief after a fashion. With Jacobitism dwindling to mere Scottish sentimentality the need for a Scottish

Secretary or, for that matter, a Scottish Office, was not apparent. In folk-memory the Union and its making were still execrated. Black be the day, wrote Robert Fergusson, that ever our fore-fathers put Scotland under the English yoke. 'Sic a parcel o' rogues in a nation' rhymed Robert Burns, reflecting on the Scottish magnates who 'fixed' the Union. But folk-memory commanded none of the 45 Scottish seats, and, as David Hume had noted in the 1760s, the Union was now accepted by educated opinion every-where in Scotland.

Yet, what the Scottish arrangements of central government still lacked was continuity. When the long life of the 3rd Duke of Argyll came to an end in 1761, so for the time being did the national prominence of his House; and there was nothing to take its place for the management of 'North Britain'. Nor was there any inclination to revive yet again the post of Scottish Secretary. However, in the 1770s the votes of the Scottish cohort at Westminster became of crucial importance to the government as its American policies floundered; and so Scottish business and patronage was entrusted to a scion of the Midlothian Dundases who by now was Lord Advocate (and, conveniently, half-brother to the Lord President at Edinburgh). Power over Scotland was safely delegated to this Dundas, skilled as he was as a man of business and in manipulating sentiment while he moved upwards through government to become Pitt's right hand man. At the Admiralty and at the Board of Control for the East India Company, Henry Dundas's power to command Scottish affairs through patronage was to become vastly extended: these were times of pressing need to find income for younger sons. Particular-ly on account of this preferment to jobs in 'John Company', both the town councils of Scotland and the landed gentry who ran the counties were bent to his will. Here was a mechanism for stifling demand for reform in Scotland, parliamentary or burghal. As Sir Walter Scott was to comment on Dundas management of Scotland *via* the India office 'No one can carry Scotland that has not the command of the Board of Control.' Formally, from 1782 Scottish affairs were the concern of the newly created Home Office, but in practice it was Dundas's views that mattered.★ His Lord Advocate successors had the responsibility for marshalling the docile Scottish members at Westminster in support of the government. 'The Lord Advocate', said one of these, tongue-in-cheek, 'should always be a tall man so that we can see whom to follow through the Division Lobby.' But the preferment and patronage that kept them in line resided with Dundas.

★So it was that in 1788 the Morayshire laird, Brodie of Brodie, interceded with Lord Sidney, as Home Secretary, that the neck of his cousin, the infamous Deacon Brodie, be spared; the Deacon, an Edinburgh town councillor who knew where the real power lay, petitioned—alas to no effect—Henry Dundas.

The Dundas years were the decades of the Scottish Enlightenment; that flowering of Scottish intellect and culture not known
before, not rivalled since. So the governmental system of management which encompassed the Scotland of these days calls for a
moment's further reflection. The contrast between Edinburgh's
intellectual ferment and the 'unenlightened' ways of Henry Dundas
may well be drawn, but like the Union itself the latter were
generally accepted, and indeed defended vigorously by 'King Hal'
himself. Why should Scotland have a manager, 'a salesman for us
like cattle', said James Boswell to his face while dining with
Dundas in London in 1783? It is better so for Scotland, Dundas
replied. The alternative was a scramble for preferment without
regard to merit. 'An agent for government' he added 'must
distribute to the best purpose. He has a trust'. In an age when
government was primarily about place and position rather than
ideas or ideals, Dundas perhaps had a fragment of a case.

On Dundas's death in 1811, another seventeen years of this kind
of management followed; his son, the 2nd Viscount Melville, as
Lord Privy Seal and later First Lord of the Admiralty stepping
into, but not quite filling, the 1st Viscount's Scottish shoes. But he
was looked on as 'minister of state for Scotland' (and a statue in
Edinburgh's Melville Street appropriately commemorates him).
However, times were changing. When Melville demitted office in
1827 and Prime Minister Canning looked for a replacement
Scottish manager in another Scottish nobleman who happened to
be First Lord of the Admiralty, there was a general disposition in
Scotland to have done with 'management'. Scottish affairs would
now lie with the Home Secretary as advised by a Scottish Lord of
the Treasury—that is, the Scottish Government whip—and by the
Lord Advocate, channelling to the Home Office the views of the
Scottish bar and bench.

This shift of power to the Home Secretary had indeed preceded
1828. So, for example, Sir Robert Peel as Home Secretary
accompanied George IV to Holyroodhouse in 1822.★ In other
ways, too, the Home Secretary had enhanced his position within
government. For all domestic affairs outwith the scope of another
minister he assumed responsibility—that is 'responsibility' as
interpreted in this the zenith of *laissez-faire*. He also maintained the
precedence over other ministers the post had enjoyed from its
beginnings.

★Papers which came across to the Scottish Office in 1885 show that from an hotel
in St Andrew Square MacLeod of MacLeod wrote to Peel on this occasion to seek a
baronetcy for himself in recognition of the (shaky) Hanoverian loyalty of the
MacLeod chief of 1745. A generation before the intermediary would have been
Dundas. (MacLeod of MacLeod was unsuccessful in his bid, receiving the same sort
of non-committal reply which down the years has been sent to importunate
honours seekers.)

The 1830s began the era of reform and change, municipal as well as parliamentary. The new Whig government appointed a Royal Commission which investigated those closed oligarchies the town councils of Scotland, exposing their widespread corruption and inefficiency. There was legislation about the courts and the universities, and there was a bonfire of sinecures. All this meant a great deal more Scottish legislation than had previously been seen. From his vantage point on the bench, the percipient Lord Cockburn saw what was needed, confiding his thoughts to his Journal.

> 'I am now clear that the only remedy is to institute a Scotch Secretaryship, and to leave the Lord Advocate to his proper duties. A practising barrister is rarely trained for a statesman . . .'

There was also the practical consideration that

> 'At present for £2,500 a year he is expected to lay out that money at the least on a seat, and then extinguish his practice by being in London . . .'

Earl Grey as Prime Minister, promised action but took none; and through the rest of the 1830s and the 1840s, 'Parliament House' government of Scotland, that is, the predominance of the Lord Advocate, continued. Then, in the 1850s, in belated recognition that with only 45 seats Scotland was grossly under-represented at Westminster in respect of both her expanded population and wealth, there was formed the National Association for the Vindication of Scottish Rights. Though it was not anti-Union or separatist it asserted the need for a Scottish Secretary. Duncan McLaren the radical Lord Provost of Edinburgh proposed at a great meeting in Edinburgh 'for the better administration of the public business of this part of the United Kingdom, and for securing to Scotland the practical benefits of a united legislature, that the Office of Secretary of State be restored.' Some fifty petitions flowed in to Parliament from all over Scotland. Then, at another crowded meeting, this time in Glasgow in the winter of 1853, Professor Aytoun, poet of a kind and Scottish romantic, proposed a Scottish Assembly 'for the direction of those matters which are exclusively Scottish.'

It was an administrative not a legislative body he had in mind, but his speech incurred the wrath of the 'Scotsman'—its then editor's attitude to Home Rule wholly governed by his perennial feud with Edinburgh's Lord Provost. There was also the wrath of the Thunderer of Printing House Square itself.

> 'There may be minor Scottish grievances that need redress, but does this constitute a reason for threatening to resolve ourselves once more into the Kingdoms of Wessex, Mercia, East Anglia and what not?'

The Ghosts of Dover House:
Lady Caroline Lamb and Lord Byron.
(Courtesy of National Portrait Gallery.)

This 'Times' comment was matched by an equally abrasive entry in Cockburn's Journals, the thoughts of an older, querulous Cockburn. Convinced as he was that Scotland's distinctive character was now all but dissolved, he was not now disposed to argue for the appointment of a Secretary of State for Scotland. His view was simply that the responsible manager of Scottish affairs 'may be the Home Secretary, or an Under-Secretary, or a Lord of the Treasury, or anything else,' but should not be the Lord Advocate. 'No sane man takes the position of Lord Advocate', he said, 'except to be well quit of it.'

By 1856 the National Association for the Vindication of Scottish Rights was no more, the enthusiasm it had generated all dissipated. Perhaps that was lost in the greater excitement of war with Russia and mutiny in India. Perhaps it was also that the 'Scotch Lord of the Treasury' was playing a greater part. Lord Elcho who held this post in the 1850s left a memoir describing what was involved. In addition to the Whip's duties to 'make a House, keep a House, and cheer the Minister', he carried Scottish legislation through the Commons. 'I carried in the House of Commons a Bill

to do away with the religious test in our Scottish universities', he wrote. 'I brought in and carried a Births, Deaths and Marriages Registration Bill, going to France to study their registration system there. I also brought in an Education Bill which was intended to extend our excellent parochial school system to our towns . . . I wrote a paper that led to the establishment in Scotland at Edinburgh of the counterpart of the South Kensington Museum . . . No change of system was required so long as the Lord Advocate and the Scottish Lord worked cordially together.'

In the quarter-century that followed, national consensus about the need for a Scottish Secretary was perhaps more apparent than real. The areas of government affecting the pockets of the propertied classes were poor relief, public health and education. As to poor relief, Scotland was free to go her own harsher way under the guidance of the Board of Supervision—that is the Edinburgh based body which since 1845 had supervised the parishes in their administration of poor relief. No need, it seemed, for a Scottish Secretary here. In legislation of the 1860s the Home Secretary tacked public health on to the Board of Supervision. But far-seeing medical officers of health wanted to do much more than merely prevent the return of cholera; and the way ahead which they foresaw was a Great Britain ministry of health to disseminate in Scotland the more enlightened ways of some English local authorities—not a Scottish Office.

As to education which, like poor relief had in the past been parish church based, this was the target of strenuous attempts at far-reaching reform in the 1850s (one of the unsuccessful measures being that introduced by Lord Elcho). But the reformers were thwarted by opposition from the established Church of Scotland, fearful as it was of losing its control of Scottish education, as much as by the votes of English members of parliament. When, eventually, with Gladstone as Prime Minister, the Education (Scotland) Act of 1872 became law, providing as it did for little more than the general availability of the three Rs, it was rightly seen as falling below the national tradition. But neither did this fuel the campaign, such as it was, for a Scottish Secretary. Here, too, many looked to London; better hope of educational progress was (wrongly) felt by many influential people to lie in closer linkage with the emerging, vigorous educationists in Whitehall. Nor had the concept of the civil spending department yet arrived, requiring the Treasury to share its control of the public purse. Educational improvement needed large sums of government money; so everyone assumed that Treasury control of educational spending must be maintained by the Privy Council in Whitehall, albeit through its 'Scotch Education Committee.' It could not be devolved to a Secretary for Scotland.

However, at Westminster, discontent among the Scottish members grumbled on. The Lord Advocate by now had consolidated his strong position, the Home Secretary invariably taking his advice; and the Scottish members—their numbers increased at last in the mid 1860s—still felt shut out. If as a member of parliament you were not also at the Scottish bar you could not aspire to the fruits of office. But the wishes of the Scottish members were modest: a parliamentary under-secretaryship for Scottish affairs at the Home Office would do. There was a brief debate in 1864 with the countervailing arguments that a Scottish appointment of this kind would introduce 'a sort of dilettante legal reformer' with 'nothing to do but interfere in Scotch affairs'. A second, equally brief, debate in 1867 was not even accorded the dignity of a government reply.

Scotland being so predominantly Liberal in her political comple-
xion it was natural that Gladstone, himself a Scot by ancestry, with
a family home in the Mearns, on coming into office in 1869 should
have set up the 'Scottish Offices Inquiry Commission.' This was a
two-man inquiry chaired by the Earl of Camperdown into the
Edinburgh based Boards which, though appointed by the Home
Secretary, were but loosely reined by him. In this the golden
period of Gladstonian Liberalism, the saving of candle-ends in
fashion, the inquiry's remit was to identify economies as well as
pacify restive Scottish members of parliament. So let us, like Lord
Camperdown, at this point have a closer look at the Boards, and at
what they did—or did not do.

The *Board of Supervision* for poor relief, the principal intrusion of
central government on the Scottish scene, has already been
mentioned. The inclusion in its membership of the Solicitor
General for Scotland and three sheriff-deputes from the judiciary in
lowlands and highlands indicated its role. The Board was to keep
the parochial boards of property owners throughout Scotland
informed and advised on what the law required of them—the relief
of the disabled poor, no less, but no more. Cyclical unemployment
of the able-bodied factory worker, by now an all too common
feature of industrialised Scotland, was no concern of theirs. Nor
was the destitution of the scores of thousands living on tiny
holdings in Highlands and Hebrides, the descendants of those who
over the previous three quarters of a century had made way for
extensive sheep grazing. Many of these had moved away to the
cities, to coal mining, to the wide world from Nova Scotia to New
Zealand. But many remained, and it was this population that the
potato blight of the 1840s and '50s had so cruelly afflicted. If the
Board of Supervision could not help the able-bodied among them
then it had to be busy warding off the demands for help from the
pauper communities. There was much work for its lawyers in all
this; and the Board's records teem with distressing incident.
The Public Health (Scotland) Act of 1867, born out of the fright
Victorian Scotland felt over the recurrence of cholera, had made
the Board of Supervision the central, and the parochial boards the
local, sanitary authorities. On the statute book it all looked
impressive enough. But progress was to be slow. The local boards
could be required by the Board in Edinburgh to appoint sanitary
inspectors and medical officers of health. Wide power was given to
the Board to deal with infectious diseases and unwholesome food.
Burgh councils were given power to build hospitals and 'public
conveniences, mortuaries and recreation grounds' with appeal to
the Board from townspeople with unwilling burgh councils. But
the legislation was in advance of public feeling. There was

something of a Scotch unwillingness to improve conditions for the next generation which had been tolerated by the present and their forebears. And it was not so long since Lord Palmerston had had to remind the civic dignitaries of Edinburgh during a cholera scare that it was better to make haste with sanitary improvement than to proclaim a national fast!

Also under the light hand of the Home Secretary, also with a membership largely from the Scottish bar, there were the *Scottish Prisons Commissioners* who had since the 1830s run as the national prison buildings erected earlier at Perth to house French prisoners of war. In addition the Commissioners inspected the scandalously inadequate county and burgh gaols. There was the *General Register Office* for births, deaths and marriages which since 1854 had been administering the national census, in years ahead to become the essential tool of social progress. This Office came under the Deputy Clerk Register who also had responsibility for the records of Scotland, housed in what had been the honey-coloured Register House but was now a building sadly begrimed by the smoke of its hundred years in 'Auld Reekie'. Over the Deputy Clerk Register stood the Lord Clerk Register, an honorific but well paid post. How honorific it was may be judged from the fact that Lord Dalhousie contrived to hold both this post and the Governor-Generalship of India (though in the stricter public morality of Victorian times he did not draw his salary for the Edinburgh post).

There was the *General Board of Lunacy for Scotland* now well in advance of current social medicine.★ There was the historic *Board of Manufactures,* dating from 1727, but with its origins in the Act of Union itself. It had moved far from its earlier purpose to develop the woollen and linen industries and now used its money to promote education in the fine arts. There was also its offspring, the quaintly named *Board of White Herring Fisheries* whose quality mark was put on the scores of thousands of barrels of salted herring exported to Europe every summer. Though they agitated for the

---

★ This is an interesting example of social reform in the mid-nineteenth century. The Poor Law Act of 1845 had placed on the parochial boards the duty of providing for the insane in properly authorised asylums. But, characteristically, the boards took a narrow view of their responsibilities. Ten years later a Miss Dorothea Dix (whose name ought surely to be honoured) waged a campaign about the neglect of the insane in Scotland. A Royal Commission was then appointed by the Home Secretary, and in 1857 the Lunacy (Scotland) Act created for the very limited period of five years a General Board of Lunacy with general supervision powers and also district local boards to build and manage asylums. The General Board under the leadership of its medical adviser now introduced many reforms and insisted upon a more humane treatment. But, all this was costly; the opposition of the local authorities was aroused; and when in 1862 the continuance of the General Board was under discussion there was an attempt made to kill it. However the value of the central authority's work and the need for it had been shown and legislation of 1862 renewed the Board on a more permanent footing.

'An old man in a hurry'—but not about the creation
of the Scottish Office. William Ewart Gladstone.
Cartoon by Harry Furniss. (Courtesy of National
Portrait Gallery.)

revival of the post of Secretary for Scotland, the radical members of parliament who appeared before Lord Camperdown, being also the standard-bearers of *laissez-faire,* argued for this Board's demise. There was also the *Bible Board* which, in its exercise of the sole remaining function of the office of Queen's Printer in Scotland, had the not very onerous task of licensing editions of the Authorised Version of the Bible; and there was that other survivor from independent Scotland, the office of *Lyon King of Arms,* master of all matters heraldic and ceremonial.

Last of all in the survey carried out by the Camperdown Commission was the post of *Queen's and Lord Treasurer's Remembrancer,* an amalgamation by the reforming Whigs of 1837 of two ancient offices. The Commission noted that 'Q & LTR' accounted for government payments and receipts. They did not mention, if indeed they knew, that he was also the Treasury's 'man in Edinburgh' encouraged to be ever watchful of the Boards, critical of the estimates of expenditure they prepared for the Treasury and of any tendency to extravagance. So it was he, not the Home Office under-secretary in distant Whitehall who made it his business to know what was going on among the Boards and to give his Treasury masters a confidential and frank appraisal. The Queen's and Lord Treasurer's Remembrancer was always a landed gentleman with a legal background and handsomely paid. As the Boards grew in the years ahead so, as we will see, did his importance.

The Inquiry's evidence gives other valuable insights. Scottish business, the members of parliament protested, was usually hurried through after midnight with insufficient debate. But the Lord Justice Clerk, a former Lord Advocate of distinction, claimed that Scottish business *was* conducted satisfactorily, that the distinctive needs of Scotland had been well understood by successive Lord Advocates whom Scottish members could readily approach, and that the burden on the Lord Advocate was heavy but not intolerable (and no doubt alleviated by the certainty of elevation to the Bench). 'Scotch members', he added, 'have been proverbial among the other members of the House not only for the quiet and efficient manner in which their business has been conducted, but also for the courtesy of manner and feeling which has prevailed in their ranks and the absence of altercation in the House, or of intrigue out of it.'

The Camperdown Report of 1869 was clear in its recommendations. It made nothing of the proposal put to it by some Scottish members of parliament that a Secretary for Scotland should be appointed to combine with the Lord Advocate and the Lord President of the Privy Council of Great Britain to form 'a sort of educational Privy Council for Scotland'—this a very tentative proposal to get round the problem already mentioned that 'the

Privy Council will not give up the key of the money chest so long as money has to be given for grants for education.' The report indeed made short work of the argument for any sort of Secretary for Scotland, and was categorical in its view that 'the Home Secretary should be in fact as he already is in theory, Minister for Scotland, having two advisers—the Lord Advocate and a civil parliamentary officer [ie the parliamentary under-secretary of state] attached to the Home Department who would consult together under the final decision of the Home Secretary.' Thus not even an exclusively Scottish parliamentary under-secretaryship at the Home Office was contemplated; and neither in the Report nor in the evidence submitted was there any suggestion that Scotland stood badly in need of greater health, social or welfare activity. Economy in government was still the watchword.

No action followed these modest recommendations of the Camperdown Report, nor were there even any parliamentary rumblings until a short debate all of eight years later 'on the neglect of Scotch business.' This seems to have been occasioned by the Lord Advocate of the day having been moved into the new Whitehall, high-Victorian, Home Office away from his own rooms off Trafalgar Square, and Scottish members now having to address themselves to a more authoritarian Home Secretary. This arrangement, the instigator of the motion contrasted unfavourably with cosy, informal custom by which, he said, Scottish members had previously settled all manner of Scottish business with the Lord Advocate in the Commons tea room!

This debate did not put the heather on fire, nor was agitation for a Scottish Secretary at all linked with new grievances which had now sailed over the horizon. One was that the body which had been set up in Edinburgh to oversee the building of the host of new primary schools had been scrapped in 1879 and all business thereafter conducted in the Scotch Education Department in London which was virtually one with the English Board of Education. Then there was annoyance that Sir Richard Cross, the 'bureaucratic, be-spectacled and energetic' Tory Home Secretary of the Beaconsfield Government had introduced, but withdrawn, a bill to create a Scottish parliamentary under-secretary in the Home Office. However, by the end of the 1870s it did indeed seem much more likely that future Great Britain-wide provision of services and controls would prevail. The creation of the post of Secretary for Scotland, still less of a Scottish Office as a recognisable department of government seemed unlikely. However much it *should* have been (had Scots been more alive to their best interests) nationally it was not much of an issue. You will, for example, look in vain in Robert Louis Stevenson's wide-ranging and often intensely Scottish correspondence of these years for any mention of it.

Meanwhile, under the Home Office in Whitehall, the development of the Scottish Boards continued. With penal servitude at home taking the place of transportation to Tasmania the reforming measures brought in by Lord Beaconsfield's government in the later 1870s included prisons legislation. This brought under direct Scottish Prisons Board control the whole variety of establishments from the antique arrangements in many a burgh to the big new prison which the North Lanarkshire County Board had built at Barlinnie. No doubt the new prisons regime would be as repressive north as south of the Tweed. There would be as much misery in the battlemented county bridewell on the slopes of Edinburgh's Calton Hill as in Oscar Wilde's Reading Gaol. But in Scotland as in England there were now unified structures of prison administration which would in time lead to less inhumanity. In 1882, Gladstone and the Liberals back in power, another act of parliament created the Fishery Board for Scotland to replace the Board of White Herring Fisheries. The advent of the steam drifter was threatening the herring fisheries just as the coming of the steam trawler threatened the inshore fisheries round the coasts of Scotland; and if stocks were to survive the new technology, regulation, the imposition of fishery limits and their policing were needed. This legislative response of 1882 was surprisingly swift; but Victorian government, however unheeding of much else, was always mindful of its need for skilled seamen from the fishing communities in time of war.

But none of this presaged the creation of a Scottish Office.

Now chance and Mr Gladstone took a hand. The sequence of events has been charted by Robert Rhodes James and by Professor Hanham; it is also seen in Rosebery's papers and in the memoirs of Charles Cooper, the then editor of the 'Scotsman'.

When his administration was turned out in 1874 Gladstone had intimated his wish to leave politics. Soon his outrage at the massacres of Bulgarian Christians by Turkish soldiery, coupled with his sense of Britain's moral mission in the conduct of world affairs, renewed his appetite for office. However, his seat at Greenwich was none too secure, and the Scottish Liberals persuaded him to stand at the possibly winnable seat of Midlothian, long the preserve of the leader of the Scottish Conservatives, the Duke of Buccleuch. The wealthy young Scottish peer, the Earl of Rosebery, intelligent as he was handsome, interested in Scottish causes as well as the Turf, nearly as influential as Buccleuch in the county, played a large part in the wooing of the 'Grand Old Man'. In the January of 1879 Gladstone was adopted as candidate, and in the ensuing electoral campaigns used as his base Rosebery's charming house at Dalmeny overlooking the Firth of Forth. Rosebery himself was the imaginative master-mind in the campaign. It was, however, the anti-militarist, brotherhood-of-man, vision in Gladstone's speeches which touched off Scottish fervour, reared as it was on the Bible and Burns. With Gladstone's oratory and moral fervour, this handsome young nobleman at his side, Scottish pride broke surface. As Cooper was to recall, 'Dalmeny became for the time being a sort of Liberal Mecca, whither the faithful flocked from all quarters to do honour to their prophet.' But there was nothing in all this about reform in Scottish affairs.

After Gladstone's victory at Midlothian and his return to Downing Street, Rosebery was offered junior office. In his annoyance that he had not been asked to join the Cabinet he refused. At the same time his standing in Scotland was enhanced by his stirring Rectorial Address at Aberdeen University on the subject of the Scottish ethos; in those days a rectorial address was an event of some importance, reported in full in the columns of the main Scottish dailies. In the winter of 1880–81 he compiled a memorandum to Sir William Harcourt, Home Secretary, arguing that the affairs of Scotland now required stronger ministerial arrangements. But his demands were modest enough; a Secretary for Scotland would be too much; an under-secretary would, presentationally, be too little. 'Take one of the old Scottish offices and attach it to the Home Office' he said, giving Harcourt the benefit of his knowledge of Scottish history. 'There is for instance, the post of President of the Privy Council of Scotland which was suppressed at the Union'. The memorandum was ignored, and Rosebery fretted.

In the June of 1881, the new-found assertiveness of Scottish opinion shewed itself in a House of Lords debate, instigated from the back-benches by Earl Fife. It was however Rosebery who shone, his speech still further enhancing his reputation in Scotland. The present system was as bad as Dundas management or indeed, he said with a smile, the days of John Knox. 'We in Scotland have been handed over to the legal rather than the spiritual arm.' Then Rosebery went on to make his claim for a Scottish post in Cabinet, this a significant advance on mere tinkering with under-secretaryships. 'It really is', he said, 'a considerable disadvantage for the country to have its chief officer permanently excluded from Cabinet'. Earl Granville, replying for the Government insisted that the Home Secretary *was* Secretary of State for Scotland, the Lord Advocate merely his legal adviser. The real difficulty he said was the congestion of business in the House of Commons. Nor was a Minister for Scottish Affairs the only new Ministerial appointment that had been suggested.

In August of 1881, Rosebery accepted junior office, being given the under-secretaryship at the Home Office on the tacit understanding with Gladstone and Harcourt that there would be organisational change to improve the handling of Scottish business. That did not come. Before the year was out he minuted to Harcourt ridiculing the lack of a permanent staff on Scottish affairs and the want of an Edinburgh office. 'People come to me on Scottish affairs and I have nowhere to receive them, except my country house seven miles from Edinburgh.' He also made fun of the reliance placed on the Lord Advocate. 'When the Government goes out of office the Lord Advocate and the [legal] Secretary disappear leaving no trace behind them. . . . The new Lord Advocate and his Secretary make their appearance on the scene and find nothing but the official furniture of their apartments.'

Nothing came of this paper—apart from a further heightening of Rosebery's exasperation. He felt strongly that Scotland (and, being conscious of his qualities, the Earl of Rosebery as well) merited recognition for the Midlothian success. In November he had another huge personal success in his rectorial address to Edinburgh University. Rosebery was now the darling of Liberal Scotland and leader of the suddenly revived national consciousness which the Midlothian campaigns had quickened. However, in December 1882 Cabinet reconstruction found no place for him. Gladstone valued Rosebery's worth but he valued seniority still more.

Now more than ever Rosebery felt cheated by the revered but slippery Gladstone, and that there must be a Scottish Secretary with the same Cabinet status as the Irish Secretary. Gladstone replied that he could see no analogy between a Secretary for Scotland and a Secretary for Ireland. In January 1883 Rosebery wrote in challenging terms. 'I entered upon office to secure attention to and a definite department for my country' he said. Gladstone replied coldly that Harcourt was the Minister for Scotland, that Scotland had received parliamentary attention, and that her legislative needs were being met. No doubt he had it in mind that a Royal Commission had been appointed under Lord Napier to ascertain the causes of agrarian unrest throughout the Highlands and Islands. There the crofting communities from Islay to Shetland were refusing to pay rent, and were bitterly resenting the huge areas given over to deer forest by sporting proprietors. However, he now had the Chancellor of the Exchequer produce a scheme for a Local Government Board for Scotland with a President in the government but not a minister of Cabinet rank. This Presidency he offered to Rosebery whose response was blunt. As reward for making Gladstone member for Midlothian Scotland was entitled to expect a Cabinet Minister. 'At any rate', he added, 'I have always been clear that I could not be an efficient Minister for Scotland without a seat in the Cabinet.' Rosebery's aspirations for Scotland and for himself had now come together.

The 3rd Marquess of Salisbury. Cartoon by Harry
Furniss. (Courtesy of National Portrait Gallery.)

In all this the Lord Advocate was no ally. He told the Cabinet
that support for change was neither 'very decided nor very
prevalent throughout the country.' What began to tip the balance
was that the Scottish Conservatives, sensing a popular cause, now
added their weight. A great bi-partisan meeting was held in

Edinburgh one January day in 1884.* From the chair, the Conservative Lord Lothian set the tone of the meeting. Though the
upsurge of national feeling was now near the surface, the day's
business was to be the sober practicalities of the better handling of
Scottish affairs. 'Gentlemen going up to London on public business', said Lord Lothian, 'do not know where to go, but are
hunted from pillar to post. And when they wish to state their
views they are received by that terrible person the permanent
official who sees everything from an English point of view, who
looks upon everything through English spectacles, and whose sole
object in view is £sd'. But with their proper Victorian concern for
economy, the meeting, while warmly endorsing the case for a
Minister for Scotland in government, debated whether the existing
cabinet post of Lord Privy Seal should not be utilised 'as the Lord
Privy Seal has nothing particularly to do.'

However the Secretary for Scotland Bill, giving this new minister of the Crown authority over the Edinburgh boards and a fair
measure of patronage to dispense in Scotland but omitting law and
justice powers in deference to opposition from the Home Office,
was introduced in the summer of 1885 by Rosebery in the House
of Lords. A few weeks later the Liberal Government fell through
the defection of the Irish members. But Lord Salisbury's short-
lived interim Conservative administration gave the bill parliamentary time; Rosebery, in these more gentlemanly times being
accorded the courtesy of remaining in charge in the Lords from the
opposition benches. (As well he might. Neither party had any
vision of this new office in government being the agent of social
change.) Royal Assent was given on August 14, 1885; the Duke of
Richmond and Gordon was appointed Secretary for Scotland; and
in November he held his Edinburgh reception in Parliament
House.

As formally set up, the Scottish Office had at least acquired a
splendid London address—the Prime Minister having been got at†
by the Lord Advocate in a railway compartment. It had also, in the
Duke of Richmond and Gordon, someone of no mean political
experience who was, as Salisbury recognised, a grandee as well. 'I

*The 'Scotsman' reporter caught the mood of the moment.
   'The doors of the Assembly Hall having been opened at 12 o'clock, ticket-
   holders forthwith began to pour into the building and were ushered into their
   places by assiduous stewards wearing rosettes in which the Liberal and
   Conservative colours were harmoniously blended. The band of the Gordon
   Highlanders stationed in the quadrangle of the Free College played, meanwhile,
   a selection of popular music. . . . The boom of the one o'clock gun from the
   ramparts of Edinburgh Castle marked the opening.'
†The late Lord Kingsburgh, who was Lord Advocate of 1885, used to tell a story
as to the manner in which Dover House was secured for the Scottish Office. He
was travelling to attend a council, and in the same saloon carriage was the Prime
Minister of the day, Lord Salisbury. The Prime Minister inquired whether a home

signed away Dover House for you to reside in . . . I wonder
Plunkett [First Commissioner of Works] did not offer you the
second pair back over a gin-shop', wrote Salisbury amusedly to the
Duke whose reply was equally light-hearted. 'You know my
opinion of the office, and that it is quite unnecessary, but the
Country and Parliament think otherwise—and the office has been
created, and someone must fill it.' There was no such princely
accommodation in Edinburgh for the Scottish Secretary; a room★ in
the Palace of Holyroodhouse had long been known as 'The Secretary's Room', but that would be a memory of Peel, Home Secretary at the royal visit of 1822.

For all that the Scottish Office had been thus handsomely
housed, both the Home Office, still holding to the view that it
could not part with its law and order responsibilities in Scotland,
and the Treasury, viewing coldly the expense, remained unhelpful.
This was no doubt to be expected of traditional Whitehall, but
north of the Tweed the Educational Institute of Scotland representing the school-teachers and the more important of the School
Boards had also been against any transfer of responsibility for
Scottish education to what they feared would be an administrative
backwater presided over by a Minister who knew nothing about
education. So a somewhat Gilbertian solution was devised and the
Scotch Education Department would not come under the Secretary for Scotland as such, but rather under the Vice-President of the
Scotch Education Committee of the Privy Council (who would be
the Secretary for Scotland!). The Secretary for Scotland was
accorded the historic dignity of being 'Keeper of the Great Seal of
Scotland'; and in Sir Francis Sandford Dover House was given a
distinguished Glaswegian from the Education Office as its senior
Civil Servant. But the Scottish Secretaryship was still a delicate
child. Even two years later the now elderly nobleman who had
been Scotch Lord of the Treasury would write to a new Secretary
for Scotland congratulating him on being 'the able holder of a
useless office.'

The whirligig of Irish affairs put Gladstone back in power in
January 1886. By now Rosebery was Foreign Secretary, and so the

---

had yet been found for the new department. The Lord Advocate replied that none
had yet been found, but that various suggestions had been made, such as a house in
Covent Garden close to the market, and others which seemed to him equally
unsuitable. The Prime Minister said that he wished the office to be well housed,
whereupon the Lord Advocate mentioned Dover House, and obtained then and
there from Lord Salisbury a note intimating his desire that Dover House should be
handed over for the purposes of the Scottish Office.' *Pages 261–2, 'Looking
Back'—by Robert Munro (Lord Alness).* But the Lord Advocate's intervention was
not wholly disinterested; he too would take up quarters in Dover House in
exchange for his cramped rooms in the Home Office!
★The west drawing-room, refurbished for Prince Albert just before his death.

first Scottish Secretary from the Liberal benches was Sir George Trevelyan, distinguished (English)man of letters, member for the Border burghs, recently and none too successfully Chief Secretary for Ireland. Trevelyan's tenure of office at Dover House was only two months. He had always been somewhat at odds with Gladstone, particularly over church matters. Now, in March 1886, Joseph Chamberlain, leader of the radicals, and he stormed out of the Cabinet meeting at which Gladstone outlined his plans for Irish Home Rule which so clearly would fail to square the circle of Ireland's place in the United Kingdom. This issue forced yet another General Election later that year at which the Conservatives were put back into office again.

As it happened, this change at Westminster saved the Scottish Office. While Gladstone—who called himself a Scot—shewed no liking for the new department, being still unconvinced of the need for it, Salisbury, the English patrician, now saved it. Perhaps it would be truer to say that Salisbury *and* the Highlands saved the Scottish Office. For throughout these years of the mid-1880s the 'land war' had continued to burn brightly in the north. The need for agrarian reform had not been part of the case for the creation of a Scottish Office; but within months of the new department's birth, Dover House had major legislation to steer through Parliament on the model of Irish land legislation of 1881. This would give the crofter security of tenure, a fixed fair rent and compensation for improvements under the administrative-cum-judicial jurisdiction of a new body appointed for the purpose, the Crofters Commission. It was a bi-partisan measure. Both parties recognised that the heat must be taken out of the Highland land problem. One Ireland was enough, and the new wider franchise which embraced the Highland crofter, had brought a clutch of radical members from the Highland constituencies. But the new legislation succeeded in appealing to both Liberal and Conservative benches only by failing to address itself to the need to give the crofters more land, and it also 'froze' crofting in its existing unsatisfactory state. At first the crofters had hailed the new legislation as their 'Magna Carta', but they and their spokesman were quick to see that the new measures would not appease land hunger, and so the rent strikes and resistance to rent enforcement went on, particularly in Skye and in the Long Island from Barra to the Butt of Lewis.

Scotland was now briefly a matter of acute 'imperial' concern— to use the language of the day. (Karl Marx had even drawn attention to the plight of the crofters in 'Das Kapital'.) Recognising this, Salisbury in 1886 put at the Scottish Office his superlatively able Scottish nephew, Arthur James Balfour, and he placed him in the Cabinet. Balfour quickly saw that the agrarian troubles in the Highlands and Islands could not be contained while police responsibilities were split between the Home Office and Dover House.

Junior though he was, he used his influence with his uncle to have the strongly held Home Office objections overridden and transfer to the Scottish Office of law and order responsibilities effected. He also called out the Marines.★ The historic letter was dated 15 September 1886 from Dover House, from the permanent under-secretary at the Scottish Office to the Secretary to the Admiralty.

'Adverting to my letter of the 13th inst. I am directed by the Secretary for Scotland to request that you will inform the Lords Commissioners of the Admiralty that it is proposed to send a military force to Skye, to support the civil authorities in the administration of law in the island.

Mr Balfour is of opinion that a body of 100 Marines acting in support of a police force of some 50 constables will be sufficient for the purpose; and he would be glad to be informed whether the Lords Commissioners would be able to send a detachment of Marines of the number indicated above to Skye in a vessel sufficiently large to convey, in addition to the Marines a force of 50 constables when sent on duty from their headquarters which will probably be fixed at Portree.

The marines will be required to be in Skye in a short time—say towards the end of the month, and to remain, as far as Mr Balfour can foresee, for a period of two or three months'.

Three thoughts arise. Despite the lone voice of the 'Scotsman' newspaper, there was in the revival of the Scottish Secretaryship no looking forward to legislative devolution. Walking with him through Dalmeny Woods to Cramond Ferry one summer's day of the mid 'eighties, the 'Scotsman' editor pressed his views on Gladstone. The Prime Minister conceded that some sort of parliament in Edinburgh might, theoretically, be possible but he quickly went on to say that the Irish problem must have prece-dence. The Irish problem was indeed soon to drown so much else in politics, including the unity of the Liberal party. Secondly, the Scottish members of parliament played little part in the run-up to the creation of the Scottish Office in 1885. Harcourt, for one, in his forthright way spoke disparagingly of them in private, and indeed, as Cooper himself conceded, 'the Scottish Liberal members did not distinguish themselves in debate.' And thirdly, if one reflects on the whole of the foregoing story, on how the Midlothian election came about, and how it led by a twisting road to Dover House, might one ask if the post of Scottish Secretary would ever have been revived, had not the Turks set to slaughtering the Christians of Bulgaria?

★However, Balfour had also sought accurate and confidential information on the hold the radical Land League had on the islands; the extent of over-renting and over-crowding; the extent to which landed proprietors were alleviating distress; the feeling about emigration; and the attitude of this Gaelic speaking people to education in English. To this end Mr Malcolm McNeill of the Board of Supervision was despatched to the Hebrides in August.

II

GOLDEN JUBILEE TO GREAT WAR

S OME LIGHT on the early years at Dover House spills over from
Dr Pellew's excellent study of the Victorian Home Office
published on our (elder) sister-department's bi-centenary in
1982. What Dr Pellew has to say of the Home Office, *circa* 1885,
will apply to its near-neighbour, Dover House, as well. A great
deal had changed since the days of 'the Circumlocution Office',
Charles Dickens' devastating parody of Whitehall thirty years
before, but much of administration was still, as it were, in the age
of sail. It was all so very small-scale. Leaving out messengers,
cleaners and the porters who fed the elegant Paine and Holland
fireplaces, the Scottish Office at the outset consisted of seven. By
1885, the Home Office, the last bastion of patronage, had only
recently surrendered to the introduction of First Division men as
the future 'intellectual' part of the office, recruited by open
competition from the universities of Oxford and Cambridge; and
to the formation of a Second Division of clerks—from staff clerks
to temporary boy clerks—for the 'mechanical' work. From the
outset Dover House was organised in this way. But every paper
coming in or going out had to go through the permanent (ie civil
service) under-secretary of state. He alone could give instructions
and sign letters, and this rule would persist for the next forty years.

The class division in Dover House would be total. The 'Oxford
men with good degrees in Greats' of the First Division were well
paid; theirs was the London of the professional and, since Oxford
men of these days had to be well-off, sometimes the social élite as
well; they also had their sights on the under-secretary's opulence of
£1,500 a year. The clerks, crawling by £5 a year from the initial £70
to £100 were poorer than, say, insurance clerks in the City. But as
they looked in the fullness of time to more than double that salary
as staff clerks, they could hope one day to become members of the
middle class, housed in a villa and with a living-in servant. But the

First Division and Second Division men would come from different backgrounds, the latter being as a contemporary description put it 'clever boys of the lower middle-class whose parents cannot afford to keep them long enough at school'.

From the outset, Dover House adopted the 'modern' custom—only that year brought into use at the Home Office—whereby new papers were put away flat and in white jackets, the front of which formed the minute sheets. Until then, as in the days of Peel, an incoming letter would be folded in four and minutes written on the blank front. The 'technological innovation' of the precedent book, supplanting those jealously guarded preserves, the memories of ageing clerks, was also now coming in. So was the copying press. But as yet there were no typewriters, still less any 'lady typewriters'. When these advance guards of the long overdue feminist revolution were first to insinuate themselves into Whitehall in the 'nineties at 18 shillings a week reaching to 25 after four years, the Scottish Office like the Home Office resisted their employment, the material to be handled on the criminal side being thought too salacious for their tender natures. The Treasury was no less blinkered; Circumlocution Office attitudes were not yet dead. 'The amount of simple copying required in the Service is not very great', a Treasury minute of the 'nineties opined, 'and it is not probable that the class of women typist will be very numerous . . . As a matter of fact, women typists will not be employed in every Department of the State, for in some instances Heads of Departments prefer Boy Typists.'

Hours were ten to four, six days a week; seven hours a day and the half-day on the sixth being, like the typewriter, innovations of the 'nineties. There was the gentlemanly privilege of two months leave for the more senior staff in the course of every summer. But what of the flavour of Whitehall life for departmental staff from the under-secretary of state to the temporary boy clerk? Regrettably the record is so meagre. Some of the Oxford men, says Dr Pellew, felt frustrated, and she records one such who on quitting the Home Office called it 'a morgue'. The confident band of administrators of the Edwardian years with their 'particular kind of impartial ability, bred by an English classical education which made them highly effective at analysing alternatives, at distinguishing points of value from irrelevancies, at ascertaining the best way of carrying out a policy, but which excluded zeal for a cause or an idea' were still in the making. As frustrated were some of the clerks when they recognised that ascent into the First Division could never be for them. But government offices are human institutions. Dr Pellew gleaned one recorded memory of clerks from the Home Office Registry tripping across Whitehall to the 'Red Lion' on thirsty summer days (and having to be summoned back); no doubt they would find there acquaintances from Dover House. And a

The Millais portrait at Dalmeny of the 5th Earl of
Rosebery. (Courtesy of the Earl of Rosebery.)

senior colleague recalls his coming across, in the 1930s, a file from
the early days of Dover House in which the permanent under-
secretary of state expostulated on a Treasury *ukase* about shorter
lunch breaks. 'If gentlemen had to return from lunch before 3
o'clock', he wrote, 'life at the office would be intolerable.'

'It should not be forgotten', wrote the Home Secretary in
September 1886 during his tussle with Balfour, 'that the proposed
delegation of powers in respect of law and order to the Secretary
for Scotland is apparently meant to include not merely the case of a
few crofters resisting the service of writs in Tiree, but also the
extreme case of a general insurrection in Scotland'. The deploy-

ment of this ultimate argument *in terrorem* showed how reluctant the Home Office would be to concede defeat, even though Salisbury had overruled it about the conduct of the police and military operation in the Hebrides. The Home Secretary would see his opportunity to regain lost ground when Balfour was given early promotion to the post of Chief Secretary for Ireland, and in his place Salisbury put the mild personage of Lord Lothian but did not give him a seat in the Cabinet. The Convention of Royal Burghs, proud of the part it had played in the revival of the post of Scottish Secretary, was quick to complain about his exclusion from the Cabinet, as did a number of town councils individually. On receipt of the last of these, Dunbar, the First Division clerk who had handled Scottish business as Rosebery's secretary at the Home Office and transferred to Dover House, minuted wryly to Cochran-Patrick, the erstwhile member of parliament become permanent under-secretary of state in 1887 (for patronage was not yet quite dead)

> 'It would be well if all the burghs in Scotland passed similar resolutions and transmitted them to the Prime Minister.'

But Lord Lothian would no doubt be reluctant to press his views against the mighty experience and prestige of the Prime Minister.

So it was that the battle to establish the position of the Secretary for Scotland in permanent fashion had now to be fought. Dunbar set to work compiling a long and closely reasoned 'Memorandum re Scottish business' about the manifest shortcomings of the Secretary for Scotland Act and the necessity that his minister have both law and order responsibilities and a general responsibility for Scottish affairs, equivalent to the traditional wide responsibility of the Home Secretary. A century later one may still recognise a piece of admirable drafting, recognise too the removal of the odd asperity, no doubt at Lord Lothian's instance, in preparing the paper for submission to Cabinet (as the Scots proverb goes, 'ne'er draw a dirk when a dunt will do.').

The upshot was the amending Secretary of Scotland Act of 1887 which in its general phrasing reflected Salisbury's statesmanlike wish that Whitehall animosity towards Dover House should cease. In addition to giving the Secretary for Scotland law and order powers, it clothed him with 'all powers and duties vested in and imposed on any of Her Majesty's Principal Secretaries of State by any Act of Parliament, law or custom so far as such powers and duties relate to Scotland'. In this the parliamentary draftsman had overreached himself, and yet another amending act had in time to wend its way through Parliament to make it clear that this did not apply to the War Office and matters military. But here was the germ of the concept which as the years went by was to assume ever greater importance for the Scottish Office—that its ministerial head was indeed 'Scotland's Minister', his remit anything of public consequence from the Mull of Galloway to Muckle Flugga.

Nevertheless, the Home Secretary remained a power in Scotland. Not even mooted as a possibility for hiving off to Dover House were the important Home Office Factory Inspectorate and Mines Inspectorate, though the abandoned proposals for a Scottish Local Government Board of 1884 had contemplated this (and on the afternoon of the Duke of Richmond and Gordon's Edinburgh appearance in November 1885 his first piece of business had been to receive a deputation from Scottish Trades Councils complaining of the inadequacy of the factory inspectorate). Administration in Scotland of these two areas of crucial importance in improving conditions at work would long remain with the Home Office, would indeed never come over to the Scottish Office. Nor was responsibility for aliens legislation given to Dover House. But, significantly, the 'industrial schools' in Scotland, where young people in trouble with the law were given a rudimentary education, were to be surrendered to the Scotch Education Department by the Home Office within a few years.

The 'standing' of a department with its Whitehall neighbours matters a great deal; never more so than in these early years with Home Office and Treasury playing the wicked sisters to the Cinderella of Dover House; the Home Office in particular now demanding that all communication with the Palace go through them. An important stage in the emergence of the Scottish Office was a handwritten letter on plain notepaper of 1887 from Sir Henry Ponsonby, the Queen's Private Secretary, to Lord Lothian.

> Buckingham Palace
> September 20, 1887
>
> My dear Lothian,
>
> I have laid your letter before the Queen. Her Majesty wishes the Secretary for Scotland to submit matters (Scottish) direct to the Queen.
>
> Yours very truly
> (Sgd) Henry E Ponsonby

The Home Office could not argue with *that;* but most sensibly Queen Victoria was to ask that the Scottish Secretary consult the Home Secretary over the exercise of the Royal Prerogative of Mercy in all cases where the law required capital punishment. Regard for precedent and compatibility of decisions were never more important than in this sombre area of administration.

If the Duke of Richmond and Gordon spent his first afternoon in office in the November of 1885 hearing complaints which had nothing to do with his new department, in the early years there were other expectations which had to go unsatisfied. The one hundred and thirty shoemakers of 'Linlithgowshire' lost no time in petitioning the Secretary for Scotland *via* the Earl of Hopetoun that the lucrative business of making boots for soldiers be restored to them. The answer from the War Office was that the Lothian shoemakers were behind the times, that army boots were now machine sewn, whereas the Linlithgow cobblers, like their forefathers, still practised hand-sewing. There was also a letter to Lord Lothian from 'Mr William McGonagall, poet' complaining that the magistrates of Dundee had put a stop to the public recitation of his compositions. It was, said the bard of 48 Step Row, an outrage, 'Queen Elizabeth, sir, allowed Shakspeare [sic] to read his plays before her at Court, and I have no doubt her Majesty Queen Victoria would allow me to do the same if I was only properly introduced to her . . .' McGonagall also enclosed some of his work, including a hand-written copy of one of his choicest pieces. The opening two lines will suffice.

'Welcome, thrice welcome, to the city of Dundee
The great African explorer, Henry M Stanley.'

'If the enclosed specimens are typical of his poetry, I don't wonder at his being gagged', minuted young Mr Dodds to Dunbar, the assistant under-secretary of state.

Now the Scottish Office was again brought into the forefront of affairs as the Salisbury administration set itself to a general reform of local government in the counties. This was sorely needed, particularly for public health provision; the parochial boards which had had public health powers placed with them in 1867 had done little towards implementation, particularly so in remoter Scotland; and with the widening of the parliamentary franchise in 1883 the running of local affairs in the countryside had now to be democratised—after a fashion—in Scotland as in England.

The Scottish version of this major legislation was the Local Government (Scotland) Act of 1889 which created county councils. So began the Office's involvement with local government which has continued to this day. But the coming of elected county councils was to be at one with the piecemeal way in which local government in Scotland was now to be put on its feet: the incumbents of Dover House of these early years lacked the standing, or the experience—were indeed too newly arrived on the scene—to bring into being a more comprehensively rational structure of local government.

The new county councils partially supplanted the 'Commissioners of Supply', that is the county committees of landowners which had been the principal local authority in the countryside since the days of King Charles II; and for each landward county there was now brought together in one authority responsibility for county roads, and for public health and for water supply (which up to now had been no one's concern). But control of the police lay not with the county council. This was placed with a Standing Joint Committee for each county consisting of equal representation from the county council and the Commissioners of Supply. Each Standing Joint Committee also had a veto over its county council's capital expenditure and borrowing; and the Liberals were incensed at the dominant position all this gave to the county gentry. The new legislation also had the effect of strictly delimiting country from town. The need for some association with the burghs was recognised in the setting up of district committees of county councils for highways with burghal representatives. Those burghs of rural Scotland which had lost their diminutive forces were represented on county councils for police business only. But these modest arrangements were in themselves not enough at a time when so many Scottish burghs were fast spreading outwards. Nor, with the solitary exception of the joining of Ross to Cromarty (where union was not to be avoided, so intermingled were the boundaries) was any attempt made to weld larger administrative areas out of the smaller counties of landward Scotland. A Boundary Commission was set up to remove anomalies and absurdities in county boundaries, but large or small as they were, the counties became the new rural authorities, with adverse consequence in future years for any broad uniformity of development as the provision of services became ever more complex and sophisticated. Some county nuptials in addition to the marriage of Ross and Cromarty could have proved equally felicitous.

Reform of burgh government began in 1892 with legislation which consolidated and added to existing measures, giving, incidentally, a curiously intimate picture of life in a Scottish burgh of the nineteenth century in its injunctions against all manner of public indecorum, even to the beating of carpets in the street and to servant lassies standing on sills when cleaning windows! (Our Scottish Office solicitors of the present day admit to a sense of wonder at the magnitude of the task that fell on the then Lord Advocate and his parliamentary draftsmen at Dover House in framing its six hundred or more sections). But it was not until 1900 that there was further legislation to put elected town councils in sole charge within their boundaries. Previously basic services— watching, lighting, paving, cleansing and water supply—had in many places been the responsibility of elected representatives known as 'police commissioners' who to the confusion of the public might or might not be the same as the burgh council.

Returned to power in 1892, the Liberals with Rosebery their curiously diffident leader had added still further to the diversity of local government by creating elected parish councils to take over poor relief from the non-elected parochial boards of landowners set up half a century before. It gave Liberal Scotland particular satisfaction that poor relief and other local functions of the new parish councils were, like education which was already in the hands of parish school boards, now given over to local bodies on which the less-well-off (but radically minded) might serve. Travel in the countryside was still largely 'pony and trap' and repayment for loss of earnings undreamt of. Was there also some political animus against the Tory-created County Councils? It would seem so, but historians have yet adequately to explore this stretch of Scottish history.

Under the new legislation the Board of Supervision was renamed the Local Government Board and given a wider role. The Board consisted of three *ex officio* members; the Secretary for Scotland, the permanent under-secretary at Dover House (now Sir Colin Scott-Moncrieff, an elderly ex-soldier with an Indian Mutiny medal and a career in colonial service) and the Solicitor General. But the work was done by the three Board members who were appointees of the Scottish Secretary, one of whom was the effective chairman, one an advocate, and one a medical man. The Board was confirming authority for the wide variety of byelaws for all manner of urban regulation now to be made by the burghs. It also guided the new parish councils, particularly in their administration of poor relief. Its major impact on the Scottish scene was, however, to be in public health. The county district committees of each county council and the burghs were now required to appoint medical officers and sanitary inspectors to the Board's satisfaction, the penalty being the withholding of government grant towards their salaries.

So it was that by the end of the century there was a tangle of local administration. In landward Scotland the county council, the standing joint committee with its half membership of country gentry, the county road board and the district committee stood alongside the parish council and parish school board. The burghs ranged from Glasgow's three quarters of a million to New Galloway's three quarters of a thousand, and in the burghs there was too the dichotomy of town council and school board. Over all—but that is not quite the right way to put it, for many of the burghs of ancient lineage did not consider themselves subject to *any* central authority—stood the Local Government Board. Over this Board, over all the Edinburgh boards as nominal president, was the Secretary for Scotland; but he was far away.

With the return to power of the Liberals in 1892 Sir George Trevelyan had became both Scottish Secretary once more (and a cabinet member). 'Gladstone', it was noted at the time, 'was keen

'Dinner at Haddo House' in 1885 by A E Emslie
showing the elderly Mr Gladstone and the young
Earl of Rosebery. (Courtesy of National Portrait
Gallery.)

to appoint Bryce [a Glaswegian, later to be ennobled and serve as
Ambassador at Washington] . . . but there was a general protest
and he was told he must give it to Trevelyan' who it was felt in the
party had not had the recognition his abilities merited. Seniority
mattered more than Scottishness.

Rosebery's eclipse, the sad, politically suicidal end to his
ambitions as he isolated himself from his Liberal colleagues, was
followed by the Conservative run which lasted through the years
of the Boer War and on up to the winter of 1905. During most of
this time the Scottish Secretary was a much respected Scottish
peer, Lord Balfour of Burleigh, and so once more Commons
business was left to the Lord Advocate. Balfour of Burleigh—to
the cartoonists of these years 'the burly Balfour' as opposed to his
Scottish Office predecessor 'the slim Balfour'—has wrongly been
written off as a 'grandee'. This is to misunderstand the man and his
times. His years at the Scottish Office saw the passing of the public
health legislation which improved on the parent act of thirty years
earlier and is still, today, the basis of much local authority activity;
also the preparation of legislation to contain the massive drink
problem of working class Scotland by regulation of the numbers of
public houses and their hours of opening; and he made an
important contribution to highland recovery.

Lord Lothian when Scottish Secretary in the previous Conservative administration had been the first of many Scottish Office ministers down the years to undertake a highland tour that he might learn for himself the dimensions of the problem. On coming into office in 1887 he had declared that 'the first step towards an immediate solution' of the crofting problem lay in 'an attractive and well-financed scheme of state-aided emigration'—as the Napier Commission had proposed—and he had toyed with proposals put to him for a highland 'plantation' in New Zealand. Nothing had come of this. But he did set up a Commission of Inquiry into ways of developing the fishing industry in the Highlands and Islands which recommended the spending of government money on the building of fishery harbours on the west coast to sustain a modern fishing industry and the financing of railway lines to transport catches to the city markets. With commendable speed their recommendations were implemented by the Western Highlands and Islands Works Act of 1891; from this would come the extension to Kyle of Lochalsh of the Highland Railway's line traversing Ross-shire and the North British Railway's construction of the superbly scenic West Highland Railway to Mallaig. Balfour of Burleigh's own contribution to the Highlands and Islands was the creation of the Congested Districts Board, with powers to assist land settlement and other development. It was in conscious imitation of the Irish Congested Districts Board set up earlier in the decade; and it seemed almost a bi-partisan approach to land hunger since more land for the crofter had been the purpose of the Liberal Government's Royal Commission on the Highlands and Islands of 1892. Although this new Edinburgh Board had no powers of compulsory purchase, had only meagre funds and even lacked borrowing powers it did succeed in creating over the next dozen years over 600 new holdings and enlargements to more than 1100 others. It was a beginning.

The advance in Scottish administration of these years is not understood if one looks only to the modest achievement of the Scottish Office. These were the years when the other occupant of Dover House, the Scotch Education Department, learned to spread its wings. Free from the sectarian strife which was now to hobble educational development in England, the Scottish Department with great self-assurance now set to the creation of good secondary schooling for all Scotland by means of government grant and a department-run national examination system. As its head was to explain to a later Royal Commission, 'elementary schooling' English-style was not recognised in Scotland; the proper phrase was 'primary schooling' which, by implication, looked forward to secondary and still higher education. The mood was vigorous, conforming to the stern intellectual tradition of the past. *'Disce puer aut abi'* was the motto of Paisley Grammar School founded in the reign of King James the Sixth; and 'learn or leave' was still the uncompromising war-cry of Scottish education. In all this too, Balfour of Burleigh was happily involved (the room tenanted by Sir Henry Craik, the forceful head of the Department was below his own in Dover House), though the shortness of the parliamentary session meant the Minister's absence on the grouse-moor or by the salmon river for months on end. For the next two decades, unquestionably it was the achievement of this Department, giving Scotland a secondary education system the envy of English educationists, which was Dover House's most striking success; the justification—if such were needed—for 1885.

Not that Balfour of Burleigh, for all the support he gave Craik and the officials of the Scotch Education Department, would have seen it that way. His affectionate biographer of fifty years ago makes it clear that foremost in his mind in his years in office was resistance to Liberal pressures—themselves due to jealous urging from the Church of Scotland's rival sects—to bring about the former's disestablishment as 'the national church'. These pressures had been particularly strong in the 1880s. Disestablishment of the Church of Scotland had indeed been more of an issue during the general elections of 1885 than the creation of a Scottish Office; and it was only as the Liberal Party fell apart in the 1890s that the issue receded. Balfour of Burleigh's constant adversary in this was Sir George Trevelyan who, while in office, had caused a fluttering in ecclesiastical doo'cots by trying to change to a disestablishment sense the wording of the monarch's message to the Church's General Assembly. It had been as if he had been proposing amendment to King James' Bible itself! Indeed, concern with Kirk matters was general in these years. The disestablishment controversy was followed by the bitter feud of the early years of the new century between the United Free Church and the Free Church over the destination of assets, a battle only ended by parliamentary legislation. All this monopolised attention and obscured the very real social problems of the day.

This 'otherness' of some of the big issues of these years before the First World War is also illustrated by the participation of the Scottish Office in another now faded cause, agricultural land settlement in the countryside. Since their failure to give the crofter more land in the legislation of 1886, land settlement generally had become a plank in the programme of the Liberals. 'We wish to make the land less of a pleasure ground for the rich, and more of a treasure house for the nation', Campbell-Bannerman, the wealthy Glaswegian about to become Prime Minister, proclaimed to a rally in the Royal Albert Hall in the December of 1905. As Secretary for Scotland he now put into Dover House his close friend and political associate, Captain John Sinclair, an enthusiast for the land settlement cause. Perhaps the astute Campbell-Bannerman also saw land settlement legislation—which the Conservative Party of the day must abhor—as a gauntlet to be thrown down in anticipation of major, coming battles with the House of Lords.

Considered lightweight by some of his party, Sinclair was an erstwhile squadron commander in the Royal Irish Lancers who had once taken part in a cavalry charge in the Sudan ('the last occasion' so his widow was to record, doubtless reflecting what her husband had told her, 'in which the lanceflag was used attached to the lance'). 'Radical Jack' Sinclair was keen for a political fight. By way of preparation he had made personal study of the small state-provided farms of Denmark, and on assuming office he sent a mission there. Sinclair correctly saw more land for the crofter as the answer to the continuing smoulder of agrarian trouble in Highlands and Hebrides, but his intention went far beyond the appeasement of land hunger in the north. He wished to extend the absolute security given by crofting tenure to the small farmer throughout Scotland, making him proof against amalgamating landlords; throughout all Scotland too he proposed the break up of big farms into large numbers of smaller ones. In this, for lowland, arable Scotland his prime purpose was nothing to do with agricultural production, and was rather—in what we today must regard as a nonsense—the reversal of rural depopulation as a countervailing measure to the degeneration in the health of the grossly overcrowded urban masses. The new land regime in Highlands and Lowlands alike was to be enforced by a Board of Agriculture and by a Scottish Land Court. Land settlement in England was to be left to the county councils, whatever they wished to make of it. But in Scotland Sinclair would not rely on them, no doubt considering them to be under the thumbs of county gentlemen acting together as Commissioners of Supply.

The Small Landholders (Scotland) Bill passed the Commons in 1907 but was savaged in the Lords; this was the doing of Rosebery, still Liberal in name but in his isolation, ever more abrasive. At his eloquent best and in lofty disregard of the crofters' genuine need for more land he ridiculed both the measure and its author.

> 'The principle of the Bill is essentially a vicious one . . . I do not believe any more vicious or more foolish principle was ever applied to land legislation. What is the crofting system? Is it the survival of the fittest? Is it the highest form of agriculture known to Scotland that we are asked to adopt? Some of your Lordships travelling in the Highlands may have seen thin sparsely cultivated strips of land, sometimes with a cottage built by the savings of children abroad, by lonely lakes, or by the shores of the sea, or on barren moors. There live men who would rather die than leave their native land, struggling against

nature, and trying to secure a precarious crop in a climate totally unsuitable for it, on soil wholly unadapted for it. Rather than leave or migrate they persevere in cultivating that ungrateful soil. All honour to them for it, I respect them for it. But I do not think that is a condition of things that we ought to work and legislate to transfer to the magnificent and fertile fields of the Lothians and the Lowlands of Scotland. I cannot imagine any responsible Minister who knows what a crofter is and what a croft is coming down deliberately to this house and proposing to apply that system to the Lowlands of Scotland. I should have been less surprised had the Secretary for War, in producing his bill for the Territorial Forces, decided that his New Army should be provided with bows and arrows for defensive purposes. What you are attempting to do by introducing the crofting system is to supersede the highest farming known to Great Britain, and perhaps to the world, by the most backward system in these islands. That is the remedy brought forward by my noble friend opposite in order that the people of Glasgow may live fewer in a room than they do now.'

Land settlement was now indeed an issue of the day in the developing national controversy over the powers of the House of Lords. It was not customary at that time for a Bill once rejected by the Lords to be resubmitted in the lifetime of the same Parliament, but as a further deliberate challenge to the Lords the Bill was so resubmitted in 1908. Once again it was rejected. Sinclair was now something of a popular hero in the Highlands, adding each summer to his considerable personal knowledge of the area by cruising in the Hebrides, first in his own yacht, then on the steam vessels of the Scottish Fishery Board—the first of many Scottish Secretaries to do so on these little ships. But it was all too much for the permanent under-secretary of state at Dover House. He was Sir Reginald Macleod of MacLeod, 27th chief of the clan; and he resigned his post that he might contest the Inverness-shire constituency in the Conservative interest (unsuccessfully).

When the Parliament Bill of 1911 presaged the clipping of the powers of the Lords, the Conservative opposition at last threw in the sponge. The Bill was passed and so the Scottish Board of Agriculture came into being, responsible for land settlement at its own hand or by arrangement with landowners, and with the stick of compulsory purchase behind its back. With it a Scottish Land Court came into being to settle resulting disputes. With this there passed from the scene the Crofters Commissioners who since 1886 had set out from their Edinburgh office at intervals throughout the year—leaving it in the care of the solitary messenger—to administer and arbitrate their régime of protection for crofters. Also wound up were the Congested Districts Boards of 1897 with its very general powers and modest achievement. The powers in regard to Scotland of the Board of Agriculture in Whitehall were also made over to the new board, excepting only animal disease responsibilities. But what the new legislation did not do was to marry afforestation with crofting as a better land use of the great areas of hill under grazing or deer forest. From the Conservative benches, Lord Lovat, who was emerging as a leader of highland opinion was a strong advocate of this; but in the highly charged political atmosphere he was not heeded.

Campbell-Bannerman had died in 1908, his last speech, as it happened, a spirited defence of the Scottish land settlement cause. Asquith who succeeded him did not share his predecessor's enthusiasm. He saw to it that the Bill went through, having put Sinclair, now become Lord Pentland, in the Lords to facilitate its passage; then in 1912, with the Bill safely on the Statute Book and the vigorous enforcement which Pentland so clearly intended about to begin, Asquith had him moved—exiled, said Lady Pentland, not mincing her words, to govern Madras. Nor did Asquith hide his disdain for Pentland.

In the years ahead, lacking Pentland's enthusiasm, there was to be no general balkanisation of Scottish farming. However, the achievement in the Highlands was real enough. Thanks to 'the Pentland Act', as it came to be known, the Scottish Office had at last the means of bringing relative content to the crofting areas. In the Board of Agriculture for Scotland it had also acquired an Edinburgh dependency on which the new, emerging, state responsibilities for agriculture, such as research and education and, later, agricultural marketing and price support could be grafted. These would, otherwise, over the years have been placed within the ambit of the Whitehall Board of Agriculture, and government involvement with farming, like government involvement with trade and industry generally, would have rested with London. This creation of an all purpose agricultural board for Scotland had its critics, including Lord Lovat. They made rather much of the expense of what was proposed, and pointed to the supposedly greater experience the London board would have. Lord Pentland would not budge, and, indeed, but for that 'most amiable, obstinate gentleman' as he appeared to his adversaries, the Scottish Office of today would probably lack its agricultural dimension. He built better than he knew.

Land settlement, which his opponents saw as an all but revolutionary proposition, was Lord Pentland's passion; but other established areas of government also received his close attention. The groundwork was done for legislation to make specific provision for the care of the mentally handicapped, as distinct from the mentally deranged. The improvement in education was perhaps the most lasting achievement of his years in office, as he worked closely with Craik's successor, Sir John Struthers. Acting without reference to its sister Whitehall ministry the Department now legislated for the schooling of the handicapped, for the care of schoolchildren's health, for teacher training and for a measure of further, post-school, education. The Education (Scotland) Act of 1908 also 'secured the maintenance from one end of Scotland to the other of a sufficient number of well-equipped and well-staffed centres of higher instruction', the words being those of Sir George MacDonald the next, just as forceful, head of the Department. (But the Liberal bias still showed. Sinclair would not go all the way with his advisers and the Conservative opposition in welding the nine hundred parish school boards into county authorities. The most he would concede were county committees for secondary education.)

In 1914 Dover House continued to be the home of the Scottish Office and the Scotch (not yet Scottish) Education Department, both looking independently of each other to the Secretary of Scotland. The building also accommodated the Lord Advocate. This was as well because the Secretary for Scotland was as yet unaided by any junior minister; and when, as from 1909 to 1912, his seat was in the Lords, the Lord Advocate had to answer for him in the Commons chamber. That they lived check by jowl in Dover House was important for smooth despatch of business, though there was some friction between Scottish Secretary and Lord Advocate over the latter's restiveness at the formers's superior role in appointing judges.

The Dover House of 1914 was in essentials the Dover House of today; a gem of a building as Paine had designed it in the 1750s, with neo-classical alterations and embellishments by Holland in the 1790s. It had been mere happy chance (and timely lobbying) that made it the Scottish Secretary's headquarters in 1885, but no more appropriate site on Whitehall could have been found, standing as it did near where had been 'the Cockpit', the court theatre of the great, rambling Stuart palace of Whitehall, in which in the summer months of 1706 the negotiations for Union between Scotland and England took place. There it had been that the English commissioners had 'opened their pack of golden ware', as a dissident Scot put it, exposing the glittering prospects of Scottish trade with an expanding empire; and there it was, seated in a great chair covered in crimson velvet and gold lace, that Queen Anne in her sweet voice had given her 'ardent, good wishes' for success in the negotiations.

Dover House was built in the 1750s as the town house of a wealthy baronet. By now the Palace of Whitehall was no longer the monarch's residence; the Cockpit had been pulled down and the house enjoyed a splendid view over St James' Park. Thereafter, it continued to go up in the world, housing the French ambassador

The Regency rotunda at Dover House.

in the 1770s. By the last decade of the century it was York House, residence of a royal duke; then Melbourne House, a centre of Whig political influence. It was also home to Lady Caroline Lamb. In the two years of their torrid relationship Lord Byron often limped up the steps under the cupola's magnificence. (That is fact: what may be legend is that the tasseled rope by the staircase was first put there to ease his climb). Lady Caroline's stormy life came to its end in her bedroom looking on to the Horse Guards Parade, to the trees of St James' Park and to the distant roof of what was then Buckingham House.

   In 1830 Lady Caroline's widowed husband, by now Lord Melbourne, found the building too much of an expense and sold it. Its grand state rooms with their elegant ceilings were now the

home of Lord Dover⋆ who became the Commissioner of Woods
and Forests, a post concerned with the upkeep of government
property rather than afforestation. Then in 1885 the building
happening to be vacant, and Lord Salisbury shrewdly recognising
that a job worth doing was worth doing well, it came to fly the
Lion flag. But Dover House could well have found a different
order of tenant. Earlier that year, Gladstone, still Prime Minister,
had been offered the building as an alternative to 'No 10'. He
declined: the grandeur of the building, he said, would 'oblige the
Prime Minister to receive' and he valued privacy.

How small the staff of the Scottish Office continued to be
through the Edwardian years! There was a running battle with the
Treasury to add to the meagre resources of the 'intellectual' part (to
use the language of the day) in view of the responsibilities that
were now accumulating. Two seniors and three juniors was the
establishment eventually wrested from the Treasury, but it could
only give very stretched support to the permanent under-secretary
of state and his deputy. The private secretaries to the secretary of
state and the permanent under-secratary were also First Division
men; and the influence of the former, then as now, would be quite
considerable. The 'mechanical' part of the Office resided with six
Second Division clerks, two 'abstractors', the copy press keeper
and four boy clerks under the steely supervision (no doubt) of the
three staff clerks. Gradations among the clerical staff were also
scrupulously maintained—even in the detail of dress; Second
Division' clerks wore spats, assistant clerks did not. As to the
door-keepers, they wore top-hats.†

In Edinburgh there was now a small sub-office‡ staffed by one
senior and a clerical assistant. It seemed to be proving its worth in
facilitating the untangling of difficulties with town and county
clerks. Then there were the Inspectorates. There was HM Inspector of Constabulary. Now that government grant was going into
the hands of local authorities for various purposes there was an
Inspector of Local Loans and Audits at Dover House. There were
three Inspectors in Scotland concerned with pollution from indust-

⋆ Better remembered as the benefactor whose wealth built the National Gallery in
Trafalgar Square.
† The late William Hansford—latterly an under-secretary in the Scottish Home
Department—used to describe his early days as a boy clerk in the Scottish Office
just before World War I. On his first day he arrived at 10 am to find the office
occupied *solely* by a splendidly-attired gentleman whom he took to be the Secretary
for Scotland, but who was in fact the doorkeeper. One of the senior officials lived
some distance from London, and each day his first action, on arriving at noon, was
to call for shaving water. Then followed the luncheon interval. All this came as a
surprise to William Hansford, who had previously been employed in a busy room
at the Customs and Excise Department.
‡ But nothing came of this first attempt to establish the Scottish Office in
Edinburgh.

rial discharge; and in Edinburgh, a legacy from the days of Burke and Hare, there was Sir James Russell, Inspector of Anatomy.

In 1914, telephones did not make the bedlam of the ministerial private office which they do today; and there were, and for long would continue to be, coal fires in the splendid fireplaces. There was no passenger lift (nor is there yet). The three ladies of the typing staff in their small room were kept well away from the clerks. Were they also kept in purdah from the male shorthand typists? And the rooms of the most senior people had screens to conceal their own personal toilet arrangements. Servicing of the building lay with eight messengers, seven charwomen and one coal porter, all under command of the Office Keeper—Mr Charles Keeping.

Not much of London has changed as little since 1914 as has the view from Dover House. In the middle of Whitehall's traffic there is now Earl Haig on his charger; but across the way is the Stuart Banqueting Hall which Inigo Jones built and Rubens decorated. Flanking Dover House on one side is the Old Treasury Building; on the other the eighteenth century charm of the Horse Guards clock-tower. In 1914 as now, from windows of the great state rooms at Dover House the eye would travel across the gravelled parade ground to the garden of 10 Downing Street, to the dull mass of the Foreign Office and on to its first floor corner windows out of which Grey of Fallodon looked with such foreboding on the night of the 4th of August.

Just before the outbreak of war, Scottish administration came under scrutiny from the Royal Commission on the Civil Service which for the previous two years had been sitting under the formidable chairmanship of Lord MacDonnell. The Scotch Education Department received nothing but praise. Sir John Struthers impressed the commissioners with his description of the marked success his department had won in building a county-based system of secondary education throughout Scotland sustained by well trained teaching staff, and culminating in uniform leaving certificate awards which were themselves a potent incentive to still greater scholastic effort and a ladder to university entrance. He also carried the day in persuading the commissioners of the rightness of the Department in confining its recruitment of senior headquarters staff to its schools inspectorate, this a highly educated body of men with teaching experience. The Department's initiative in having opened an Edinburgh office to facilitate liaison with the nine hundred or so parish school boards in Scotland was likewise commended. But the board system in Edinburgh as practised in the Local Government, Fishery and Prisons Boards and by the new Agriculture Board was given something of a slating. By now these stood on their own as anachronisms; for the Boards of Education, Agriculture and Fisheries, Trade, Works and Local Government in Whitehall were now orthodox government ministeries in all but name.

In appearing for the Scottish Local Government Board before the Royal Commission, its vice chairman, Sir George McCrae, made an inglorious shewing. He was a Princes Street hatter who had been an able enough City Treasurer of Edinburgh, had sat in Parliament for an Edinburgh constituency, had been knighted and then been given by Lord Pentland the post of vice chairman of the Board (the Secretary for Scotland was the nominal chairman). Sir George told the Royal Commission that the Scottish Secretary invariably accepted the Board's advice; but then he was reluctant to express his own views. He was also rather negative about the possibility of employing women.

Q. 'Have you ever thought at all of giving the girls [ie typing staff] any clerical work of a higher character to do; not merely typing but such work as your junior second division clerks could do?

A. No. I must say that has never been officially considered by the Board.

Q. Do you see any objection to it?

A. I do not know.

Q. You do object, I infer, that girls and young boys should be together in the same room?

A. Certainly, and, after all, I think they have a different way in tackling their work.

Lord MacDonnell would not let Sir George off with this, but it was to no avail. His inflexibility would raise no eyebrows in Edinburgh, but perhaps it did not endear him to the members of the Royal Commission. His description of the Board at work as if they were merely the partners of an Edinburgh law firm may also have had its effect.

'*Sir George McCrae* What really happens is that there is no constituted meeting unless for some very important and specific purpose. A file on an important question is sent up from the Secretary [of the Board]; it goes first to the medical member, and he writes a minute on it. Then it goes to the legal member, and he writes a minute on it, and then it comes to me; and if there is any divergence of opinion they come into my room and talk it over. There is very seldom a formal meeting.

Lord MacDonnell But when there is a divergence of opinion between the three of you on some matter of great importance, what happens?

Sir George McCrae Then it comes up to London.

Lord MacDonnell Does it never happen that you have a constituted meeting, to use your own expression, of the Board?
Sir George McCrae Rarely, unless the Secretary for Scotland is
up in Scotland, and there is some very important question that
we want to decide. The normal condition of business is that we
have no Board meeting.'

With over three hundred staff and thirty four posts commanding
the then handsome salary of £1,000 a year or more, the Boards
were a sizeable enclave of the Civil Service. (The other end of the
spectrum was £50 a year and free boots for a female prison warder
at Greenock.) It was however the archaism of patronage in top
appointments to the Board which the Royal Commission most
deplored, though Dodds, now Permanent Under Secretary of
State at Dover House, sought to reassure them that the Scottish
Secretary would always be diligent in making the best possible
appointments. When with such obvious success senior administration elsewhere had become the province of career civil servants the
Commission could see no reason for exceptions in Edinburgh; and
Sir George McCrae was not much of an advertisement for the
Scottish system. For all his attempted defence of the *status quo,*
Dodds half conceded that he was defending the indefensible; and
the Royal Commission in their Report were quick to pick this up.

'We believe that the time has now come when this system of
Boards should be reconsidered, for the following reasons:—
    In the first place the evidence which we have received
indicates that the Board system is less effective in securing
responsibility for official action and advice than the system
followed in the office of the Secretary for Scotland.
    In the next place, the Board system, as it exists in Scotland,
must tend to weaken in some degree the important distinction
between the qualities, and the methods of selection, which are
suitable for political, and those which are suitable for permanent
appointments.
    Our third reason for reconsidering the Board system is that
the higher business of administration is apparently sometimes
performed by men who bring to it no special knowledge of the
work. Members of Scottish Boards are usually appointed by
patronage from outside the Civil Service; and in the early years
of their service they are learning their duties. The system affords
no room for that type of selected and trained permanent
administrative official which is represented by the Administrative Class. "The Edinburgh Boards," we were told, "take the
place of the Higher Division in London offices." In our belief,
however, this arrangement is not satisfactory; and we recommend that the Scottish Departments be no longer deprived of

the advantages which would come from employing officers of the Administrative Class . . .

We therefore recommend that Your Majesty's Government should take such steps as may be necessary to substitute the organisation which prevails in the Scottish Office for the Board system as the normal form of organisation in the Edinburgh Departments.'

The MacDonnell Commission's contention was that with top appointments awarded to 'establishment' figures in Scotland as a sort of perquisite to politicians or members of the Faculty of Advocates, the Boards were backwaters of administration. But, then in cosy Edinburgh everything, though not exactly provincial, *was* rather small scale. To be frivolous for a moment: should the heavens have opened on the day of a Royal Garden Party at Holyroodhouse and the great event be cancelled, a Lion flag was hoisted at the Nelson Monument: everyone who was anyone in Edwardian Edinburgh lived within eyeshot of the Calton Hill!

The system of independent boards had been general throughout Great Britain in the nineteenth century, but now survived only in Scotland. The English Local Government Board was now virtually a government department with its political head in parliament. There was however something of the fashion of the moment in the MacDonnell Commission's praise of the generalist administrators of the higher civil service. (In the same way half a century on, there was something of mere fashion in the undervaluing of the generalist in the Report of the Committee on the Civil Service of 1969.) Patronage in Victorian administration could mean good appointments. The truly able man could be placed in a position of influence without a long and daunting climb by the ladder of seniority. Debilitating adherence to the practice of 'Buggins' turn' in promotions to top posts could be avoided. Lord Polwarth, Chairman of the Scottish Prison Commissioners, typified the virtues of the system; he had been given the post after distinguished work against slavery in Africa, and was a truly enlightened administrator. What then was so wrong with the boards? Edinburgh was mystified by the Royal Commission's outright condemnation.

It was Sir George McCrae's Local Government Board which Lord MacDonnell's Commission had in its sights. They rightly sensed its inadequacy: we for our part can see it all too clearly when we consider the Board's inaction over the often deplorable and generally worsening state of Scottish working-class housing in the years before 1914. This is an episode of Scottish history which was to have both a profound effect on the shape of Scottish administration and a malign and enduring consequence for our social history. For these reasons we must now look more closely at the Board's record, and first reach back briefly to the years of its predecessor, the Poor Law Board of Supervision.

Had he been brave enough to attempt the steep slope of the Advocate's Close to the historic High Street of Edinburgh, the visitor to Edinburgh of a hundred years ago would have had difficulty in discerning in the squalor all around the erstwhile handsome capital of the Enlightenment. There was a similar heart of dereliction in historic Glasgow, now bearing little resemblance to Daniel Defoe's 'cleanest and beautifullest and best built city in Britain': the descendants of Bailie Nicol Jarvie had long since quitted the Saltmarket. As the nineteenth century had advanced, round this putrescent centre a great rash of building had been thrown up to house the scores of thousands of incomers from rural Scotland, the Highlands and Ireland. Much of it was in tenements, not as tall as the Edinburgh lands but, like them, one family to a room—the whole business of family living and dying in one room. It was much the same story in all the manufacturing towns of Scotland; Dundee with the rapid growth of its jute mills was perhaps the worst. A third of all families in that city lived in single ends, and when the city's social conscience began to stir, it was seen that in these families two children out of every five died in infancy.

Yet in Edinburgh of the 1860s and 1870s the City Improvement Trust, a sort of improvement committee of the Town Council, had had great swathes cut through the old town, in this assault on Jacobean Edinburgh sweeping away three thousand houses of the poor. But it did not seek to replace them—that was seen as a task for private enterprise. In Glasgow, perennially inclined as it was—as it is—to be rather more ambitious in its civic projects, the Improvement Trust which came into being in 1870 likewise set to the demolition of much of her historic past, displacing some thirty thousand people. But when the Trust proposed rating for replacement housing this was successfully resisted by the Glasgow ratepayers. Glasgow had put its hand in its pocket to finance the brilliant achievement of piped water to the city all the way from the highland hills, and it would lead the world in the creation of public parks and in civic transport; the rehousing of the poor was another matter. In Kelvinside, as in Morningside, the general view does seem to have been that the poor positively preferred the single end as a way of life.

The year in which Dover House became the Scottish Office saw the Scottish Report of the Royal Commission on Housing of the Working Classes which was chaired by the radical Sir Charles Dilke. The tone of this report of 1885 was bland, as was the evidence given to it by the chairman of the Board of Supervision.

As to urban housing, 'we have,' he said with surprising complacency 'no great anxiety about the large towns'; and he went on
to tell Dilke and his colleagues that it really was as much the
inability of the workman to appreciate the comforts of a better
dwelling as any inability to pay more rent which was the root of
the problem. 'Much evidence', the Royal Commission reported,
'was given by witnesses from large towns to the effect that a
considerable proportion of the labouring classes in Scotland would
be able to house themselves in far greater comfort if it were not for
the large sums they spend on drink . . . many of them might live
in better houses if they kept more sober.'

The Royal Commission took note that the great urban clear-
ances of the Scottish cities were of little benefit to the poor, only
'the more respectable artizans' finding new and better houses. But,
as the report went on to say, it was Scottish opinion itself that had
warned them off the obvious remedy of local authority rehousing—the remedy which the Disraeli government had put on the
Statute Book in 1876 for such town councils throughout Great
Britain as cared to use it.

> 'In all Scotch towns there seems to be a general feeling that there
> is no obligation to re-house people turned out. The Legal
> Secretary★ to the Lord Advocate said that "he had never heard
> of inconvenience from that cause". The Clerk to the Edinburgh
> City Improvement Trust went further and said that "Sir
> Richard Cross's Act [the 1876 Act] is very heavily handicapped
> by the provision that artizans' dwellings must be provided upon
> the areas operated upon: I think it is most amply done by private
> enterprise." The President of the Edinburgh Trades Council,
> speaking on behalf of the working classes, strongly opposed the
> town council in any sense becoming responsible for the housing
> of the people.'

Similar views prevailed in Glasgow.

> 'The opinion of Bailie Morison on the subject is that the
> functions of a corporation are of destruction of bad property,
> not of reconstruction, unless it can be done in the way of
> purchasing land in large quantities and retailing it to private
> builders, preserving open spaces, making sanitary improve-
> ments, and letting the land under restrictions.'

Despite all this—and the somewhat surprising views of the
President of the Edinburgh Trades Council, 'speaking on behalf of
the working classes'—the Royal Commission members were

★This was Mr Donald Crawford who in the July of that year was to enter into a
divorce action against his young wife, citing Dilke as co-respondent. This murky
episode with its possibly political overtones is studied in Roy Jenkins' biography of
Dilke.

unhappy as they came to a conclusion. They recognised 'the
pressure on already overcrowded space, in consequence of demoli-
tions . . . seeing that whenever operations on a large scale have
taken place accommodation had been provided for only a very
small proportion of the number displaced, and frequently the new
accommodation has not been of a character to suit the very poor
who previously inhabited the locality'. But, this said, Dilke and his
colleagues washed their hands of the matter. Subsequent legislation
of 1890 for Scotland as for England reiterated that local authorities
might assume power to rehouse the displaced poor if they chose to
do so. But none did so, despite the exasperated advocacy of some
medical officers of health who saw all too clearly that even if the
poor did prefer the single-end, so did the tuberculosis bacillus.

Legislation for the Scottish burghs of 1892 contained power to
town councils to banish in town tenements the abomination of the
dry closet, and further legislation in 1903 dealt with the introduction of building byelaws. During the years around the turn of the
century, unceasing efforts by medical officers of health did indeed
ensure that landlords equipped much of the better working class
housing with water supply and improved sanitation. But there was
no clamour by local government for grants from central government for council housing. There were no representations from the
Local Government Board to Dover House. Nor was there any
move by the Scottish Office to involve itself. In 1909 the Liberal
Government brought in for all Britain legislation which at last
required local authorities to assume power to build working class
housing, rate financed. The Secretary of State was quick to
delegate oversight of this to the Local Government Board in
Edinburgh and to leave it at that. For their part, Scottish local
authorities changed their stance not a whit.

Not that there was any lack of public discussion of 'the housing
problem'. Rosebery had spoken on the issue, linking it to the
advancement of Britain's imperial dream. In Glasgow, a Mr
William Burrell as chairman of the Health Sub-Committee of the
Corporation had been much concerned with it before he turned
back to art collecting. And, indeed, how could it be ignored when
some of the vilest slums in Scotland were almost a hundred yards
(or less) distant from Lorimer's glorious new Thistle Chapel at St
Giles, opened with fitting ceremony in 1909? It was simply that
public debate still largely saw the issue as one which abstention
from strong drink on the part of the working classes could solve. If
there was a legislative remedy—so ran the thoughts of many—it
lay in the Temperance (Scotland) Act of these years which sought
local prohibition of the sale of liquor if communities wished it so.
The poor lived in slums and they always would. Even where the
assumed fecklessness of the poor could not be made the scapegoat,
government seemed paralysed; as in 1909, when the Local Govern-

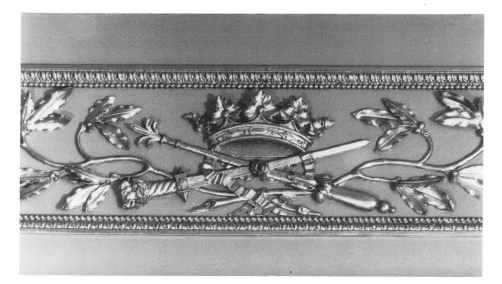

Detail above a doorway at Dover House
The Duke of York's coronet: the crossed sword and
baton show his military rank (for this was 'The
Grand Old Duke of York who had ten thousand
men . . .')

ment Board could do nothing to persuade the Lewis District
Committee of Ross and Cromarty County Council to tackle the
hovels of black houses that disfigured the island. The local
authority said that they were at their rating limit; it was not for the
Board in Edinburgh to amend this; that was for Dover House, and
Dover House did not move. There the matter rested.

From Lady Pentland's memoir of her husband, it seems that
when it came the belated Scottish Office initiative over the nation's
housing was almost fortuitous. In 1909 Lord Pentland had con-
sented to receive a deputation from the Scottish Miners Federation
about the squalor of so many of the miners' rows owned by the
colliery companies of Lanarkshire, Ayrshire and Fife. Her husband, Lady Pentland tells us, had always had a soft spot for the
Scottish miner: and so he moved the Local Government Board in
Edinburgh to institute a study of miners' housing, the Board in
turn calling on county medical officers of health to make enquiries.
Their reports to the Board were eloquent of the general squalor,
but no action had been taken two years later when a further
deputation from the Scottish Miners Federation was received, nor
by the end of 1911 when there was a further one from the
members of parliament for the mining constituencies. The following October, Lord Pentland having now been summarily moved
to the governor-generalship of Madras, his successor, MacKinnon
Wood, an abrasively effective politician, had a Royal Commission

appointed to report on all working class housing in Scotland. Now at last it was beginning to be recognised that private enterprise could not build houses with the space which decency required and with the water supply and sanitation which medical officers of health demanded—that is, could not build at rents which the lowest paid could afford. For the private builder this was no doubt deterrent enough, but there was also the abiding disincentive that in Scotland, unlike England, the rates burden bore on the owner as well as the occupier. The former would seek to pass it on to the latter by way of increased rent, but he could not be sure that it would be possible for him to do so, particularly, when, as then, municipal expenditure was on the increase, and so, consequently, was the rates burden. Lastly, there were the disinclination of working class Scotland to give as much priority in household budgets as their English counterparts to rent, and the disinclination of the Scottish builder to build in brick. (England had 'Coronation Streets' by the thousand to take the edge off her lesser housing problem: Scotland had none.)

It took the Great War to force recognition that a socially disastrous, indeed potentially revolutionary, situation had been brought about by neglect of housing. That the Royal Commission, after being suspended on the outbreak of war, should have been reactivated as the conflict dragged on was in itself indicative of the new mood of the nation. To read the impassioned paragraphs of the Royal Commission's historic majority report as it finally appeared in 1917 is to be sharply aware of the background: the swathes of Cameron dead at Loos or of Royal Scots on the Somme.* The mood was now so clearly a determination that *something* good must come out of all this. So it was that the opening paragraphs of the majority report voiced sentiments little heard in Edwardian, unknown to Victorian, Scotland.

> 'The housing ideal which we keep prominently before us is—How to provide a healthy and comfortable dwelling for every family in the land.'

And again

> 'The conscience of the nation has been awakened in regard to this and many other social problems. We believe that the nation will never again tolerate the apathy which has obtained hitherto in regard to the conditions of life of a great part of the population of the British Islands . . . We have come to the conclusion that a wide and sweeping change is required in the provision of houses, and have framed our policy and recommendations accordingly.'

*Including their 16th battalion, raised and commanded by Sir George McCrae, which lost half its strength on the first day of the battle. Sir George was awarded the DSO for rallying the remnants.

That a change in the nation's attitude to the housing of the masses was indeed taking place is corroborated by the words with which Balfour of Burleigh, called out of retirement by MacKinnon Wood in 1915 to chair the enquiry into industrial unrest in shipyards on Clydeside, had accompanied his report. In common with so many, the war had struck cruelly at Balfour of Burleigh; he had lost his son, the Master of Burleigh, with the Argylls at Mons the previous year. Now 'B of B' said bluntly that the nation which had failed to give the Clydeside workman decent housing for his family had no right to expect other than poor labour relations, and addiction to drink and red revolution. It was indeed a sentiment all but unthinkable while he had been Secretary for Scotland.

Embodied in a massive document of over three hundred thousand words, the recommendations of the Report of the Royal Commission on Scottish Housing of 1917 covered every aspect of house building and improvement in city, burgh, landward lowlands and crofting highlands; and it demanded a break with the past. The state should explicitly accept a direct responsibility for the housing of the Scottish working classes. To meet this responsibility there should be placed on local authorities by central government a definite obligation to provide a sufficiency of houses.

Accompanying the passionate recommendations of the majority was a good deal of firmly worded dissent by five members led by Lord Lovat in intervals snatched from army service (for, like Sir George McCrae he too had raised his own body of men for the colours). The report by the minority he led was comprehensive in its dislike of the majority's proposals. Sixty-five years on, the minority's counter-arguments still have force.

While the need for extensive rehousing of the working classes was accepted, the minority argued that much too large and novel a responsibility would be thrown on town and country councils were they to become the agents of house building. The indirect effect, they contended, would be to devitalise private enterprise building, with dire consequences in the long run for Scottish housing generally. Unlimited municipal housing they said, would also in time mean that there would be towns and urbanised counties where most householders were local authority tenants— and, they said, think what that could bring! Government should confine itself to subsidising the private enterprise builder directly to the extent of the rise in interest rates since 1914 and the higher building costs which the scarcities of war-time had brought. In any event, the minority concluded, the housebuilding effort should be concentrated on 'moving-up', ie that everything should be done 'to promote in open suburban surroundings the provision of dwellings for the better paid artisan, so that the houses vacated by this class may become available for those poorer tenants who may lose their dwellings through closing orders or improvement schemes'.

In the appetite for change of the later war years and the resolve to build 'houses for heroes' the majority's views quickly became the basis for a government financed housing policy. The Housing (Scotland) Act of 1919 was to commit the Scottish Secretary, as it did the burgh and county councils of Scotland, to a new, interventionist course; and from now on, year in, year out, local authority house-building would be a major concern of central government in Scotland.

But there was now a leeway in housing which could not be made up. And as central and local government sought to catch up, all would have to be done in a great hurry. There would be no gradual build-up of experience in design for working-class housing. If only in these pre-war years it had been possible to enlist the genius of Charles Rennie Mackintosh in fashioning new styles and imaginative layout of Scottish working-class housing which would also look well to the eye!

The majority's report had one final recommendation.

'We consider that the Local Government Board, as central authority for public health and housing, should be formed into a substantive department of the same status as the Scotch Education Department . . .'

For the task now to be done, they found the Board operating on its own to be not enough. The Scottish Office was nominally responsible to Parliament for the Local Government Board, as it was for all the Edinburgh Boards, but actual responsibility in central government resided much more in matters of expenditure and staffing with the Scottish Office's Whitehall neighbour, the Treasury. That department was still advised with great frankness and total confidence about the Boards by its 'man in Edinburgh', the King's and Lord Treasurer's Remembrancer. (For example, it was the Treasury, not Dover House, who, had they cared, would have been alerted by K & LTR in 1914 to the implications of Sir George McCrae's new-found military role, and that his management of affairs—at a time when there must have been much to do—was limited to what could be achieved by his 'rush into the LG Bd about every other day for the matter of five or ten minutes, but no more'.) And so responsibility was dangerously diffused. Some awareness of performance is the necessary feedstock of the strategic overview. While the latter was supposed to reside with the Scottish Office, the former lay with the Treasury. Would it be 1980s insolence to suggest that any one of today's bright young management consultants would have quickly recognised what was wrong?

The Slim Balfour and the Burleigh Balfour

'The Slim Balfour and the Burleigh Balfour'.
Cartoon of about 1900 of A J Balfour and Lord
Balfour of Burleigh. (Reproduced in 'Lord Balfour of
Burleigh' by Lady Frances Balfour.)

In areas of fairly settled administration where change through
politics was not called for, the Edinburgh board system could, no
doubt, serve well enough. But, for housing, change *via* Westminster alone would suffice—and here the board system as it was
operated seems to have had the effect of obscuring the problems
from the politicians and distancing those grappling with the
problems from the political solutions so desperately needed. And
yet this distancing of the politicians from the problem should not
have happened; the appointment of a political figure in Sir George
McCrae to lead the Board should have ensured that there was a
link with Westminster. So one comes back to the blinkered view
taken by most Scots in Edwardian Scotland of the housing
problem. As soon as the legislation of 1909 was in the Statute
Book, the English Local Government Board had been quick to
prod their local authorities about the necessity of their using the
reaffirmed powers in the 1909 act about municipal house-building;
and indeed some there was, notably in London, Sheffield and
Liverpool. With a housing problem so much worse than that south
of the border, was the Scottish Board supine? It seems so, but
judgement must await more research.

Neither the closing recommendations of this great report of the
Royal Commission on Housing nor the denunciation of the board
system in the Report of the Royal Commission on the Civil
Service which Lord MacDonnell chaired succeeded in ending the

independent life of the Scottish Local Government Board. This is the more surprising in that the powerful voice of Lord Haldane was also raised against the Scottish Boards in the magisterial review of government departments which he carried out for the the Ministry of Reconstruction in 1918.

Yet some change there was to the Board. As further floors to its edifice there were added the functions of the National Health Insurance Commissioners in Scotland who also supervised the Lloyd Georgian old age pensions; since their inception in 1911 there had been separate Scottish administration for this, probably in anticipation of the expected measure of 'Home Rule' for Scotland as well as Ireland. There was also added the Highlands and Islands Medical Service; and this was a truly enlightened reform accompanying the introduction of National Health Insurance in 1912. The still impoverished crofting population of the north and west did not fit into the concept of health insurance for the employee; and so the Government financing of a general practitioner service in the highlands and islands was proposed. (The committee of enquiry which made this proposal was a Treasury, not a Scottish Office committee; one would so much wish to know what hand Dover House had in its creation.) These additions made, in 1919 the Board was renamed the Scottish Board of Health. At Dover House a new parliamentary under-secretary post was created to oversee its work.

The Local Government Board's report for 1919 was something of a valediction; and it allowed itself a little reflection on the changes in attitudes over the years. It owned up to having relaxed the former rigidity in poor law administration. For the Board had reached the commonsense conclusion that if you are able-bodied but starving, you will not long remain healthy; and Poor Law administration was now belatedly based on this commendable assumption. It was also in contradiction of some Victorian attitudes that the Report should add 'we recognise that what is wrong with the poor is their poverty . . .'

This final report of the Local Government Board looked back on what had been achieved generally in the domain of public health, particularly since the major public health legislation of 1897 had stirred local authorities into action. It noted with satisfaction the increase in the number of hospitals for infectious disease, as much a rural as an urban necessity as revealed by some gruesome vignettes in the Board's earlier reports. As to housing, the Board conceded that the recent report of the Royal Commission 'had revealed an appalling shortage of working-class housing in Scotland, and made manifest the urgent duty of the State to step in where private enterprise had stopped, and to carry out an extensive programme of rehousing the people of Scotland.' For the Board was it something of a death-bed repentance?

III

BETWEEN THE WARS

ONE EVENING in 1922, Robert Munro, Liberal member of parliament for that Scottish anachronism 'the northern burghs', former Lord Advocate and now for the past six years Secretary for Scotland, spoke with satisfaction to an Edinburgh audience on the state of Scottish administration.

His views would find ready acceptance particularly since the achievements of the Scottish Education Department, as it had now renamed itself, were widely praised south as well as north of the border.

The coping stone of the educational arch had been the legislation of 1918 which replaced the nine hundred or more parish education boards and county committees for secondary education with comprehensive education authorities, one for the entire school population, burghal as well as landward, within each county, and one for each of the four Scottish cities. Munro was justifiably proud of this achievement, although, to secure the passage of the Bill he had had to pull back from the full integration of education with the rest of local government; the concentration of fire from entrenched interests was still too strong. Nor was the demise of the parish education board everywhere applauded. At the burgh of Kirkintilloch near Glasgow, Tom Johnston, a town councillor in his thirties making his name in socialist journalism and in diatribe against the landed gentry took a jaundiced view of the new regime—and to the end of his days was to feel (perhaps unjustifiably) that an experiment in local democracy had been strangled.

'In the old School Board days the teaching profession—at least its more vocal and clamorous elements—continually demanded wider administrative areas in education. . . . They said they had all the experience of democratic control they could suffer. . . . But when the teachers got their County Area Education

Authorities they were speedily disillusioned, the remote controllers showing no more (if as much) concern for the status and remuneration of teaching than the local and proximate councillors had done. But there was a substantial increase in the administrative payroll.'

Like the School Boards they supplanted, the new education authorities were elected bodies; and to safeguard minority interests election to them was by proportional representation. Of these minority interests the one clamouring for attention was the Roman Catholic community from which came one child in every seven of school age—and how much higher the proportion must have been in the industrial west where that community was largely concentrated. Here—as in housing—it was possible to effect change which would have been anathema to many in pre-war years; and so the generally impoverished Roman Catholic schools were brought within the national education system, and the inequity of catholic ratepayers supporting schools they could not use was ended. As his nephew recalls, it was Munro, though son of a Free Church manse and reared in a sectarian atmosphere, who personally forced through this change, and took pride in so doing. The school-leaving age was also to be raised, and in the new era of hope and opportunity there was to be compulsory part-time education at least up to the age of eighteen for all. Here was the vision of Sir John Struthers at work. That dominant personality, 'with a certain brusqueness of manner' as Munro was later to recall, had consistently had these ends in view as he worked in his spacious ground floor room at Dover House, its walls decorated in the high Louis Seize style fashionable in the 1790s, ducal coronets in gold over the doors. The influence of the highland born Secretary for Scotland may also be detected in the removal of another wrong of too long standing. The Act required the new education authorities to make provision for the teaching of Gaelic. Sadly it had been no part of the vision of the fiercely energetic administrators of the Scotch Education Department to save the Gaelic language in those earlier decades when it could still have been possible to do so.

For the department itself, the consequences of the 1918 Act were to be a great deal more than the replacement of 'Scotch' by 'Scottish'. When it had close to a thousand parish education boards to lead into the light, the Department and its spokesmen of the Inspectorate had necessarily taken on an authoritarian style. Now, there were to be professional Directors of Education in each of the new county and city authorities: something less forceful, more persuasive, was needed. But the change was to be slow in coming. Sir George MacDonald who succeeded Struthers in 1922 was another strong administrator; a stern one as well, as is caught by his portrait now in an Edinburgh gallery. But MacDonald made an

The Calton Prison (on the site which has been
occupied since 1939 by Old St Andrew's House).
The view from the playground of the former Royal
High School of Edinburgh. (Courtesy of *The
Scotsman*.)

outstandingly practical contribution to Scottish administration—
just as he did for his private passion, Roman antiquities, by tracing
the line of the Antonine Wall—in that it was he who moved the
effective headquarters of the department from London to Edinburgh.

That evening in Edinburgh, Munro also spoke of the Scottish
Boards, so let us consider how they then stood.

Across from the offices of the Scottish Education Department
the *Board of Agriculture* was now established at Edinburgh's
Queen Street. The name of the office was York Buildings,
something of Empire France in its lines. It had been built as
stock-brokers' offices with tobacconists' shops and such-like under
the archways of its frontage. For the Board the cause of land
settlement had for the moment found a new impetus—as a means
of rewarding soldiers back from the war who wanted to become
dairy-farmers in a smallish way. It was also meeting difficulties.
Lord Pentland, languishing in his Indian governorship, might still
be revered within the Scottish Liberal Club for his land settlement

legislation. It was otherwise amongst the country gentry in the New Club, a few doors along Princes Street. The land settlement schemes hatched by the Board and its newly recruited corps of 'lands officers' were leading to endless wrangling and expensive arbitrations, as landowners generally persuaded themselves that the new Scottish Land Court would not give them a fair price for land taken. Sir Kenneth MacKenzie of Gairloch, the King's and Lord Treasurer's Remembrancer, as the Treasury's man in Edinburgh from 1900 to 1921 had also kept up an effective sniping fire. All the top jobs in the Board had gone to 'politicians and members of the United Free church',★ he informed his masters. Extravagance, he continued, ranged from big matters ('The Board just goes on spending regardless of estimates or money at its disposal') to lesser ones ('What I have constantly objected to is the provision of a limousine in which the members of the Board can joyride round their experimental farms and small colonies'). Sometimes he was merely silly in his criticism of the Board. A school had been established to train island girls for domestic service, and Treasury approval had been sought to its taking on a gym teacher. 'I never look for gymnastic skill when employing scullery maids', growled Sir Kenneth.

However, with a Liberal Secretary for Scotland in office, the barbs of the King's and Lord Treasurer's Remembrancer could not halt land settlement. Where, it seems from the records, his influence may have been felt was in the government decision of 1919 that forestry in Scotland should cease to be within the scope of the Board of Agriculture and instead be placed with a Forestry Commission for Great Britain over which, regrettably, the Scottish Secretary would for the next twenty-five years have no influence. Munro and the Scottish Office fought hard against this creation of an independent Forestry Commission, but Lord Lovat was an increasingly effective spokesman for it, and was, indeed, to become its first chairman. This divorce of forestry from agriculture might, perhaps, not have taken place had the Board of Agriculture, as Lovat had proposed, blended afforestation with crofting agriculture in the highlands.

Since the Board had been taking such stick, let us pause to look more closely at the events of these days which brought it into the headlines, those of the London 'Times' as well as of the 'Stornoway Gazette'. This was its celebrated conflict with the Lancashire millionaire Lord Leverhulme. Moved by his own personal vision of the Hebridean future which would have a big local fishing fleet and extensive island fish processing factories, Leverhulme had taken all Lewis and Harris under his wing; and he had an

---

★A minute by one of these stalwarts commenting on an applicant for a small-holding was long remembered. It ran 'Wee Free. T.T. A good man—and so is his wife'.

instinctive distaste for the crofting agriculture which the Board and the Secretary for Scotland wished to reinforce in the Outer Hebrides as elsewhere. When some Lewis ex-servicemen, taking the law into their own hands, carved small-holdings for themselves out of island farms which Leverhulme now owned, the latter made progress with his fishery and other schemes for Lewis dependent on the Secretary for Scotland turning against the land raiders. In writing in the 1950s his history of the clash that followed, Nigel Nicolson was given access to the Scottish Office and Board of Agriculture papers of the time. As Nicolson brought out, Leverhulme was unnecessarily a prisoner of his own prejudices against crofting, while Munro, as Scottish Secretary, was constrained by the prevailing enthusiasm throughout all Liberal Scotland for land settlement. Sir Kenneth MacKenzie's fairer-minded successor as the Treasury man in Edinburgh reported that the authorities were indeed 'in a blue funk' about the land raiding which would surely follow failure to create small-holdings. 'All up the west coast', he reported, 'where the population went to the war to a man the people are relying on the Government's promise that land would be provided for them on their return.' Even so, as Nicolson recognised, in deference to Leverhulme's views Munro did hold his hand over the breaking up of the few large farms on Lewis to which 'Lord Soapsuds' (as he was derisively known to his critics) objected. But it was to no purpose. A dip in the commercial fortunes of Lever Bros. caused Leverhulme to delay his plans, and in the delay the land settlement squabble broke out anew.

As we in the Scottish Office of the 1950s looked through these old papers in the wake of Nicolson's researches, the testy missives from the Lancashire millionaire, the emollient replies from the Scottish Secretary, there *seemed* nothing for us to regret in that, as we can now see, disturbed trading and changed tastes were soon disastrously to weaken the market for Minch herring—Leverhulme or no Leverhulme. Yet a haunting doubt remains. Leverhulme's hopes for a large scale exclusively *herring* fishery Stornoway-based would probably have proved illusory in any event. But under the continuing tutelage of Lever Bros., had that been secured, the Isle of Lewis (like scores of islands along the Norwegian coast) might have learned the sooner to adapt to modern fishing. It was to succeed in so doing in the 1960s in response to initiatives from the Scottish Office and the Highlands and Islands Development Board, but by then forty years had been wasted.

But that is speculation. Neither the Scottish Office at Dover House nor the newly fledged Board of Agriculture was equipped to evaluate ambitious highland development schemes. A family bereavement prevented the Secretary for Scotland from visiting Stornoway when he was set to do this. And so Munro, throughout the worst of the conflict, did not visit the islands and could not test for himself Lewis opinion, could not find out at first hand if it indeed was the case (as was asserted afterwards, though insufficiently so at the time) that opinion on the island was all for Leverhulme and against the land raiders. Neither, incidentally, was Dr Murray, the member of parliament for the Western Isles, able to help adjudge the reality of local opinion, whatever that was; and this for the contemporary reason that in these days members of parliament had to meet their own travel costs to and from their constituencies—and Murray was not a rich man.

In the working of the Board, fervour for land settlement dominated all else. Munro told his Edinburgh audience that he saw the three Scottish agricultural colleges founded before the war as ancillary to the establishment of small-holdings: the colleges would teach the small-holder how to farm. But the colleges themselves had a somewhat wider vision of the future of agriculture, as had the three agricultural research stations established in this decade by local farming enterprise and by the help of government money channelled through the Board. Pre-eminent of these was the Rowett Research Institute at Aberdeen which was to win fame (and is currently earning new renown for its work in nutritional research).

Looking across the garden valley to Edinburgh Castle from their offices at 121 Princes Street—which the King's and Lord Treasurer's Remembrancer had sourly reported to be too grandiose—there reigned *the Scottish Board of Health,* successor since 1919 to the Local Government Board for Scotland, with a staff of close to four hundred. The members of the Local Government Board, including their Vice-President now returned from France, had been continued in office in the new Health Board, though Sir George McCrae was to retire in 1922.★ Every Thursday evening of the session at Westminster saw the parliamentary under-secretary for Health making his way from Dover House to King's Cross for the night sleeper to Waverley so that he might chair the Friday meeting of the Board. The roll call of the Board of Health's concerns was impressive. It had now been given responsibility for the schemes of health insurance for working people under the legislation of 1911 and for the administration of old age pensions. The introduction of old age pensions had eased poverty for many, but poor law administration remained. A new, more determined stage in the war against the national scourge of tuberculosis was now beginning, as against other infectious disease. The Board was also dedicated to the improvement of hospital services, still under the control of local authorities or voluntary bodies; and of maternity services. Legislation for these last dated from the middle

---

★ Sir George thereupon returned to Liberal politics and Parliament. He died in 1928.

of the war, and was another aspect of the social progress the national tragedy accelerated; the carnage in Flanders, it was said, had pricked consciences about the appalling infant mortality nearer home. The Board's concern extended to child welfare and school health administration. But central to it all was housing: everything depended on progress in this crucial sector, as the Board now conceded.

The Prisons Board, still under Lord Polwarth's distinguished chairmanship, kept up its movement away from the Victorian concepts of penal servitude—silence, hard labour, and bare conditions. The imitation gothic establishment on the Calton Hill was now closing its ponderous doors (a little local difficulty having been surmounted in rebutting the claims of Edinburgh's Town Clerk as to the ownership of this valuable site). The new Edinburgh prison, a building beyond the city's western outskirts, reflected more enlightened concepts: it was, indeed, the first twentieth century prison built in Great Britain. *The Scottish Fishery Board* was now back to normal; its flotilla of fishery cruisers had returned from war service, and its Secretary had given up the unauthorised wearing of the uniform of a Royal Navy Paymaster-Lieutenant which had so incensed K & LTR; but it was viewing with dismay the collapse in the herring industry's prosperity with the non-revival of so many of the pre-war export markets. *The General Board of Control* for the supervision of the mentally ill and handicapped; *the Registrar General's Office* and *the Scottish Record Office,* both still under the Deputy Clerk Register; and *the Board of Trustees* which Lord Pentland had established for those glories of Edinburgh, the National Galleries of Scotland; these made up the remainder of this 1920s version of control in Scotland of Scottish affairs.

At Dover House, its modest numbers working closely with the Secretary for Scotland, the Scottish Office was emerging from a period of acute concern at industrial trouble on Clydeside. The troubles at Fairfield's in 1915 had been followed by more general unrest during the war. Whitehall had looked with apprehension at the unrest on the Clyde, and had no great confidence in the ability of the Scottish Office to cope (if we may judge by the memoirs of Lord Addison, then parliamentary under-secretary at the Ministry of Munitions). Equally alarming had been the rioting in Glasgow that followed the end of the war. On this the War Cabinet minutes of 1919 record that somewhat excitedly:

> The Secretary for Scotland said that, in his opinion, it was more clear than ever that it was a misnomer to call the situation in Glasgow a strike—it was a 'Bolshevist rising'.

The Scottish Office was also now coming in for disquieting criticism over the case of Oscar Slater, convicted for murder at

Glasgow in 1909 on shaky evidence. Solely on account of this, for the murder had been brutal, Lord Pentland had commuted the sentence to life imprisonment. Slater went to Peterhead Jail; but outrage at his sentence still boiled up, particularly in the London newspapers, despite a half-hearted enquiry by the Sheriff of Lanarkshire which Pentland's successor had commissioned in 1914. Basically, what was wrong was the lack of a criminal appeal court in the Scottish judicial system; and the significance of the case of Oscar Slater in our legal history was to be that it would soon play its part in the making good of that huge defect.

To a modest extent Dover House officials linked up with the Edinburgh Boards, except for the Board of Health where the Parliamentary Secretary chaired weekly meetings. With land settlement raising so many hackles, the Board of Agriculture had been required to communicate with the Secretary for Scotland on policy matters through the Scottish Office (and this had been the reason for Munro's personal involvement in the Leverhulme episode). But, generally, the Boards remained answerable directly to the Treasury for their moneys and staffing; and since the Treasury still relied on the King's and Lord Treasurer's Remembrancer rather than on Dover House for advice on the Boards, the Scottish Office still did not become involved in their day to day affairs.

So—did the Secretary for Scotland really feel the complacent satisfaction he voiced to the Royal Philosophical Society of Edinburgh that evening of 1922 about the role of his office? Perhaps not altogether so. He had, as we have seen, lost the important Cabinet battle about control of the Forestry Commission. He had also now seen responsibility for roads and transport centralised in London with the new Ministry of Transport. He was acutely aware that the Scottish Secretary lacked status, for all that his powers, duties and staff had increased so very much since 1885. The convention that the Secretary for Scotland was indeed 'Scotland's Minister' with a voice to be heard on all Scottish matters, in whatever department of government they might reside was now accepted; and, thanks to the influence and perhaps the Scottish sympathies of Bonar Law at the Prime Minister's right hand, the creation of an inner war cabinet in 1916 did not wholly shut out the Scottish Secretary. However Munro, rightly, saw that nothing less than elevation of the post to the dignity of 'one of His Majesty's Principal Secretaries of State' would do. In 1921 Birkenhead speaking in the Lords had committed the Government to make this change; but in 1922 hope was still deferred.

In these years of the early 1920s the strictures on the Scottish Boards of the Royal Commission on the Civil Service of 1914 had merely been ignored; they had not been defused. Viscount Haldane's influential report of 1918 on the organisation of Government had endorsed them. By the later 1920s Sir John Gilmour, Secretary of State for Scotland—the long deferred upgrading having at last been effected in 1926—was convinced that the Boards had had their day. No doubt the Treasury, with their overall concern with the machinery of government, prompted him to this view.

So it was that in 1927 Gilmour presented his Reorganisation of Offices (Scotland) Bill to transform the Scottish Boards of Health, Agriculture and Prisons into three departments, answerable to him and, broadly similar to the Scottish Education Department. There was to be an end to patronage, and, in its place recruitment of university-trained men from the First Division of the Civil Service. But the Bill ran into difficulties, and when it became clear that it would not go through 'on the nod'—to use Westminster parlance—it was withdrawn for reintroduction the following year. The barrage of criticism that descended on the Bill when it was debated on the floor of the House came from the Opposition led by Tom Johnston and, less nimbly, by that sturdy erstwhile miner, William Adamson; but it was also reinforced by a very able Conservative dissentient in Noel Skelton who within a few years was to be a junior minister at the Scottish Office.★ Dissent ran thus. The Boards *are* efficient, and, in particular there is a world of difference between the workings of the Scottish Board of Health and those of its predecessor. Surely it is better to have a *Board* view of business, so often technical and involved as it is, rather than the attempted distillation of controversy by the senior civil servant sitting in isolation a-top each departmental pyramid? For all his Oxford education (no doubt in classics) he would in all probability know little about health, agriculture etc, etc. He might even be English! Given the wide range of responsibilities on the Secretary of State's shoulders, much wider than that of any of his colleagues at Westminster, it is essential that advice proffered him comes from men who really know what they are talking about. The Board system is the best means of ensuring that. Lastly, here is a means of keeping in Scotland the effective control of Scottish affairs and satisfying the national aspiration. To transmogrify the Boards into departments will be to subjugate them to Whitehall!

In debate, the Secretary of State and the Lord Advocate reminded the House of the emphatic recommendations of the MacDonnell Report of 1914. Gilmour stoutly maintained that the opponents of the Bill had misrepresented its purpose and were all at sea in their predictions. There are, he said, many Scots in the

★His father had been Secretary of the Board of Supervision from 1868 to 1892 and chairman of this and then vice-president of the Local Government Board until 1897.

Higher Civil Service in Whitehall who would be happy to have an opportunity of serving their native land. For the Liberals, Sir Archibald Sinclair supported the Bill, but this, he said, was because the Board of Agriculture was not proving sufficiently competent in pushing on with land settlement. However Tom Johnston and his colleagues on the Labour benches were not persuaded. James Maxton—as you read the Hansard record, you can picture his eager face and flowing hair—pleaded for a free vote of Scottish members. But the government whips saw the Bill through.

Thus a new style Scottish administration was welded into being. Had the post of Scottish Secretary not been upgraded in 1926, then in Whitehall as at Westminster where status matters so much, it would have lacked the persuasive force it was to need in stormy days to come. For example, had the post still lacked higher status, Walter Elliot would not have moved to it from the Ministry of Agriculture in the mid 1930s; and that would have been a grave loss. Equally, this transformation of boards into departments in 1928 was effected just in time. The range of government activity in so many areas of national life, social as well as economic, was to widen fast in the next two decades. Had the Secretary of State's domain not been organised in a way which was 'compatible'—to use the word in its computery sense—with the rest of government it would assuredly have missed out.

To look back over the 1920s, it can be said that in these years the Scottish Office, as it were, came of age. With the upgrading of the *castellan* of Dover House to the dignity of 'one of His Majesty's Principal Secretaries of State', with the transformation of the three principal Edinburgh boards into departments of government, the Scottish Office was now set for what was to become its historic role—to be spokesman for Scotland.

As the first Secretary of State for Scotland to be appointed since the 'Forty-five, Gilmour was in no doubt about the significance of the upgrading—even if the Treasury, somewhat miserably, would not as yet concede the salary appropriate to the post. In Gilmour's eyes the upgrading finally put to rights what had been lacking in the governing of Scotland. To honour the happy outcome he prevailed on their noble descendants to gift to Dover House the portraits, some by Kneller, of the Secretaries of State from Scotland under Queen Anne and the early Georges. The upgrading had this further practical consequence in that it now enabled Walter Elliot, who had begun his ministerial service at the Scottish Office in 1922, to be redesignated Parliamentary Under Secretary of State for Scotland with deputy authority over the full range of his chief's responsibilities.

Other milestones of importance in the development of the Scottish Office were passed in the 'twenties. Chief of these 'firsts' was the wresting from Government of more money than the

'The jam-factory': the rejected design for Old St
Andrew's House, as exposed by *The Scotsman* in
1929. (Courtesy of *The Scotsman*.)

arithmetical proportion of eleven to eighty fixed by Mr Chancellor
Goschen in 1888. This happened over housing where the Scottish
need was manifestly greater, and it merits a closer look.

The Housing Act of 1923 which Neville Chamberlain, as
Baldwin's Minister of Health, had piloted through Parliament was
a 'Great Britain' measure. It had as its main thrust the re-housing of
working people by means of direct subsidy to the hands of the
private enterprise builder. As such it was dismally inappropriate
for Scotland where the building industry was so very much

weaker and, with close to half the population still confined in the single room or the room-and-kitchen, the need for houses so much greater. However, the energetic Minister for Health was deaf to representations from Dover House. This being a 'Great Britain' bill, the Parliamentary Secretary for Health at the Scottish Office was given the task of winding-up, and in his speech Elliot did not conceal his view that Scotland had been badly treated. Nor was Lord Novar, the Secretary for Scotland after Munro, able to give Elliot effective support. Novar, isolated in the Lords, was an erstwhile Liberal Imperialist like his mentor Rosebery; and for all that he had recently been an outstandingly successful Governor-General of Australia he was without much influence in the party he had so recently joined.

In the brief Labour government of 1924 John Wheatley, the Clydeside member of parliament appointed Minister of Health, successfully put through legislation placing central government support to local authority house-building on an improved basis. Thanks to the Wheatley Act, there was now the necessary, solid basis for progress in housing, but still more help was needed in Scotland. With the Conservatives once more in power the more influential Gilmour, as the new Scottish Secretary, now prevailed on Baldwin, as Prime Minister, to visit Glasgow privately to see for himself the awfulness of the Cowcaddens and the Gorbals.

Elliot accompanied the Prime Minister on this visit. No doubt the outcome was foreseen, but the stage management was well done, if we may read between the lines of the 'Glasgow Herald' of October 1st, 1925,

> 'Major Elliot said that housing was a subject engaging the closest attention of the Prime Minister and the Secretary for Scotland, and he hoped it might be possible, especially after Mr Baldwin's visit to Glasgow, to get the justice of the Scottish claim admitted, namely that we in Scotland had a special problem and should, if necessary, be allowed special considerations in dealing with it.'

That evening, in Glasgow, Baldwin announced more Government support for local authority housing in Scotland!

This victory was the more remarkable in that it included government money for an ambitious programme of pre-fabricated housing, essential if quick inroads were to be made on the Scottish housing shortage. This angered Chamberlain at the Ministry of Health still further. The Scottish Office, he wrote to his sister, 'will always make a bungle of it, if it is possible to do so . . .', and he went on to berate Elliot outrageously.

Chamberlain's opposition had indeed been characteristically vigorous. A fortnight after Baldwin's *incognito* visit to Glasgow the Minister of Health swept into Dundee, there to inspect the slums of the notorious 'Blue Mountains', extol the virtues of owner-occupation, and at the City Chambers that evening speak not at all playfully of the need of his department to be 'exceedingly watchful' that the Scottish Office got no more out of Government than its due share. But Elliot knew what had been achieved, and the press cuttings of the episode are carefully preserved in his papers. Speaking that winter at a by-election in Tom Johnston's Kirkintilloch he hammered home the point that Baldwin's had been 'the first Government to admit the justice of the claim that Scotland had a special case in the matter of housing, and to make special provision for it'.

Another 'first', precursor of many in the years ahead, lay in using the breadth of the Scottish Office to identify in one field the solution to a problem lying in another; and again it was largely Elliot's doing. The puny growth of too many Scottish schoolchildren was recognised as a national disgrace by the Board of Health in Edinburgh as by the Scottish Education Department. At the Rowett Research Institute at Aberdeen Boyd Orr, world leader as he was becoming in nutritional science and a close friend of Elliot, urged on him the improvement which could result from milk being made freely available to schoolchildren. When, with his new status as Parliamentary Under-Secretary of State, Elliot was made a member of the new Empire Marketing Board for Agriculture and chairman of its research committee he was quick to get money for trials among Scottish schoolchildren to prove Boyd Orr's point. This joint initiative by the Research Institute director and Elliot was to have the happy outcome in 1930 of legislation he introduced with all party backing. So school milk for Scottish schoolchildren of the thirties, so many of them poorly fed as they were, came into being; and with it a more general recognition that nutrition is the handmaid of education. Dairy farmers did not do too badly out of it either.

The major Scottish legislative achievement of the 1920s was, however, the ambitious reorganisation of local government passed through parliament in 1929. This took place in the face of vigorous resistance from opposition benches; Tom Johnston had never lost his affection for small scale local government. In England as in Scotland the burden of local taxation was to be lightened on depressed industry and, as it then was, equally depressed agriculture. On to the Scottish measure giving effect to this, Gilmour tacked the far-reaching and fundamental reforms Elliot and he had had in mind for years. (No preliminary committee of enquiry, on whose recommendations ministers might lean, be it noted!) So it was that the Local Government (Scotland) Bill of 1929 abolished parish councils; stripped the smaller burghs of much of their autonomy; did away with those rural anachronisms, the county commissioners of supply; and established well-knit county government. Only the four cities and the score of burghs with populations over 20,000 remained outwith the new county system of local government, and, as regards the latter, not so for education.

It was as Elliot put it, 'the countification of the five great semi-national services—police, roads, health, education and poor law'.★ The parish pump did not feature in his vision though, as a sop to representations from both sides of the House, the setting-up of District Councils, but with trifling powers, had had to be included in the Bill at the last minute. Overall, the imperatives of efficiency seemed to have been married to the claims of community. It seemed at last an enduring structure of local government. This was not to be. But of that more, much more, later.

The 'twenties were a decade of real achievement for the Scottish Office; but Scottish politics, particularly among the mid-week expatriates of Westminster, was now often conducted in a raucous tone. It was a far cry to the serenity of the Victorian years when 'Scotch' business was conducted quietly late at night in an all but deserted debating chamber. For example, the prefabricated housing programme—the prefabrication being of steel—was noisily misrepresented by the cohort of Clydesiders in the Commons as the deliberate supplanting of Scottish bricklayers by the less skilled and lower-paid. Back in his Glasgow constituency, Elliot seems to have had to endure some caustic comment from his right flank about the allegedly palatial standards to which the councillors of George Square were rehousing the working classes. The officials of the Board of Health, for their part, were experiencing winds of politics which had never blown on the Local Government Board for Scotland.

Seen from nearly sixty years on—but, no doubt those with memories going back that far recall it differently—it appears an unhappy unconfident time; the war of the trenches proudly remembered by 'poor men in stinking pubs' as in that memorable passage of Linklater's 'Magnus Merriman', but the thousand war memorials going up in burgh and parish evoking very different feelings. It was also a decade of returning uncertainty about the Scottish identity, despite the long-awaited re-unification of the Church of Scotland in 1929. In his papers, Elliot kept a newspaper report of a sermon of these years by a fashionable Glasgow divine on the theme that 'the country was being anglified in the upper strata and Irishised in its lower strata', and that the ancient national virtues of thrift and sabbath observance like the old Scots tongue itself were now in desuetude. None of this jeremiad would reflect

★Powers given by the Act to the Secretary of State in respect of 'excessive and unreasonable expenditure' by local authorities were to lie dormant for some forty years before being invoked and used.

Elliot's cheerfully courageous approach, but no doubt it was delivered to a receptive congregation in Glasgow's West End.

But, by now, one thing had been put to rights. Oscar Slater was free, pardoned and compensated after a fashion. It happened that 1927 had seen a revival of interest in the case, stirred this time by a Glasgow journalist and Sir Arthur Conan Doyle. Gilmour first ordered Slater's release, and then in setting-up a Scottish Court of Criminal Appeal legislated retrospectively so that it could look anew at Slater's case nearly twenty years after the trial of 1909 which had gone so grievously wrong.

In 1929 the Conservatives lost the General Election and a minority Labour government came into power. This introduced Tom Johnston to office as Parliamentary Under-Secretary of State at the Scottish Office with Adamson, the veteran miners' leader, as Secretary of State. It had indeed been Ramsay Macdonald's intention to place Adamson as Secretary of State in the Lords, leaving all House of Commons business to Johnston, until he learned, just in time, that Adamson had a son. As Johnston wryly commented in his volume of reminiscence it would never do for a socialist prime minister to create a peerage for which there was an heir! Tom Johnston had not long to make his mark at Dover House but he did so well enough to be singled out for membership of the group of ministers to devise national employment schemes, and to be promoted to the post of Lord Privy Seal in Cabinet. Then came the world financial crisis of 1931, the formation of a National Government with Ramsay Macdonald as premier but with most of his party—including Tom Johnston—holding aloof, and severe economies in government. So both 1931 and 1932 saw a slowing up all round to Scottish Office activity; withdrawal of the housing subsidies and continued deferment of the higher school-leaving age promised thirteen years before.

In the autumn of 1932, there was a Scottish Office milestone in the allocation to Scottish affairs of a day in the debate at Westminster on the King's speech which, as always, opened the new session of parliament. Could it have been that the business managers thought the diversion of a debate on Scotland no bad thing, soldiering it out being the general response to the depression that had settled on industrial Britain? More probably the occasion had to do with the apparent surge of nationalist feeling in Scotland which had recently moved the students of Glasgow University to make Compton Mackenzie their Lord Rector, moved the Duke of Montrose to convene a group to agitate for a measure of self-government, and in turn moved Mackenzie to declaim against 'moderation and devolution'. If one may judge from Hansard, this upset at Gilmorehill seemed to disturb the back benches just as the

notorious pacifist resolution by Oxford students was to do two
years later. And indeed it was clear that Scottish nationalism
1932-style was of a different order altogether from the 'Home Rule
all round' proposals of the Asquith government in pre-war years.
Though the quietening of Ireland had been their main purpose,
these proposals of 1914 would in the passing—and with remark-
ably little public debate—have also installed a parliament in
Edinburgh to legislate on the then narrow confines of domestic
policy. The new wave of feeling, by contrast, was born out of
industrial depression and challenged the concept of Union itself.

The why and the wherefore of nationalist feeling in Scotland
then and subsequently is not the subject of this book, but in this
debate of 1932 the surge of nationalist sentiment in young Scotland
was, as it were, a disturbance in the wings affecting the stage
performance as speaker after speaker from the government benches took the (unrepresented) nationalists to task. However the
Scottish Office as it was, rather than Scottish Home Rule as it
might be, was also discussed at some length in the eight hours of
debate into that November evening; and if it was one best-selling
novelist outwith parliament in the person of Compton Mackenzie
who seemed to be dropping lighted matches in the Scottish
heather, it was another, John Buchan, prolific author of thrillers,
since 1928 member for the Scottish Universities, who was the star
of this debate at Westminster. He would be listened to the more
keenly because of the measure of enhanced self respect he had
recently given his countrymen from the refurbishing of their
national heroes, the Marquis of Montrose and Sir Walter Scott, in
his popularly acclaimed biographies.

Buchan began in sombre tones. Something must be done, he
said, and done soon, if Scotland was not to lose her historic
individuality. 'It seems to many', he said, 'that we are in danger
very soon of reaching that point where Scotland will have nothing
distinctive to show to the world.' The root of the malaise, Buchan
continued, and the source of the nationalist surge, was a passionate
feeling particularly among the young that Scotland should not lose
her personality; and while changes in the machinery of government could not of themselves effect a cultural revival they had a
part to play. Thus, he continued, the government's modest
proposals for transferring to Scotland consideration of Private Bills
with local impact such as proposals for burgh boundary extensions, electricity schemes and other such useful social advances
were to be welcomed. Then, he said, 'we should get rid once and
for all of the entirely indefensible system of tacking Scotland on to
English measures in one or two interpretation clauses which are
usually obscure and sometimes quite impossible to construe'.
More importantly the scope of government in Scotland should be
widened. 'Agriculture, education and health are already adminis-

tered in Scotland, and I think that other problems of Scottish administration should be administered from Edinburgh, and that Whitehall should be no more than a London office for the Scottish Secretary.' With these and other reforms, some seemingly trivial, some obviously important, Scotland would cease to be regarded as an administrative backwater and would be seen as a sister nation 'with her own compact and organic system of government'.

Next, Buchan itemised the need for an 'outward and visible sign of Scottish nationhood' through the building of a dignified and worthy centre for Scottish administration in Edinburgh, so picking up a point which the senior Scottish conservative Sir Robert Horne had made at the outset of the debate. The piecemeal growth of Scottish administration, said Buchan, had resulted in a scatter of offices throughout the New Town, and this did nothing for its efficiency, cohesion, or for the convenience of visiting county clerks and the delegations they brought with them. On his visits to Edinburgh the Secretary of State still had to make do with a darkish room in Parliament House from which the regular occupants had been temporarily evicted.* In John Buchan's mind as in others was the possibility of using the southern slope of the Calton Hill where the forbidding presence of the 'Calt'n Jile' had now disappeared. Lastly, in a vision of what the departments under the aegis of the Secretary of State for Scotland could be, he spoke of what might be achieved.

> 'There is a third point which is more important still. We want a Scottish policy. We have never had one. While agriculture, education, health and other branches have many points in their problems which are common to English problems, they have many which are individual and idiomatic. The mere fact that Scotland is constitutionally to a large degree a distinct unit gives us a chance of planning ahead in Scotland that is not possible for any other part of Britain.'

The future Lord Tweedsmuir and Governor-General of Canada was no great orator, and had indeed, as his biographer records, a rather high pitched voice with a nasal tone. But here he spoke for Scotland, having seen in brilliant clarity that nothing less would serve than a more unified Scottish Office which was also capable of growth.

Some share of the honours of the day must also go to a short speech by a Tory textile industrialist, Sir Samuel Chapman, the member for South Edinburgh. Sir Robert Horne who had once been Chancellor of the Exchequer had said bluntly that government was powerless to help depressed Scotland; Sir Godfrey Collins, the Secretary of State, distinguished businessman and a

---

*No 6 Parliament Square. On the lintel the wording 'Secretary for Scotland' can still be discerned.

former Liberal Chief Whip, said that recovery must wait on a future revival of world trade; and while Lord Dunglass, the young member for Lanark who was one day to be Prime Minister, had urged Government to use its international bargaining powers in defence of industry he spoke only of the traditional industries of Clydeside. Chapman, by contrast, spoke of the four factories of lighter industry which despite the Depression he personally had helped establish in central Scotland by 'selling' it as a location to foreign industrialists. With the tariff fence now round Britain, there *is,* he insisted, new industry to be attracted from abroad; Scotland *can* take her share. This was to be a recurring Scottish Office theme in the future, but like his namesake in the Keats sonnet it was Chapman who was the first to 'speak out loud and bold'.

'Compact and organic' the fief of the Secretary of State for Scotland was not yet, even though the boards had now been transmuted into twentieth century departments. But Collins could now lay claim to a significant extension of government activity in Scotland. This came from the legislation of 1934 which appointed Commissioners for the industrially depressed areas of Britain. For the paralysis which had gripped government in the nation's financial crisis was now easing just a little. Something—though, at Treasury insistence, too little—was to be done for the traditional areas of heavy industry and their dereliction, human as well as industrial. But while the English Commissioner was appointed by the 'Great Britain' Minister of Labour, and looked to his Ministry as parent department, the Cabinet agreed that the Scottish Commissioner should be appointed by the incumbent of Dover House and work closely with the Scottish Office and the Departments of Health and Agriculture in Edinburgh, as well as with the Scottish representatives of the Ministry of Labour. This switch to Scottish Office paternity was the more significant in that the cautious 'Investigation into the Industrial Conditions in Certain Depressed Areas' throughout Great Britain which preceded the appointment of the Commissioners had been firmly in the hands of the Ministry of Labour. However, Collins had established his position in Cabinet by successfully fighting for fair treatment of the long-term unemployed through the new Unemployment Assistance Board which supplanted Poor Law relief; and this had raised his stock.

The appointment of a Scottish businessman, Sir Arthur Rose, as the initial Scottish Commissioner, could be said to be a reversion to the patronage which the legislation of 1928 had been at such pains to abolish. But *this* 'board' did not isolate the problem from the politicians. Sir William Goodchild, a senior official with former service in the Scottish Office, acted as Rose's deputy. At Drum-

Looking down on Old St Andrew's House from the top of the Calton Hill in 1974. Flags at half mast to mark the death of a head of state. (Courtesy of *The Scotsman*.)

sheugh Gardens, as an important step in the building of a more effective Scottish administration, an Edinburgh office of the Secretary of State had opened its doors in 1935; and there was day to day contact between its staff and those in the regency house on the other side of Edinburgh's New Town accommodating the Scottish Commissioner.

Once it was underway, the effort to remove the blight which spread across Scotland from West Renfrewshire to West Lothian, from the pit-heads of Douglasdale to the jute mills of Dundee achieved something, and had a permanent effect on the Scottish Office. This calls for a closer look. At Chamberlain's insistence from the Treasury the initial legislation of 1934 was cautious to the point of triviality, eschewing direct help to industry. The public utility schemes promoted, such as long overdue work so that the filth of Paisley no longer flowed into the Clyde, were marginal to the problem. However, on Sir Godfrey Collins' death in office in 1936 he was succeeded by Walter Elliot, his prestige high from the work he had done as Minister of Agriculture in building an enduring edifice of controlled agricultural marketing and support. With Elliot's advocacy and the support of his friends in Cabinet, there was amending legislation in 1937 to extend the boundaries of the 'special areas', and empower the Commissioners to build industrial estates, to let factories, subsidise new industry, and widen the range of public utilities to be helped.

Economists have pointed out that the industrial ventures set afoot by the Commissioners in these years of the later 'thirties did very much less to reduce unemployment than did the involuntary Keynesianism forced on government by the necessity of rearmament. But here at last was the concept of government assistance to industry in selected areas. (The funding of government money in 1934 to restart work on the giant Cunarder at Clydebank was, in the eyes of Chamberlain, not so much regional aid as a means of promoting the desired merger of the Cunard and White Star Lines for a more competitive British presence on the North Atlantic.) So the 1937 legislation was indeed an important beginning for Scottish and for British administration.

But it was only a beginning. A coherent regional industrial policy depended on government's willingness to force the new industries—the industries of the future—to look north, away from the south-east of Britain to which too much had already gravitated. Watching from the government back-benches, Harold Macmillan felt vehemently that this was so. The Commissioner's annual reports to the Secretary of State for the later 'thirties show that in addition to industrial retraining and factory building, and an imaginative touch in money for the making of films on Scotland, there was financial impetus to many capital improvements; from assisting the Clyde Navigation trust to remove awkward bends in the river to the supply of electricity to Lanarkshire villages; from aid to hospital building by town and county councils to land improvement schemes supervised by the Macaulay Institute of Soil Research; and in welfare projects great and small from the building of summer camps for the families of the unemployed to—the construction of a toddlers' playground in sadly congested Greenock! But they failed to point out the necessity of guiding industry northwards.

However one might see in the fertility of ideas a more general stirring of the 'thirties. This was born perhaps as much of the greater ease with which in motor cars and buses, bicycles and hob-nailed boots Scots could now get around their native land, H V Morton's sprightly travel books in hand, as from the much talked of literary 'renaissance' of these years. This slow return of confidence may also be seen in the work of the Scottish National

Development Council which, to the inspired suggestion of a Glasgow businessman (an importer of American typewriters, not a captain of industry) had been formed by leaders in Scottish industry, commerce and finance in the depth of the economic winter. In co-operation with the Scottish Office, the Council in turn formed in 1936 a 'Scottish Economic Committee' representative of industry, finance, transport and labour. Goodchild, who had been the Commissioner's deputy, was its secretary-general. Sir Steven Bilsland became its chairman; and here, thanks to the patriotic vision, charm and persistence of this west of Scotland industrialist began that close collaboration between the Scottish Office and the leaders of the nation's industrial and financial life which was to become a continuing and essential feature of Scottish administration. For it was at Bilsland's suggestion, through the Scottish Economic Committee, that Elliot had persuaded his Cabinet colleagues to countenance the establishment by the Special Areas Commissioners of industrial estates to bring in new growth industry.

The reality as we will shortly see, was that inroads were being made into the housing problem in these years of the mid-'thirties; that organised marketing and subsidy now promised a better future for farming just as the setting up of the Herring Industry Board did for the east-coast drifters. But overall Scotland was still in a frightsome condition. Walter Elliot sought to convey to his Cabinet colleagues the alarm he felt at Scotland's continuing depression in industry and social backwardness, and he called for a programme of special action well beyond what was already being attempted. He did not succeed, Chamberlain now being Prime Minister and Sir John Simon at the Treasury.

Yet *brio* there was. The more so since 1937 had been Coronation year, and Elliot took great pleasure in seeing to Scottish participation, though greatly to his chagrin the cautious Office of Works vetoed his plans for a Coronation ball in Holyroodhouse; the flooring, they said would not stand eightsome reels. Then 1938 was the year of the Empire Exhibition which, in the grand style of international exhibitions, so magically transformed Glasgow's Bellahouston Park throughout that rainy summer and seemed to succeed in heralding the return of confidence; it was no mean feat in still 'depressed' Scotland. The Scottish National Development Council took the lead in organisation, but the Scottish Office were also involved. Elliot who had visited the Paris International Exhibition of the previous year contributed his imaginative energy to the enlisting of support in London as in Scotland; and from the Treasury the essential preliminary of a guarantee against loss was secured. Overall, the recollection of those who were closest to him—and it is one which has not faded with the years—is that so much was owed to Elliot's questing, argumentative mind in the

imparting of a sense of purpose and cohesion in the sectors of
Scottish administration over which he presided. He continued and
enhanced the many initiatives Collins had begun. And he was
grievously disappointed when the Prime Minister moved him to
the Ministry of Health in Whitehall that year. To Elliot this was no
promotion; rather it seemed to him an exasperating interruption in
what he hoped would be his continuing work for Scotland.

Alongside the imposing 'Palace of Engineering' and other
signposts to the future, the Empire Exhibition included a reminder
of the other Scotland, a replica-clachan of the old *Gaeltachd*.
Fittingly so: although the black house was now becoming a thing
of the past—building grants to crofters from the Department of
Agriculture were seeing to that—the hobbled economy of the
north and west demanded attention. But now, in the general
revival of Scottishness of these years an important beginning was
made towards what was to become a continuing commitment of
the Secretary of State's departments—the comprehensive economic development of the Highlands and Islands. Among the
Secretary of State's departments there was as yet no co-ordinating
mechanism for this. The Department of Agriculture at their Queen
Street headquarters in Edinburgh maintained their particular concern for the crofting communities—the islands from Tiree in the
Southern Hebrides to Unst in the north of Shetland, the desperately
small holdings along the serrated coast of the western highlands,
and the bigger, more improvable crofts of the eastern highlands.
But crofting was only a part of highland agriculture, just as
agriculture was only a part of the highland economy. State
afforestation in Scotland now getting into its stride particularly in
Argyll, was not in any way the responsibility of the Scottish
Office. The Fishery Board in Edinburgh observed the continuing
decline in the Hebridean fishing effort but felt powerless to arrest
it, and indeed had problems enough on its hands with the
difficulties of the main east of Scotland herring and white fish
fleets. As to sea transport Dover House in concert with the
Ministry of Transport had seen to it in the later 1920s that the
MacBrayne shipping services to the west coast and the Hebrides
would not founder, and had persuaded a railway company and the
major coastal shipping concern to take it over—with a guaranteed
return on their money. But few yet looked on improved transport
as a weapon of highland development, and with the guaranteed
return for their investment they enjoyed from government neither
the London, Midland and Scottish Railway Company nor Coast
Lines had the incentive to use it as such.

Now, in 1937, the Development Council's Scottish Economic
Committee, with some support from the Secretary of State's

departments, set up a committee to look into the overall development and social needs of the Highlands and Islands. The example
of what was beginning to be achieved in the distressed industrial
lowlands was clearly in the Committee's mind; and its chairman,
Professor Hilleary, and his colleagues proposed a development
authority for the Highlands and Islands with executive powers, a
solution which seems to have appealed to Elliot. They also sought
an attack all along the front; on forestry and fisheries as well as on
agriculture; on the development of tourism with the possibilities
which the motorised age was bringing; and on industrial development where this was possible, including the harnessing of the huge
sleeping resource of water power. In this last the committee took
issue (as Elliot also had done) with the bizarre alliance at Westminster of sporting land-owners and coal-mining representatives which
had squashed recent industrial proposals for hydro-electricity.

The coming of war was to still the discussion which the Hilleary
proposals had begun to generate. But after the war they were to
lead to a comprehensive and integrated approach to highland
development by the Secretary of State's departments with, ultimately, the adoption of the development board solution which
Hilleary had advocated.

'The glass is falling hour by hour,
The glass will fall for ever,
But if you break the bloody glass,
You won't hold up the weather.'*

This was the famous verdict of the 'thirties poet, Louis MacNeice,
on optimistic planning for Highlands and Hebrides. There were
now those in Scotland—with just a tinge of quixotry as it seemed
to disbelievers in Edinburgh as in London—determined to change
the climate.

Throughout the last three years before the war Edinburgh
looked with curiosity at the new government offices now a-
building on the side of the Calton Hill; and the Secretary of State's
departments in London and Edinburgh awaited, and then debated,
the document which was at last to unify them after a fashion. After
attempting unsuccessfully to persuade Stanley Baldwin to give the
Scottish Office an additional parliamentary under-secretary, and
just before his untimely death, Sir Godfrey Collins had all but set
up a Committee to review the relationship to each other of all the
bodies that came under his control; and indeed Sir John Gilmour,
who had been Home Secretary after his stint as Scottish Secretary,
had already accepted chairmanship. This Committee quickly set to

*From 'Bagpipe Music' in *Selected Poems* by Louis MacNeice; Faber and Faber.

work, and so 1939 was to see a new style Scottish Office as well as a new Edinburgh headquarters.

But 'Scottish Office' would have been a misnomer for the regime that this second stab at reorganisation was now to create to the design of the Gilmour Committee as it was published in the autumn of 1937. That Committee's recommendations were at pains to preserve, indeed deepen, the independence of the Secretary of State's departments, one from the other. All but ministerial work and parliamentary and liaison activity were now to move to Edinburgh—that is, in plainer English and respectively, all but the London office during the parliamentary session for the Secretary of State, his junior ministers, the permanent under-secretary of state, and all their private secretaries; a desk for someone versed in the curious ways of the Commons and the Lords; and a small group of officers on the telephone to Whitehall ministries when not on the telephone to Edinburgh. At first only this depleted Dover House would continue to be known as 'the Scottish Office'. However, with the changes in attitudes and organisation of the decades since then, the title has also come to apply to nearly all of the Secretary of State's direct responsibility in Scotland. 'The Departments of the Secretary of State for Scotland' which sticklers for departmental independence would insist was the proper title, could never be so convenient, nor so catchy.

The transformation in 1928 of the Health, Agriculture and Prisons Boards into departments more directly under the control of the Secretary of State had aroused misgivings that control in Scotland of Scottish government business was at risk. These fears had proved unfounded. But while the reorganisation of 1928 had gone a long way towards recognition that, constitutionally, a Minister and his department are inseparable, in the face of opposition it had failed to go the last mile in that it kept the new departments seemingly independent of the Secretary of State. This had not yet led to difficulties, but it could do so. There had been the cautionary tale of the Fishery Board's embarrassing *refusal* to accept a *refusal* by the Secretary of State to confirm one of their fisheries byelaws which ran counter to wider policy. If such Gilbertian scenes and resulting public mystification were to be avoided, further change was necessary. There was also this further point, which the Gilmour Committee foresaw, that it might be necessary for future Scottish Secretaries to make still further reorganisation of their commands, and that they ought to be able to do so without the delay of resort to parliament for new legislation.

The Scottish departments now about to be realigned by government's acceptance of the Gilmour recommendations differed a good deal from each other in temperament as in history. Any marshalling of clans raises points of precedence, and while the new

William Adamson—the first Labour Scottish
Secretary (Secretary for Scotland 1924; Secretary of
State for Scotland 1929–31.); by Tom Curr (at Dover
House.)

regime implied that no department, was, in Orwellian terms, to be
'more equal than others', the cool reception given in 1935 by some
in the Edinburgh departments to the local government division of
the Scottish Office when it moved north with the new Edinburgh
office of the Secretary of State did not augur well. 'Frankly, we

thought ourselves a cut above the Edinburgh departments' is the recollection of one who took part in this move to Scotland. 'And they', he added reflectively 'thought us rather a dilettante lot'. Wartime exigencies would soon put paid to much of this, but the departments were not quite yet a band of brothers, although the opening of the office in Drumsheugh Gardens was intended by Sir Godfrey Collins to be a step of major significance in the development of Scottish administration.

Of the four departments as they stood at the beginning of 1939, Health now with a staff of eight hundred—double its initial muster—was the biggest. Although the patronage-appointed members of the Board of Health had demitted office in 1928, it was not until the mid-thirties that the department's structure was reorganised on civil service lines with the import of a small cadre of young university-trained generalists destined to move into the senior posts in the years ahead. For the present, the stalwarts of the old Board held many of the top posts and continued to give the Department much of its sinewy character.* The Department's success in navigating the housing legislation of 1935 and 1938 through parliamentary shoals had enhanced its self-confidence. The government commitment to the relief of the generally severe overcrowding in working class housing as well as to slum clearance was now permanent. There was now more generous subsidy to local authorities, higher in Scotland than in England. There was the supplementary work of the Scottish Special Housing Association which the efforts of Walter Elliot and Sir William Douglas, the Secretary of the Health Department had established. All this was accompanied by unremitting pressure on town and county councils by the Department and its ministers; and so there was now the heady prospect of a Scotland without slums by 1942. A Scotland without rural slums as well, for there was now legislation to require much better standards of housing for the farm-worker and country-dweller; with his agricultural background Elliot was insistent on this.

Equally enthusiastic was the Department's Health Services Division. Nineteen thirty-seven had seen important legislation on local authority maternity services. It also saw the publication of the report of the Scottish Health Services Committee which had been set up in Collins' time. This ambitiously proposed a national health service for Scotland, involving a new structure of medical and allied services and an extension of the general practitioner service to all, that is to the families of the health-insured worker. As much as

* One of these was Miss Muriel Ritson who had come into the Board of Health in 1919 as an Insurance Commissioner and now, as a woman assistant secretary, was unique in Scotland. She is still fondly recalled by some who knew her as 'neatly dressed and correct in bearing, but very ready to extend a welcome to the new female entrant'.

in its recommendations the significance of the report lay in its thorough review of the basic factors of heredity, nutrition, education and environment and its detailed study of the family doctor, maternity, hospital, nursing services and so on. At the blast of its trumpet, the walls of Jericho did not tumble, but it stimulated thinking. When, ten years later the post-war government set itself to the creation of the National Health Service for all Britain, the Department of Health for Scotland would be unchallenged in its right to plan a health service to match Scottish needs and conditions.

Meanwhile poor law administration by local authorities, to oversee which the Department's ancestor had been created close to a hundred years before, was now on the wane. With unemployment assistance now a responsibility of central government, by 1937 local authorities had ceased to be responsible for all but a small residue of the able-bodied poor and met only the welfare needs of the sick, the aged and the infirm. Administration of the pensions schemes still rested with the Department and accounted for many of the Department's eight hundred, but it would soon cease to do so.

Welfare for the poor would soon go, but the Department was now receiving the first infusion of new strength with the beginnings of more effective town planning. As with housing, the business of planning was seen to be the responsibility of the cities, the county councils, and the larger burghs; but the Department's role was to encourage as well as confirm. It was, however, as yet limited to promoting the better layout of urban development. Regional planning (e.g. a bringing together under leadership from the centre of all the local planning authorities from bridge-building Motherwell to ship-building Greenock so that more sense might be made of Clydeside) was as yet below the horizon. But there were those among the planners now being recruited by the Department who recognised that it must come.

Vastly different in character was the Scottish Education Department. It was now for the greater part based in Edinburgh, but was still less than a hundred and fifty strong, and still drawing its intellectual strength exclusively from the sixty or more of the Schools Inspectorate. As in the days of Craik and Struthers it was also from the Inspectorate that the Department's administrative posts were filled. However, as the historian of the Inspectorate was to record, the Department was having difficulty in maintaining the momentum of innovation of previous decades. Perhaps it was that the traditional role of the Department in supervising a system of primary and secondary schooling had been so largely taken over by the county education authorities, and that the Department had not yet found its way to a new role. Perhaps it was that classics-based elitism was no longer quite what it had been.

Perhaps it was simply that government had not yet provided the money to implement either the raising of the school leaving age which the Act of 1918 had envisaged or the development of further education.

> 'At the end of the 1930s there were problems in all areas of Scottish education . . . the over-emphasis on academic instruction in the secondaries; the failure of the post-primary courses for the less gifted pupils to win public acceptance; and the unwillingness of young people to take advantage of opportunities in further education. The Department and its inspectors were conscious of the problems, however, and were attempting to find solutions to them, even if these solutions were not always those that we should favour . . .'

No doubt it was in its preoccupation with these problems that the Department kept its sights on school education rather than on new horizons. When legislation came in 1936 for the payment of government grant to local authorities and others for the provision of playing-fields, swimming pools, village halls and so on, it was the Scottish Office at its new Drumsheugh Gardens office, not the Scottish Education Department, which stretched out to take the central responsibility—though the Board of Education saw no difficulty in assuming responsibility in England and Wales.

Viewed from fifty years on, this temporary loss of vision in the Department—if that is what it was—might, indeed ought, to have been corrected by tighter ministerial control. It was not at all that, say, Collins was a lesser man than Balfour of Burleigh or Sinclair, but simply that with the transformation of the Edinburgh boards into departments of the Secretary of State, and with the widening of the horizons of government he had such a great deal more to do than his Edwardian predecessors even though he was now assisted by a parliamentary under secretary. Collins had sought unsuccessfully to obtain Baldwin's approval to the appointment of a second junior minister.

The Department of Agriculture was growing in its own distinctive way. Now five hundred and fifty strong, it was participating with the Ministry of Agriculture in Whitehall in the establishment of agricultural marketing schemes and the beginnings of price support for the farmer. It was broadening the science-base of farming through the three agricultural colleges and the four research institutes it funded. Its seed-testing station was promoting crop improvement. Like Health, it was not until 1935 that it had taken on any young university men from the Civil Service First Division competition, though the Department's chief, Sir Patrick Laird was from 'first division' Whitehall and indeed had joined the Scottish Office in 1911. The Department's unique character was however maintained by the professional Lands Staff, enthusiastic as ever for land settlement. They were a robust corps, usually themselves of farming stock, much given to the wearing of Harris tweeds and travel on Messrs MacBrayne's steamers. Any plan to break-up the Scottish lowlands into a Danish pattern of smallholdings had now long been abandoned, but the schemes establishing ex-servicemen in modest dairy farms had been successful enough; and in the north and west, scene of the Department's main land settlement activity, its social purpose held firm.

In the 'thirties, land settlement seemed to find a new relevance in supplementing the 'depressed areas' work of the Special Commissioner with the creation of minute holdings of 5–10 acres, a 'department bungalow' and an implement shed for each, as an employment creating device in the vicinity of cities and industrial towns. The Department set to this work with a will. The target was a thousand of these new holdings for poultry and pig production or the growing of raspberries and strawberries. It was attained, and the fulfilled sense of mission shines through the Department's Annual Report for 1938, justifying the mighty effort.

> 'As compared with the farm or industrial employee, the small holder is his own master and this gives him a satisfaction which is reflected in his bearing and in his standing among his neighbours.'

The Commissioner in his annual reports spoke only of this as giving a number of unemployed men something to do and a little more money; the Lands Staff would have it that they were bringing into being a new breed of agriculturist. But this was soon to be revealed as swimming against the economic tide.

Last in this review of the pre-1939 arrangements, there was 'the Scottish Office' at Dover House, now by the Gilmour proposals about to be reunited in Edinburgh with its Local Government Division, to have added to it the Prisons Department and the Fishery Board, and to be renamed the Scottish Home Department—thus making still more diverse a departmental range of activity which was already very wide. There were the parallel responsibilities to those borne by the Home Office, particularly in law and order. But the Scottish Office also shaped a parallel course to the Ministry of Health in its concern with local government, particularly in finance and rating, and to the Lord Chancellor's Department in maintaining the Scottish courts of law. Though its numbers fell short of a hundred, the Scottish Office had also to sustain the Secretary of State in his general role, in and out of Cabinet, as 'Scotland's Minister'; for example, the autumn months during which the Gilmour Report was received found the office busy drafting a paper on 'Fundamental Problems of Scotland' for Elliot to submit to Cabinet. Month in, month out, in regard to such as the Ministry of Transport or the Board of Trade, the office had both to be consulted on matters affecting Scotland or seek out the offending department and ask to be heard. There was also, the Gilmour Committee noted, the Scottish Office role in supervising the Commissioner for the Special Areas in Scotland, though the Committee did not appear to envisage the special area activities as being a permanent feature of government. In this, perhaps, they reported just too soon; the amending legislation of 1937 for the Special Areas, which was to include the highly significant power of selective aid to industry, was still going through Parliament while the Committee were sitting. So the Gilmour Report could make no place in the revised organisation for the future exercise of these powers after the temporary presence of the Special Commissioner was no longer there; and near to forty years were to elapse before the Secretary of State recovered powers himself to give selective assistance to Scottish industry.

The Department of Agriculture would now link directly with the Whitehall Ministry of Agriculture, a role which Dover House had discharged since the days of the Board; and the Department of Health would take over the responsibility which, just as surprisingly, it had not had up to now for the General Board of Control for the mentally ill. (It would now be the only survivor of the Edinburgh boards—this no oversight but a recognition of its good name.) But this was more than balanced by the taking into the new Scottish Home Department of the Fishery Board, rather unhappy at losing their seeming independence, and the Prisons Department, now, incidentally, developing borstal training for young offenders at Polmont in Stirlingshire. The care of children in trouble and the after care of prisoners through the Scottish Juvenile and After Care Office in Edinburgh was another area of growth. But the able young administrators of Dover House and Drumsheugh Gardens who were now about to be brought together in Edinburgh did not look askance at the daunting variety of their work. The Home Office tradition had been that theirs was a general responsibility for all domestic matters affecting government which did not lie within the province of other newer departments. The Scottish Office had shared this viewpoint; so would the new Scottish Home Department.

The Gilmour recommendations and the implementing legislation in the spring of 1939 met the second of John Buchan's *desiderata* in that they could make easier the natural growth of the office. Did they also produce a compact regime? Outwardly this was so, despite the invisible barriers between departments in their new Edinburgh home. All departments were to be equal in the eyes of the Secretary of State. However, in their anxiety that departmental independence of each other in their relationship with the Secretary of State should be absolute, the Gilmour Committee

Walter Elliot (Secretary of State for Scotland
1936–38.) (Courtesy of *The Glasgow Herald*.)

rejected the *via media* later adopted, that of common staffing with
ready interchangeability of staff between departments to provide a
stronger community of effort. Thus from the outset the new
regime nurtured strong, sometimes fierce, departmental loyalties;
sense of identity and continuity with the past was carefully
preserved. The price was the distancing here and there of work
that might be better run in double harness. An assistant-principal
coming fresh with his university laurels, say, to the Scottish Home
Department and placed there in its Local Government Division
could not acquire first hand experience of the close relationship of
the Scottish Education Department and the Department of Health
with those twin heartlands of local government—education and
housing. And when, in the 'forties and 'fifties, regional planning
burgeoned in the Department of Health, and linkage with the

Board of Trade's regional distribution of industry policies rested
with the Scottish Home Department, some interchange of staff
between Health and Home, had it been possible, might well have
been advantageous. But too much should not be made of all this.
At last the departments that made up the Secretary of State's
domain were housed—if not quite under one roof—at least all in
one city. Nothing but good could come of it.

In this re-ordering of Scottish administration John Buchan's
imperatives were further promoted by the retention at the Secretary of State's side of an official of the highest rank as his personal
adviser with something of the chief of staff/ambassador-at-large
about him. With these attributes this unique mandarin was able to
scan the Whitehall horizon and thus both warn and intervene over
issues which, though not strictly, or even not at all within the fields
of the Scottish departments, might be of burning concern to the
Secretary of State as 'Scotland's Minister'. As we have seen, this
penumbral role of the ministerial incumbent of Dover House had
been implicit from the beginning; now, with Government pervading so very many aspects of the economy and national life, its
importance was crucial.

This role of the Secretary of State's right-hand man, the
permanent under-secretary of state, was enhanced by the fact that
in accordance with the Gilmour concept of direct departmental
relationships with the Secretary of State 'PUS of S' did not
interpose himself between department and minister. Nor was
co-ordination of work where there was marginal overlap of
departmental responsibility ever to be a major role for him;
departments would always prefer to sort things out directly
between themselves without recourse to his exalted level. But he
had to be kept at all times, in Field Marshal Montgomery's
favourite phrase, 'in the picture'. And so from his rather lonely
eminence the permanent under-secretary of state could see, as it
was his role to see, what was going on in the Scottish departments
in Edinburgh as in the great departments of Whitehall. But it all
depended a great deal on his personality; his 'power base' was not
the solid foundation with which permanent secretaries of government departments are usually favoured.

The new Edinburgh home for the Secretary of State and his
departments was conceived years before the Gilmour Committee
was set up. Since then, the departments, particularly Health and
Agriculture, had grown in numbers, and the Gilmour proposals
implied that room had to be found for nearly a hundred staff from
Dover House. So, even at the outset, St Andrew's House as the
new building was named, was not big enough. When Edinburgh
got over her panic that the new building would desecrate the
Calton Hill it was seen that the architect, Thomas Tait, had done

rather well and produced 'by far the most impressive building erected in Scotland between the wars'.

Architectural reviews would also call it 'a composition of Egyptian monumentality', and indeed the Edinburgh public, peering at the new building from tram-cars swinging along the curve of the Regent Road, might find the cliff-like facade of the north front rather severe. The carved stone heads (Agriculture, Fisheries, Health, Education, Architecture—and Statecraft!) high above the main doorway they might think just a shade forbidding. But the visitor looking up, say, from Clarinda's grave in the Canongate Churchyard far below, or indeed the civil servant himself looking down on the building from the top of the Calton Hill as he took a lunch-time stroll, would have no difficulty in seeing what Tait was after, and how well he had fitted the great building into the hillside.

But the new building could have turned out so differently. The choice of Tait as architect was made on advice from an independent panel of 1934. Five years earlier the Office of Works in London had produced plans of their own which they pushed through the Edinburgh Town Council but, high-handedly, refused to divulge to the public. Smelling a rat, the 'Scotsman', in an intrepid piece of journalistic enterprise succeeded in copying the plans and letting their readers see how the proposed new building would look. 'Scotsman' readers were not slow to denounce it as 'looking like a jam factory', the Royal Fine Art Commission were of the same mind; and after some huffing and putting the offending plans were withdrawn.

The staff were ready for the new building; the new building was ready for the staff. A date had been fixed for a royal opening. But this was the late summer of 1939. By the morning on which St Andrew's House first opened its elegant bronze doors the nation was already at war.

IV

THE SECOND WORLD WAR:
YEARS OF OPPORTUNITY

FOR ANYONE able to remember something more of the Empire Exhibition than its delectable fun-fair, the autumn of 1938 will forever be the autumn of Munich, the months of international crisis culminating in the meeting in the Bavarian city of Prime Minister, Premier, Führer and Duce to avert European war—but only for a year. For civil departments of government, as for military, the imminent prospect of havoc from aerial bombardment was a searing experience. 'The bomber will always get through', Stanley Baldwin had informed the nation only a few years before (this also the fervent hope of our own Bomber Command). So the prospect of war called for all the energies and ingenuity that civil servants possessed to meet the expected calamity.

Planning in earnest had begun the previous year. There would, it was assumed, be huge numbers of civilian wounded; and in the spring of 1938 the Department of Health had surveyed the hospital resources of Scotland including what use might be made of hotels and private schools to see where beds could be got for air-raid casualties. The need for unified command was quickly recognised; and so the Department planned to assume responsibility for the whole of this, the Emergency Hospital Service, organised into five regions, in each of which a medical officer from the Department would work closely with local authorities and their medical officers of health.

With the imminent threat of war that autumn, both planning and the amassing of hospital equipment accelerated; and the momentum was kept up throughout the succeeding winter months as the Munich agreement was recognised for the false dawn it had been to so many. By the end of 1938 the Department had also taken over from the Home Office Air Raid Precautions Department in London the oversight of local authority arrangements for ambu-

lances and first aid posts. The whole casualty service was now
within the Department of Health's responsibility.

To lessen the number of expected casualties from the expected
onslaught from the air many would have to be evacuated from the
cities and towns at greatest risk. Here again the first instinct of
government had been to arrange everything from the Home Office
in London; but, come September, 1938, they were glad enough to
leave the arranging of evacuation in Scotland to the Scottish
Department of Health. Now it was decided that effort must be
concentrated on getting the schoolchildren away to safety, if need
be; and billeting surveys began, supervised by the Department. A
Scottish Advisory Committee on Evacuation was appointed, representing local authorities, educational interests and—not least—the
Women's Voluntary Services. How different it all was from the
halcyon months that had preceded the Kaiser's War!

Bombing would burn as well as kill and wound; and so an
Auxiliary Fire Service was brought into being throughout Britain.
In Scotland, as organised from Dover House in close collaboration
with the Home Office, it supplemented the very uneven fire cover
by the local authority fire brigades—still provided in separation
from each other and without any central supervision within the
thirty-three counties and one hundred and ninety-one burghs.
Indeed it was not until legislation with an eye to the coming war
was passed in 1938 that there had been any general obligation on
local authorities to provide official fire brigades. Until then these
had been the Cinderellas of local government 'housed in the burgh
yard', as a senior member of the Home Department recalls, 'along
with the cleansing department and often without a telephone'.
Lastly, there was the maintenance of government itself should
enemy bombing paralyse the life of the nation. For this, in Scotland,
there was to be a Regional Commissioner and his staff in Edinburgh, working with District Commissioners and their staffs.

Close co-operation between the Secretary of State's departments
would be essential in coping with the myriad upheavals which war
would bring. So it was well that the concentration of the four
departments in St Andrew's House coincided with the outbreak of
war. By and large all now went according to plan in these
September days. The Emergency Hospital Service became a reality,
as did the Emergency Medical Service to staff it; so did the
Auxiliary Fire Service and the Regional Commissioner's 'shadow'
administration; and that historic first weekend of September 1939
also saw enacted the administrative miracle of spiriting away a
hundred and seventy thousand schoolchildren and mothers from
Glasgow, Edinburgh and Dundee; also from Clydebank, its
renowned shipyard making the burgh an obvious target.

Except for one autumn afternoon of 1939 when cruisers of the
Royal Navy were bombed at their anchorage above the Forth

Bridge—and all Edinburgh buzzed with the story of the Heinkel chased 'at roof-top height' over a city suburb—the various emergency arrangements were not tested in these opening months of war; to the chagrin of those in charge, there had not even been time to sound the air raid sirens before the raid began that golden September day. So it was that over the winter some three-quarters of the evacuees returned to their city homes, this posing great problems for the local education authorities and the Inspectorate of the Scottish Education Department alike. There were also complaints from douce Scotland of the counties and small burghs over the cleanliness of some urban waifs, and, indeed, in the whole trauma of wartime, nothing was to change Scottish social attitudes so much as the first impact of evacuation. That is the view echoed by Alastair Dunnett★ then with Glasgow's 'Daily Record' and soon to serve in the wartime staff at St Andrew's House. 'The evacuation of the children', he has written, 'revealed in a clash of thunder the social conditions and deprivation of a great part of our population and the level on which they lived'.

Meanwhile, there was steady development in the Emergency Hospital Service with new hutted hospitals being built for the Department of Health by the Office of Works, the 'Great Britain' department with a Scottish presence which had seen to the building of St Andrew's House. At Ballochmyle in Ayrshire, Law in Lanarkshire, Killearn in Stirlingshire, Bridge of Earn near Perth, and Stracathro in Angus, these were a massive addition to the hospital resources of Scotland; to serve them, within the Department at St Andrew's House there was a large hospitals supply branch. There was also need for a great deal of ancillary effort, as in the creation of blood banks for blood transfusion to meet everyday needs as well as those arising from air raids. It was recognised—wisely, since the whole community would have to be persuaded to give of their blood as well as of their money—that this was a field for voluntary effort; and so, with the bolstering of government grant, the Scottish National Blood Transfusion Association came

---

★As tragi-comic illustration to this, Alastair Dunnett kindly permits me to repeat his story of evacuation day in genteel Callander.

> 'Families had turned up and taken, in ones and twos and threes, the various little groups of children who had been dumped on the station platform, until there were only two left, two extremely grubby and unprepossessing little boys, a slightly older brother and a young brother whom he was holding by the hand. The young brother was crying and the older fellow, perhaps just eight or nine years, was trying hard not to cry. Nobody wanted them. They were too appallingly dirty and undesirable, and as the platform cleared except for them Jimmy [the 'Daily Record' reporter and Dunnett's colleague] saw the older boy lead the wee fellow up to a dubious adult and say 'We can wash the close and go for the messages and we can run along the railway line looking for coal.'

('Among Friends': an autobiography; by Alastair Dunnett; Century Publishing, London, 1984.)

into being. Participation rather than dictation was also the theme in the deployment of medical manpower. The re-allocation of doctors, dentists, pharmacists and opticians throughout Scotland was done by their own professional bodies; and under the Scottish Board of the Royal College of Nursing a register of nurses was compiled and new nursing staff enrolled. Lastly, the great voluntary hospitals of Scotland were supported financially by the Department from the outset of war.

The coming of war transformed the Department of Agriculture, as it shifted its main weight from land settlement to the production of food from the land. Here, too, planning had begun some years before, but it would have been to less avail had it not chimed with Walter Elliot's work in the pre-war years, both at the Ministry of Agriculture and at the Scottish Office to increase the acreage growing grain. Between the wars over half-a-million acres of arable Scotland alone had been put down to grass, as much of agriculture throughout Britain became 'dog-and-stick' farming. The recovery of the arable acreage had still a long way to go, but recovery was well begun before 1939; farmers were once more expansion-minded thanks to the subsidies for grain crops, liming and fertilisers.

In the 1914–18 war, enemy U-boats had not critically threatened the nation's imports of food until unrestricted under-sea warfare reached its peak in 1917. In the renewed struggle with Germany, the danger was foreseen, and right from the outset the complex local administration of war-time agriculture was delegated. Participation by leading farmers, all 'substantial men'—to use rural parlance—had been canvassed since the previous year; and so the movement of the Department into its glossy new quarters in St Andrew's House on the September morning following the declaration of war was accompanied by the springing into being of forty Agricultural Executive Committees throughout Scotland, each with a secretary and an executive officer drawn usually from the Agricultural Colleges which in Scotland were also the agricultural advisory service. The Department supplied members of their technical staff to act as liaison officers with the committees, and, generally, to work closely with them. So the committees set to their task of persuading farmers to increase the overall acreage under crops that the nation might be fed, and at the same time to increase home grown feed for livestock in substitution for the tonnages which the Merchant Navy could no longer carry (or the U-boats permit).

To run ahead of strict chronology at this point, the agricultural departments—the Department in Edinburgh participating in full with its big sister in Whitehall Place—were to fight a six year campaign which, though bloodless, was as continuous and as crucial as the Battle of the Atlantic itself. As shipping losses soared in 1941 and again in early 1943, they called for still further acreages under tillage (an acre of grain or potatoes feeds a vastly greater number than an acre of grass) and better use of the grassland that remained to produce more milk. This gave the Scottish Department its opportunity; with the acreage of low ground grassland diminished it made sense to look to the immense sleeping resources for meat production of summer grass on hills and uplands. The hand of the Department of Agriculture for Scotland may be seen in the introduction of hill sheep and hill cattle subsidies in 1941 and their supplement by the Marginal Agricultural Production Scheme of 1942—though the Department lived to regret this title, in later years a red rag to Treasury economists. In securing the necessary swift compliance by farmers with these developments of policy, in enforcing the rationing of feedstuffs to livestock producers, in encouraging good farming practice and coming down with a heavy hand on the laggard, little could have been attained without the enthusiastic and unremitting work of the Agricultural Executive Committees. But the Department itself had also completely reorganised itself, diverting staff from land settlement that they might manage the labour force, including the Women's Land Army, which was needed for the huge expansion. It also now ran a Tractor Service—it was in the war years that the splendid Clydesdales became rarities on Scottish farms. It instructed farmers in the use of other machinery. It paid out subsidies; and it increased the farmland resource by land drainage schemes, bracken eradication and pest control. The seven hundred staff of 1939 had doubled by the war's end.

By the summer of 1940 the new rhythm of administration had set in throughout St Andrew's House. Modifying the tendency to fierce departmental independence of the four tenant departments of St Andrew's House, some members of the Scottish Education Department's Schools Inspectorate now found themselves administering the Emergency Hospital Service; and there were historians seconded from Register House and senior staff from the National Library and the Royal Scottish Museum grappling with war-time problems elsewhere in the building. For those whose day had ended at five in happier times with, as like as not, a game of golf to follow, there would now be fire-watching, the Home Guard, and makeshift beds in the basement. The imminent threat of invasion flooded the Police Division of the new Home Department with work, as much of Scotland became an armed camp. St Andrew's House remained open for business till seven every evening with some typing staff remaining still later so that the Iron Duke's maxim might be observed and 'the business of the day done in the day'. (Even Lyon King of Arms was said to be contemplating the appropriate uniform for himself should he be obliged to fulfil his historic role of emissary to the enemy: his heraldic tabard, he felt, would be altogether too much for the battle-dressed 'forties!)

It might seem odd that with the Scottish departments now concentrated in Edinburgh it was thought necessary to have a Regional Commissioner there. What was the police service, for which the Department did have responsibility, but the 'emergency' service *par excellence*? And was it any good reason for the dichotomy that the Regional Commissioner was now preparing for the worst eventuality of invasion and a collapse of civil administration? But the arrangement had been agreed in pre-war planning, and, as things turned out it did not greatly matter. Tom Johnston as Regional Commissioner and Sir Steven Bilsland as District Commissioner in the west were 'kent faces', and the relationships they and their staffs had with St Andrew's House were easy. Meanwhile, throughout that autumn of 1940 and the winter of the blitz, the liaison staff at Dover House were in the front line which total war had made of central London.

Then came the night in March 1941 when Matthew Wilson—a veteran survivor from these days—as Duty Officer in the bowels of St Andrew's House took a telephone message from the Department of Health's General Inspector at Clydebank to let him know that the town was under intensive air attack. With anti-aircraft artillery the only defence, and that as effective as 'shooting at a blue-bottle in the dark with an air pistol', there seemed every reason to think that the systematic bombing of Scottish towns and cities had begun; and so a determined attempt was made by the Department of Health and the Home Department and by the Regional Commissioner's organisation to improve all aspects of civil defence. With such a torrent of destruction and death, the need to give immediate and strong support to the local authority concerned seemed a main lesson from Clydebank's two nights of ordeal; so was the need to improve on the billeting of the homeless. Consequently, when the next major raid came on Greenock in the month of May, a team from St Andrew's House was on the move within hours; and this was as well because the vicious nature of the air raid and its shattering of local services posed fearful problems. One such was the need to evacuate Greenock before the expected second night of terror came. The Department of Health's representative organising this as best he could on the afternoon of the day following the raid still recalls the awfulness of the moment as nightfall approached and the buses commandeered were seen to be all too few for a frightened and angry mob of townsfolk.

The expected second raid on Greenock did not come. Nor, as the Luftwaffe was redeployed in eastern Europe, were there any more massive air raids in Scotland. But planning and re-planning to cope with extensive bombing, or worse, went on; and a high state of preparedness was maintained. From early in 1941 the Home Office and the Scottish Home Department took over from town and county councils the running of their fire brigades, and with the Auxiliary Fire Service formed a comprehensive National Fire Service. The establishment, equipping and training of this great service was now run from St Andrew's House, like the Emergency Hospital and Medical Services run by the Department of Health. As with the army itself in the Home Commands preparing for the return to Europe, large scale exercises to test civil defence arrangements were frequent, and taken very seriously. 'It was no joke', recalls one member of the Home Department, 'to be woken up in the middle of the night by a telephone call to inform you that German parachutists had seized Edinburgh's North Bridge—and why hadn't the police been armed?'

Meanwhile Dover House had been abandoned in favour of Fielden House among the Georgian red brick of Westminster's Great College Street. This was a stronger, steel-framed building put up between the wars and likely to be less susceptible to blast damage. It had been taken over from the joint parliamentary branch of the four main-line railway companies,* for in one of the raids of early 1941 a bomb had fallen on the adjacent Treasury building to Dover House, and Sir Matthew Featherstone's fine mansion was severely shaken, so badly so that it was pronounced unfit for further use. For the rest of the war Dover House had a sort of half-life, some of it being used, but not by Scottish Office staff. The great rooms, empty of their fine furnishings, had a distressed appearance. A lady serving with one of the government organisations then squatting in the building recalls going by night into what had been the Secretary of State's room. Her torch light disturbed a rat on Tom Johnston's desk!

In reality, Scotland herself was also now at the nadir of her fortunes. The heady excitement of these days could not alter the fact that the war had every appearance of being both a social and economic disaster for her. A social disaster, primarily because the great house-building programme which had offered a prospect of a slum-free Scotland within a few years had stopped abruptly with the completion of those houses a-building at the outbreak of war. Each year added to the decrepitude of the tenements thrown up in the earlier Victorian decades—let alone what additions to the housing backlog would result from German bombers. An econo-

---

* Sir Charles Cunningham recalls that the address given the building was 10 Great College Street, although the door was in Little College Street. This change of address was made because Fielden House was built on the site of a house notorious for its Oscar Wildean connections, and the railway lawyers did not value the link!

mic disaster because more and more Scottish labour was being
drafted south to the factories of the English Midlands which were
the scene of Britain's main war-time industrial expansion; and with
this expansion went a contraction in civil industry engineered by
the Ministry of Supply. All too often, concentration of production
meant the short-sighted close-down of factories in Scotland. But
these were the very factories where when peace returned growth
potential would reside. The Clyde now rang once again to the
sound of the riveters at work, but the dismal sequel to the
ship-building boom of the Great War was all too clearly remembered. Though Rolls-Royce were now at the Hillington Industrial
Estate making aero engines, this was still seen by the Company as
a temporary, war-time arrangement. Nor would the new Ferranti
factory at Edinburgh to manufacture the gyro-gunsight designed
by the Royal Aircraft Establishment at Farnborough have itself
been enough to reverse the southward drift. To far too great an
extent Scotland's role seemed to be that of providing labour for the
new English factories, and the mere storage of what they produced.

But the hour had brought forth the man in the person of Tom
Johnston. He was now sixty, feeling that his parliamentary career
would soon be over, indeed fervently hoping this would be so
because night sleepers to King's Cross or Euston were always a
sore trial to him. However, his tenure of the post of Scottish
Regional Commissioner had given him a firm understanding of
the new style Scottish Office. He had been able to take its measure
and that of its civil servants; and they, for their part, had had an
opportunity to get to know and like him. He was also remembered for his fertility in ideas during his sojourn at the Scottish
Office from 1929 to 1931, and for his long-headedness. One
anecdote from these earlier days was remembered in particular. A
distasteful necessity of 1930 had been the evacuation of distant St
Kilda, its population by then reduced far below the level of
viability. The onset of over-harsh religion in the 19th century and
the further subtle corruption of island values by the more frequent
visitors from the mainland in the 20th were largely responsible for
this, but evacuation of the farthest of the Hebrides was indeed an
emotional topic of which the journalists, understandably enough,
were making much. The danger was that their ignorance of the
true reasons for St Kilda's plight would lead them to lambast the
Secretary of State for general 'neglect' of the Highlands and
Islands. So when the proposal came before Johnston, as parliamentary under-secretary, that a film company should be permitted to
join the team of Department of Health officials in the old
MacBrayne steamer organising the evacuation he sagely minuted
that he did not think that the poor St Kilda people 'should be put to
the embarrassment of having their farewell to the island filmed'.

Tom Johnston (Secretary of State for Scotland
1941–45); by James Gunn (at Dover House).

Expediency chimed with humanity, and the Department thought
the more of him for his adroit decision.

Churchill in his Cabinet reconstruction in early 1941 appointed
Johnston to be Secretary of State for Scotland, in place of Ernest
Brown who was moved to the Ministry of Health in Whitehall.
There was some surprise that the Scottish post had not gone to
Walter Elliot (and indeed those who had worked closely with
Elliot in pre-war days felt—and it must be said, still feel—that his
exclusion from all office in the National Government was regrett-
able indeed). Moreover, as Johnston amusedly recounts in his
reminiscences, there was also many a Scottish laird who had not
yet forgiven him for his assaults on Scottish landowning in his
journalistic days; TJ's diatribe, 'Our Noble Families' was still

sharply enough remembered to keep him out of the Caledonian Club in fashionable London, even though he had now received the Great Seal of Scotland from the monarch and taken up duty as Secretary of State in a Coalition government. But from the outset, St Andrew's House knew that in Tom Johnston it had a chief with whom it could show its paces.

For Johnston had genius in turning adversity to advantage. Although he was to claim that he was 'hypnotised' by Churchill into accepting the Scottish Secretaryship, it is difficult to believe this when by his own admission he ventured to Downing Street so well armed with conditions of acceptance. As he recalled it, his conversation with the Prime Minister about the chief of these was brief and to the point.

> 'I had mustered up sufficient sense to table prior conditions.
> "What are they?" I was asked.
> (Me): "First, I should want to try out a Council of State for Scotland—a council composed of all the living ex-Secretaries for Scotland, of all parties; and whenever we were all agreed upon a Scottish issue, I could look to you for backing!"
> (The PM): "That seems a sort of national government of all parties idea, just like our Government here. All right, I'll look sympathetically upon anything about which Scotland is unanimous." '

And now began a sequence of events to which Scotland still owes an enormous debt of gratitude.

The 'Council on Post-war Problems' as it was entitled at the outset, under Johnston's Chairmanship as Secretary of State consisted of all four surviving holders of the office. Ernest Brown; Colonel Sir John Colville who had succeeded Walter Elliot in 1938 and was himself a prominent industrialist; Elliot himself; Sir Archibald Sinclair, leader of the Liberals, who had briefly been Secretary of State for Scotland in the National Government of 1931. There was also Lord Alness last met as Robert Munro, Secretary for Scotland from 1916–22, and who, though now retired from the Scottish Bench, was as precise in his thinking as ever. Here was a mechanism which neatly brought together Labour, Conservative, Liberal and National Liberal, which turned to advantage the important posts at the Health and Air Ministries respectively held by Brown and Sinclair, and secured the maximum co-operation between the parties on proposals brought before it. Lastly—but perhaps this had all along been foremost in Johnston's mind—the authority of this Scottish 'Council on Post-war Problems' or 'Council of State', as it came to be called, and its known endorsement by the Prime Minister could be used as a sort of political jemmy to prise out of Whitehall the concessions that Scotland so sorely needed.

Political initiatives in Whitehall are an enduring Scottish necessity. So is systematic policy stimulation by Ministers, and it was perhaps as a means of regular review of the policies of his departments by the Secretary of State rather than for any new ideas it generated on its own that the Council had its chief importance. Throughout the years of its existence, attendance of officials at the Council of State was kept small. This was not, as might be thought an attempt from the Chair to 'outgun' them, for Johnston's rapport with most of his senior advisers was outstandingly good; and he came to each meeting armed with ideas and proposals which in the preceding weeks had already been tossed backwards and forwards between his office on the fifth floor of St Andrew's House and the departmental secretariats below. The reason for its small size was that, experienced hand in the ways of government as he now was, Johnston recognised that beyond quite a modest level of numbers the efficiency of a committee is usually in inverse relationship to its size. The other aspect of the Council's existence to be noted is its regularity of meeting from its first in September 1941 to its last in February 1945 as the end of the European war—and of the Coalition Government—came in sight. So without more ado, and by means of the excellent minuting by Dr Christopher Macrae, the Council's secretary, let us watch Tom Johnston and his colleagues at work, at this critical period in the history of the Scottish Office.

Treading warily, Johnston began the first meeting by stating the general purpose to be consideration of post-war Scottish problems, and he invited suggestions as to their identification. He also produced his own list. These were: hydro-electricity in the Highlands, the herring industry, hill sheep farming, the regionalisation of water supply, and the unification of hospital services, this last, with war-time demands and the development of the Emergency Hospital Service, now seeming less distant a prospect than in pre-war years.

Nevertheless, this was a modest enough shopping list, kept modest, perhaps, for sound tactical reasons. It was Elliot who was left to speak of housing as Scotland's greatest post-war problem which if unsolved might stultify progress on all fronts; and it was left to Colville, as a leading industrialist, to point to the burgeoning of new war-time industry south of the Trent, and its relative absence north of the Border.

By the Council's third meeting in December it was into its swing. The Council's various initiatives had all this in common, that they required the setting up of strong committees of enquiry, with remits and membership agreed with Whitehall ministers; so, at its second meeting the Council had discussed membership. Now by early December, from the chair Johnston was able to say that all the enquiries were now under way; and so he moved on to the subject Colville had raised—the dearth of war-time industry in Scotland and the concentration of surviving civil industry in England. By the next meeting in the early days of January 1942, matters had progressed a great deal further. Johnston said he had taken up direct with the President of the Board of Trade their offending instruction that five hundred girls be recruited from Scotland each week for war factories in the Midlands; also the significant case of two Scottish pottery firms which were to close under the 'concentration of industry' policy. But something more systematic was needed. 'It might be of assistance', said Johnston to the Council, 'if the Convention of Royal Burghs and the other local authority associations could be induced to co-operate with the Scottish National Development Council [which like its Scottish Economic Committee had with war-time become rather inactive] to form the nucleus of a new body which could be strengthened with the addition of representative businessmen and influential trade unionists to compose an industrial committee or council.' This body could be a guarding lion both to Scotland's immediate and long-term industrial interests. 'I would emphasise' said Johnston, looking closely, one may imagine, at his ministerial colleagues 'the need for getting hold of early information about developments'. They would know what he meant. By the March meeting of the Council of State, Johnston was able to report that 'The Scottish Council on Industry' had already gone to battle stations with an Emergency Committee led by the impressive presence of Lord Provost Will Y Darling of Edinburgh and with Sir Steven Bilsland in support.

In succeeding months and years, Johnston would use the Scottish Council of Industry and his own Council of State as weapons for both hands, the activity of the former assisted by the authority of the latter. Over individual issues, Johnston as Secretary of State would seek out the erring Whitehall minister. But the real weapons, rather than dirk and claymore, were reasoned argument and patient advocacy by himself, by his supporting officials of the Home Department, and by Bilsland. For example: the Ministry of Supply had been on the point of running down the important, long-standing carpet-making industry of the West of Scotland in the interests of 'concentration', so closing the factories and making other use of their workers; and the Scottish Council for Industry was properly alarmed. But Johnston was able to announce to the Council of State that he had received from the Minister of Supply an assurance that the factories would be kept in being and turned over to war production. So it went on throughout the remaining war years, the ball passing purposefully between Council for Industry and Council of State. Whether Whitehall ever learned that Dr Christopher Macrae was Secretary to the former as well as to the latter is not clear!

Hydro-electricity had come first in Johnston's initial shopping-list. Turning war-time to advantage he saw in it circumstances producing a broader unanimity of thinking in Scotland about the role hydro-electricity should play. Since the defeat of the Caledonian Power Scheme in 1936 agitation by those with vision to discern the possibilities had continued. The Hilleary Committee of 1938 had said bluntly that hydro-electricity was a prerequisite to Highland recovery; and in Edward McColl, the Regional Manager in Scotland of the Central Electricity Board, the concept of 'power from the glens' had a vigorous advocate. However the omens were not good; in September 1941 the House of Commons had rejected the Grampian Electricity Supply Bill, yet another private bill embodying a commercial proposition which would have put to use the potential for hydro-electricity of lovely Glen Affric in Inverness-shire. Once more it was an alliance from Left and Right which blocked the Bill; after a long and heated debate the member for Govan, for example, finding himself in the same lobby as the member for Twickenham. However, for proponents of hydro-electricity the gall of this defeat was sweetened by the thoughtful intervention of the Secretary of State for Scotland. Left had objected to exploitation of the water resources of the Highlands by commercial development. Right, despite the very full enquiry into the Bill at Edinburgh under the improved Private Legislation procedure, was still concerned about loss of amenity. Johnston scotched the objection about the supposed harm to the Highlands; there was 'not a solitary crofter and not a sheep in Glen Affric, and only a working population of five stalkers and two gardeners'. It was right he asserted 'to debate in the middle of a war plans for post-war development'. But he hinted that something better might be in the offing and that government might 'bring forward their own proposals for the co-ordination of the hydro-electric resources of this country.' This, as Johnston no doubt intended took some of the heat out of the debate, and deterred the digging of entrenchments, particularly by some of his party colleagues, which could be obstacles for what he had in mind.

A Committee on Hydro-Electric Development in Scotland, chaired by Lord Cooper, the brightest star in the Scottish judicial firmament, was now appointed. Its remit was to consider the practicability and desirability of hydro-electric development, and by what type of authority it should be developed; and also to keep in mind both Highland interests and the safeguarding of the landscape. Despite these hefty terms of reference, the Committee reported unanimously, and in favour, within nine months. Keeping up the momentum, Johnston told the Council of State at their September meeting that he would approach Whitehall Ministers 'while members are considering the Report'; and so the Council meeting on 1 December 1942 was informed that 'government approval had now been given for a Bill embodying the principles of the Report'.

Meanwhile, there had been representations that the proposal of the Hilleary Committee of 1938 for a Development Commissioner for the Highlands (with what would amount to a sort of Highlands and Islands Development Board) should be adopted. Some of the Highland County Councils also gave it their tenacious support. Johnston was against this. Better, he thought, to have individual action on the various fronts the Council had demarcated, hydro-electricity, hill sheep farming, herring fishing, and now land settlement as well. 'It was so like Tom', said one who remembered these days, 'that he should concentrate on making the best, long-term use of what was to hand. It was always the eminently practicable, never the romantically unattainable.' Nor would it, said Johnston, ease the now long-standing Highland malaise to designate the Highland counties as a 'depressed area'. However, these rumblings from the north were appeased when the Bill presented to parliament in 1943 to set up a North of Scotland Hydro-Electric Board gave prominent place to its role in Highland development; support of the region's economy was to be generated as well as electricity. This Bill went through the House of Commons unopposed, and was skilfully piloted by Lord Alness through the hazards of any continuing opposition in the Lords.

As one looks through the successive minutes of the Council of State, as drafted by Christopher Macrae and endorsed by Sir Horace Hamilton, the Permanent Under Secretary of State, one sees Johnston using the Council as something much more than the initial, declared, concept of a 'Council on Scotland's Post-War Problems' (and indeed that limiting title was soon dropped). Papers presented to the Council are clear and purposeful, obviously the result of close collaboration by the departments, though couched in the first person singular. Membership at meetings dwindles; early on Colville leaves to become Governor-General of Bombay; Elliot in 1944 takes on a government mission to West Africa; and their own pressing departmental business necessarily makes Sinclair's and Brown's attendance fitful. But taking cognisance of major topics as they arise, whether of immediate rather than post-war significance, the mechanism of the Council whirrs on, even if it means Johnston sitting with only old Lord Alness for ex-ministerial company. The Council was now an integral part of Johnston's personal sway over the Scottish Office.

Indeed, a great deal was happening. The pretensions of the powerful Office of Works in London to set itself up as the post-war Housing Department for all Britain was resisted, and, instead, the Scottish Housing Advisory Committee was reconstituted as to membership and purpose. The evident ambitions of Lord Reith at the new Planning Ministry in Whitehall to run the broader aspects of town and country planning in Scotland as in England were also thwarted. The formidable ex-Director General of the BBC was not only handed off, Murrayfield-style; the Department of Health for Scotland now stepped up recruitment of its own small corps of planners, and, with the score of local authorities concerned, launched a planning survey of the economic and development needs of the Clyde Valley region; more of this later. The Hill Sheep Industry Enquiry had pointed to the scope for afforestation in Highlands and Southern Uplands alike as a valuable adjunct to hill-farming if properly integrated with it. A lengthy battle was now begun to bring the Forestry Commission into proper relationship with the Scottish Office, the outcome being the Commission's reconstitution under the ministerial direction of the Secretary of State for Scotland and, for England and Wales, the Minister of Agriculture. Legislation was prepared to bring about better co-operation over water supply between Scottish local authorities, particularly in the central belt; and, as the war moved towards its end through the winter of 1944, sites were identified for the rash of post-war housing which would be needed. Early on, Johnston had seen to it that the Emergency Hospital Service was put to use in clearing the backlog of civilian patients for the local authority and voluntary hospitals; and indeed it was the need to put to permanent post-war use the supplement they provided, as well as to feel a Scottish way towards a National Health Service, that a committee had been set up under the chairmanship of Sir Hector Hetherington, the strong-minded Principal of Glasgow University.

Looking back from the 1950s on all that had been achieved, Johnston was to voice exasperation that he had, as he thought, made so little headway with the Scottish Education Department. The Education (Scotland) Act of 1944 did succeed in going some way to realise one of his ambitions, to restore local delegation in county administration of schools; but one of his other educational ambitions—to widen the school curriculum—got nowhere. 'I had a bad flop over the teaching of citizenship in the schools', he wrote. 'Despite backing from the Council of State—and especially from Lord Alness—I failed to make any serious headway in importing into our school system what I thought was, or should be, the first necessity of all education, a culture of good citizenship. True, we got an advisory council on education and recommendations about the prime necessity of turning out good citizens; we produced a splendid pamphlet on the subject; but the polite, although obviously reluctant, acquiescence of the do-nothings, and the Petronella dance-like side-stepping of the pundits filled me with foreboding that we were not going to break far into the existing codes.' This was hitting hard and it has to be said that others besides the Department had doubts about the teaching (or teachability) of 'citizenship'. But the curriculum was in need of fundamental overhaul, particularly for those not academically inclined. In this matter of teaching 'citizenship' as in his equally unrewarded campaign to have schools teach youngsters the proper cooking of simple Scottish food, we can see Johnston groping towards a clearer view of the need for curricular change.

Other ingrained attitudes would not budge. Continuing rent restriction, along with the requirement that owners share the rate burden with their tenants, had killed house-building for letting before the war and brought about widespread deterioration of rented housing as property aged. With this abiding anxiety about the state of Scottish housing, in the Council of State Elliot insisted that 'some way out of the mesh of obligations on property owners had to be found'. By the end of 1942 a Committee on Rating had been set up under the chairmanship of the Dean of Faculty, one part of its remit being to consider the case for limitation of owners' rates; and by the date of the Council's last meeting in February 1945 it had reported unanimously about the need to limit owners' liability. But this was too late for legislation under the protecting guns of the war-time coalition; nor were its findings welcome to the stalwarts of the old Independent Labour Party, particularly George Buchanan who was to have responsibility for Scottish housing in the post-war government from 1945. The Council of State was not a magic wand.

But, overall, the achievement was massive, particularly in the build up of industry in Scotland. This is not at all to belittle the part played by the Ministries of Supply and Aircraft Production and by the Board of Trade, for, essentially, the task of the Scottish Office was to bring pressure to bear on these departments; and much was owed to their receptiveness. Even by the end of 1943 the meagre 3½ per cent of war production carried out in Scotland had risen to 13 per cent involving over 50,000 workers in three hundred and seventy projects in new, reopened or extended factories. And if the Council of State could not survive the return of party government, in the Scottish Council of Industry a sword had been fashioned to defend the gains that had been made.

While the close collaboration between Johnston and most of his officials has been emphasised, the small staff of the Scottish Information Office deserves special mention. It was the means by which Johnston added to the range of opinions he could sound, and it was used to disseminate his plans and his hopes to the Scottish public. Walter Elliot had been the first to see the need for good publicity and to enlist a press officer, but the Scottish Information Office did not come into being until the beginning of the war when it also acted as the Ministry of Information in Scotland. In Johnston's years at the Scottish Office it did a great deal to make the people of Scotland look to the future—whatever the difficulties of the post-war years might be—with hope and courage.

None was closer to Johnston than the late William Ballantine, the Director of the Scottish Information Office whose influence spread far beyond his room on the ground floor of St Andrew's House. The tale is now well-known, indeed it is recounted by Johnston himself in his already quoted volume of autobiographical reminiscences, of the visit to Britain in 1941 by Harry Hopkins, President Roosevelt's special envoy sent to assess the durability of Britain's purpose. The envoy was unimpressed and ominously silent on the closing evening until he was moved to paraphrase the Old Testament ('Wheresoever thou goest we go, thy people shall be our people, etc etc') bringing Winston Churchill and everyone else present to the verge of tears. This transformation of the aloof American, with its mighty implication for future Atlantic accord, had been triggered-off by Johnston as host—for the dinner was in Glasgow—making an inspired and timely reference in his Scots burr to Hopkins' grandmother having come from the Perthshire village of Auchterarder.★

'And who do you think it was', Willie Ballantine would say, a mischievous glint behind his spectacles, 'who was it that passed the note to TJ suggesting that grannie in Auchterarder was worth a mention!'

There has lastly to be special mention of the war service of the Scottish Home Department's small fishery protection cruisers and their ships' companies. On the outbreak of war all eight of these from forty year old *Brenda* to spanking-new *Minna* went over to exacting, hum-drum work with shipping convoys in the Firths of Forth and the Clyde. 'The monotonous duties of the service were enlivened from time to time by enemy aircraft coming into the Firth of Forth to lay mines, but as the vessels were only armed with an old 12-pounder gun at this time, frequently the aircraft was out of range before the gun could be brought to bear. Many rounds were fired off from Lewis and Browning machine guns as well, but no aircraft was known to have been brought down.' *Minna* was mined in 1940 off Fidra, and a year later bombed and all but lost. Repaired, she had still more hazardous times ahead, for she spent the rest of the war smuggling agents and saboteurs into

★According to Martin Gilbert (Winston S Churchill, Vol VI, p 991) Churchill's doctor recorded in his diary: 'I sat next Harry Hopkins, an unkempt figure. After a time he got up and, turning to the PM said "I suppose you wish to know what I am going to say to President Roosevelt on my return. Well, I'm going to quote you one verse from the Book of Books in the truth of which Mr Johnston's mother and my own Scottish mother were brought up: 'Whither thou goest I will go; and where thou lodgest I will lodge; thy people shall be my people, and thy God my God'." Then he added very quietly: "Even to the end." I was surprised to find the PM in tears. He knew what it meant.'

North Africa and the South of France, Normandy and Norway. So useful did she prove to be for these clandestine missions that, but for the abrupt ending of the war with Japan the later months of 1945 would have found her doing similar work off the Malayan coast.

For Scotland, it had been anything but a quiet war. The battle of the Atlantic had been fought from the Clyde and the airfields of the Hebrides. Rosyth to Scapa, Leuchars to Shetland, the Royal Navy and Royal Air Force had had operational bases along the east coast. All manner of soldiery had trained for battle, from the Commandos in Lochaber to the gallant Poles in Fife, to the 1st Army in Ayrshire preparing for the North African landings.

But there had only been one Clydebank, one Greenock. Had there been many more such disasters, had the buzz-bombs and V bombs of 1944 held Scotland within their range, the social fabric would have been so stretched that the Scottish Office would probably have had its hands too full coping with the general distress to plan, still less initiate, post-war measures. Relative to England, for the first time this century Scotland had been lucky. A commentator of these days saw 'the sky of Scotland mackerelled with hope'.

V

'FORTIES TO 'SIXTIES

WITH THE break-up of coalition government soon after the end of the war in Europe, Tom Johnston demitted office. To many of those who worked with him at St Andrew's House in Edinburgh, or at Fielden House, to which the Secretary of State had shifted his flag in 1941, he was something of a hero-figure. For the most part he had achieved the near-perfect integration of a minister and his staff. But he was now in his middle-sixties; his dislike of London was undiminished; and though he seemed as adroit as ever in getting his own way he professed to those closest to him a distaste for political in-fighting. So it might well be thought that he was happy to go. But Forsyth Hardy of the Scottish Information Office of these days, and so his travelling companion on many a long journey, has an intriguing recollection from the spring months of 1945 when the break up of the Coalition was seen to be inevitable. This is of Johnston toying with the thought that he might continue in a new government after the war as Secretary of State for Scotland, but in the House of Lords. As Hardy recalls, one of the political columnists thereupon was induced to 'fly a kite'; but nothing came of it. The convention that the Scottish Secretary ought to sit in the Commons had been prayed in aid by Mr Asquith in removing Lord Pentland from the post in 1912, and by Mr Baldwin in 1924 in explaining to Lord Novar why the latter's hopes of reappointment to Dover House had to be disappointed. But even had he become Lord Johnston, as Secretary of State, 'TJ' could not have avoided the twice-weekly cabinet meetings which were to be the norm of government from now on. 'Ordeal-by-sleeper', the fitful slumber on the 'Night Scotsman' between Waverley and King's Cross which he so loathed, would still have had to be endured.

On the break up of the Coalition, and its succession by the Churchill 'caretaker' administration in the run-up to the General

Election of 1945, Johnston was succeeded by a peer in the person
of the war-time Regional Commissioner, Lord Rosebery, son of
the 'founder' of the Scottish Office of 1885. Had there been a
Conservative victory at the General Election, would Rosebery
have been continued in office and the convention broken that the
Scottish Secretary should be in the Commons? Perhaps he thought
so. 'Haven't been the best Secretary of State', he said in his gruff
way to his private office staff on demitting office. 'Haven't been
the worst.' Then after a silence he added, 'Haven't had time'. It
was during these summer months of 1945 that the legislative
achievement of the Education (Scotland) Act 1945 was put
through. Among many other reforms to catch up with the
educational advance of the great 'Butler' Act of 1944 in England
and Wales, it provided at last for the raising of the school-leaving
age to fifteen. Though the Department had been at odds with
Johnston during his tenure in their reluctance to accommodate his
ideas on the curriculum, they had in the latter war years been busy
in preparing this major legislation.

With the Labour victory, the new occupant of the big room on
the fifth floor of St Andrew's House with its fine walnut panelling,
blue leather chairs, and dramatic view of the ascent of the Royal
Mile from Holyroodhouse to Edinburgh Castle, was Joseph
Westwood. Once a miner, Westwood had served in the war years
as a likeable junior minister at St Andrew's House; and he was as
big a contrast as could be to Rosebery's physical presence,
background and style. Johnston had not stood for re-election to
Parliament. 'It was a great regret to me' Attlee was to write of
Johnston 'that he decided at the end of the war to retire from
political life'. (But if Attlee had been closer to Scotland he might
not have put it quite that way: TJ's new career as chairman of the
North of Scotland Hydro-Electric Board and also as chairman of
the Scottish Tourist Board was no retiral from 'politicking'.)

The post-war years of the Attlee administration are often
represented as something of a revolution in government. With the
fruition of the Johnstonian initiatives, they were, for the Scottish
Office also years of continuity. However these years are also
remembered for the agonies of frustration endured as the business
of implementation got under way. Shortage of physical resources
hobbled so much of what was being attempted. The nation-wide
rationing of resources was as complex as it was absolute, and it
involved a great deal of high level wrangling in Whitehall committee rooms. Sometimes rationing had to be applied almost to the
point of absurdity. If for any particular project a local authority,
hospital board or whatever could be allotted by its matching St
Andrew's House department the requisite share of an abstraction
known as 'capital investment', then, subject to the usually doubtful
availability of labour and material, construction could begin. If

not, not. So in 1947 one Border burgh pled with St Andrew's House that the steel for a new footbridge across the Tweed was (somehow) already in the Burgh Surveyor's yard, that its workmen were not otherwise employed, and that from South Africa a millionaire son of the burgh had donated the cost. All this was to no avail: the requisite 'capital investment' was lacking for central government to authorise the work! It gave the officials at St Andrew's House no pleasure so to administer scarcity.

But standing back, as the hard-pressed staff were little able to do at the time, we can see that these were years of achievement over most of the Scottish Office spectrum. Those who joined after service in that most far-flung of wars quickly recognised what a ferment of activity there had been and that it showed no signs of abating; there was to be no return to pre-war hours. Of all this, the creation of the National Health Service might well be singled out for further mention, partly because it was the only one of the major nationalising measures which involved the Scottish Office at first hand; also because it was brought into being by the Department of Health independently of—though in consultation with— the Ministry in Whitehall. And here the task of integrating the hospital service was particularly formidable. The great city hospitals with their long associations with the medical schools of the universities; other hospitals also in pre-war days supported by public donation; the few general hospitals and the many mental hospitals run by local authorities; the cottage hospitals in the burghs; and lastly, the whole war-time Emergency Hospital Service; all these with their differences of tradition and outlook had to be speedily blended by the department into the one unified service administered by five regional hospital boards. The need to go our own independent way as necessary was bluntly, and successfully, asserted; for the Department had itself been running an Emergency Hospital and Medical Service since 1939 while the Ministry of Health in Whitehall had not. Nor was the planned exclusion of London's great teaching hospitals from the national hospital service in England seen by the department as any good reason why Edinburgh's Royal and such-like, should be left out of the Scottish regional hospital boards, whatever the 'embarrassment' this might be said by Whitehall to be causing south of the Border. Throughout, good relations with the medical profession were maintained; this, as is recalled, due in no small measure to the personal qualities of Sir Andrew Davidson, the department's Chief Medical Officer. Indeed, down the years the continuing development of the Health Service was to see a close partnership between the department's administrators and its doctors reflecting the equality in Civil Service ranking of the Department's Secretary and its CMO.

Local Health Executives which would give general practitioner cover to all the population had also to be set up with speed to take over from the pre-war Local Health Committees whose scope had been limited to the insured employee, and did not embrace his family. There had also to be new divisions of staff in St Andrew's House to deal with the dentists, pharmacists and opticians. The differences in these professions between Scotland and England were not great, but in the interests of the department's full coverage of the health service in Scotland some duplication of effort was tolerated. Overall, the measure of Scottish control of Scottish health affairs enjoyed by the Department under its ministers proved to be a major factor in the relatively smooth development of the National Health Service in Scotland.

The war time suggestions from London that post-war housing in Britain should become the province of the Ministry of Works having been beaten off, the Department of Health remained in charge in Scotland. The agents for the huge rehousing tasks now being resumed continued to be the town and county councils supplemented in the areas of greatest need by the Scottish Special Housing Association strengthened and expanded from its pre-war beginnings. There was major legislation in 1946 to set new and higher levels of housing subsidy. All building proposals by local authorities or the Association were given detailed examination by the Department of Health's architects, quantity surveyors and administrators. In 1944 the Scottish Housing Advisory Committee which Johnston had reconstituted had produced a stimulating report on design, layout and standard of construction entitled 'Planning our New Homes'; but the role of the Department's housing divisions was now to apply strict standards so that the available supplies of bricks, timber and so on might go further. With the lack of skilled labour a constraint everywhere, and following the success of the government's end of war programme of temporary pre-fabricated houses of which there were 32,000 in Scotland alone, the Department also put a great deal of effort into promoting the partial factory construction of houses and the acceptance of these 'non-traditionals' by the local authorities. It was more than a little ironic, old hands observed, that the factory made house, so decried in Walter Elliot's time, should now be seen as a means of salvation by some of its erstwhile critics.

Planning was another burgeoning area. Here again, as we have seen, there had been during the later war years successful resistance by the Department to London's centralising tendencies. The town and country planning legislation of 1947, complex to the point of bafflement as it was, had its distinctively Scottish version; and with the concept of planning including the New Towns Act of 1946 East Kilbride became Britain's as well as Scotland's first New Town. Development through New Towns conformed to the emerging creed of *regional* planning and, in particular to the Clyde

Valley Regional Plan which Tom Johnston had commissioned in
the war years and which was published in 1946. In retrospect, it
would be difficult to over-estimate the importance of the Clyde
Valley Plan. The team, mostly from the Department of Health,
which produced it under the leadership of Sir Patrick Abercrombie
and Sir Robert Matthew had carried out a comprehensive review
of the physical, social, recreational and economic development
possibilities of the entire region from Carrick to the northern tip of
Loch Lomond, from the headwaters of the Clyde to the Tail of the
Bank. The report did more than call for development through
New Towns with their better prospects of attracting new industry.
It pointed uncompromisingly to the need drastically to reduce the
three-quarters of a million huddled in three square miles of central
Glasgow, and to the approaching exhaustion of the great Lanarkshire coalfield (which had been the subject of a special Scottish
Office inquiry at the instance of Tom Johnston). It was equally
firm in its insistence that steel making in Lanarkshire, for its own
long term good, ought to move to an estuarine location. In the
then boom conditions for the shipyards, when no one else was
facing the facts, it asserted that within a few years shipbuilding on
the Clyde would have sunk to something lower than the worst of
the inter-war years. Lastly it said bluntly that Clydeside needed a
regional authority for the immense tasks to be done. Neither the
steel industry nor the shipbuilders and the shipbuilding unions
heeded what the report had to say: and the local authorities, who
had combined well enough in the preparation of the report but
were now somewhat in a huff as they read its far-reaching
proposals, made difficulties about paying for its publication. Yet,
there was not the like of the Clyde Valley Plan elsewhere in
Britain, and in time it would have its full effect. To read it today is
to be struck by something more—the depth and warmth of its
affectionate regard for Clydeside and Clydesiders. (I Corinthians,
13 applies to great tasks of economic and social recovery as to
everything else.)

The Department of Agriculture continued to grow in numbers;
by 1948 it had topped the two thousand mark. With the national
balance of payments deficit taking over from the Battle of the
Atlantic as the determinant of policy, the maximisation of farm
production was still the order of the day. Despite the disbandment
of some of the war-time activities many controls were still in
existence. Rationing of animal feed was to continue into the 1950s
as did the paraphernalia of control administration. (In 1951 there
was still in existence a body known as the Waste Food Board, the
feeding of pigs its purpose in life.) But by 1948 the close
surveillance and disciplining of farming by the forty war-time
Agricultural Executive Committee had been succeeded by guidance and encouragement from eleven bodies, similarly named,

which divided Scotland broadly by distinctive farming areas: one for the Borders; one for the Lothians; one for the north-east; one for Caithness, Orkney and Shetland and so on. To these committees was also delegated the determination of farmers' eligibility for the grants governments now gave to 'marginal' upland farming and, at a still higher rate, to hill farming. In so judging their peers the Committees did good work; no other bodies could have done it so well. In these years the department also began to be better able to manage its now considerable funding of agricultural research in Scotland. *In* Scotland, but by no means entirely *for* Scotland: the Rowett Institute at Aberdeen where Boyd Orr had reigned, the Hannah at Ayr on dairy farming research, and the Institute near Edinburgh doing pioneering work on animal diseases, particularly in sheep, had established a world-wide prestige. But the generosity of their founders within and outwith farming had now been succeeded by government funding, and there would soon be other institutes to be financed for the crops side of Scottish farming. While scientific research was in most other fields financed by 'Great Britain' bodies, agricultural research in Scotland was (and still is) an exception. But the department's involvement in this blended well with its long-standing association with the three Scottish agricultural colleges which it also funded. All this widened the department's horizons.

The Scottish Education Department had its hands full with school building programmes, many linked to the spread of new housing, and with digesting the increased responsibilities brought about by the raising of the school leaving age. There was new thinking for the department in the reports on secondary and primary schooling by the Advisory Council on Scottish Education which Johnston had reconstituted under the distinguished chairmanship of Sir James Robertson, Rector of Aberdeen Grammar School. These were massive and penetrating reports. Drastic changes in the examination procedure for the higher classes of the secondary schools were recommended which would lessen the grip on 'the Highers' exercised by the Department's Inspectorate since the days of Sir Henry Craik. Still less acceptable to the Department was the Advisory Council's unsought criticism of the traditional role of the Inspectorate. 'The hurried, routine inspection of a succession of classes followed by a stereotyped report seems to us a time-wasting practice yielding profit to no one' was the blunt verdict of Sir James and his colleagues. The Inspectorate ought, they said, to include men and women with actual experience of teaching in primary schools. Even their name should be changed to that of 'HM Education Officers'. The upper reaches of the Department were not amused.

This brings us to the Scottish Home Department which was exerting itself all round in what has well been described as 'an enthusiastic and revivalist spirit'. An efficient National Fire Service was now successfully handed over to large groupings of town and county councils. The Department was closely involved with the new arrangements for centralised training and inspection, and for national aspects linked with the Home Office in Whitehall. Police training and equipment were being modernised at the department's instance and the prison system humanised in many ways. The Probation Service was reorganised. There was new work and a strengthening of the child-care inspectorate to implement the historic Children's Act of 1948 which at last made proper provision for homeless children by bringing together under central supervision the work of local authorities and of the voluntary bodies. The genial presence of W. Hewitson Brown, the department's chief inspector for these matters, is still remembered: he was tireless in his persuasion of all concerned 'to make the Act work'.

With the changeover of war-time factories to peace-time use the Industry Division worked closely with Bilsland's Scottish Council—to give it its full title, the Scottish Council (Development and Industry)—formed immediately after the war out of the war-time Scottish Council for Industry and the pre-war Scottish National Development Council. The Division redoubled its pressure on the Board of Trade and the Ministry of Supply to ensure that Scottish opportunities were not let slide. And in its dealings with the Hydro-Board the department was itself now intimately involved in building up a new industry. Controversy over hydro-electric development had faded away after public enquiries, held under the aegis of the department and presided over by Mr John Cameron KC (later Lord Cameron) into the first two major constructional schemes, at Loch Sloy in the Argyllshire hills and the valley of the Tummel in Perthshire, had come down in their favour. But it fell to the Secretary of State, as advised by the Department, to approve each of the many new construction and distribution schemes emanating from the Board's Edinburgh offices. The Department had also to argue the case for each project in order to secure Treasury guarantees of the Board's large borrowing. It had to see to it that, amid so many competing claims, the Board got the army of labourers and great quantities of building material it needed. Lastly, the Department had the major hand in the safeguarding alike of the beauty and of the salmon fisheries of the highlands about which such a very great deal had been said in parliament and public enquiry. All this conferred experience for the many tasks in the fields of industry and development of the years ahead.

These too were the years of rebuilding the inshore fishing industry, and here the department led the Ministry of Agriculture and Fisheries in Whitehall. Unlike agriculture, where much of the workforce had exemption and by the end of the war the industry was incomparably stronger than it had been at the beginning, the inshore fishermen—as always—were the first to go to war. By 1945 their elderly steam drifters and trawlers had fallen victim to rust and Admiralty service. But, thanks to the report of the war-time committee on the herring fishing industry which Walter Elliot had chaired, complemented by one on the white fish industry which had been chaired by that redoubtable Shetlander, Sir Basil Neven-Spence, legislation was soon prepared for schemes to enable fishermen to encompass a better future from the drift netting of the herring shoals as they progressed round Britain and the seine-netting of white fish at other seasons. For the new boats there were harbours round the Scottish coast to be built with grant from the department and from the Development Commission in London, and to designs approved by the department's civil engineers. Like agricultural research, fisheries research in Scotland also looked to St Andrew's House for funding and support. Lastly, there was a close relationship with the industry's own bodies, the Herring Industry Board in Edinburgh and the White Fish Authority and its Scottish Committee. Leading this concerted effort was John Aglen, who was to dedicate his great energy to the rehabilitation of the industry and the well-being of the fishing communities for which he had so high a regard. But the outcome of the initial post-war measures was unexpected. With their smart new 'dual-purpose' boats financed under 'Herring Fisheries' legislation, the east coast fishermen from Eyemouth to Lossiemouth quickly swung the balance of their catching effort towards haddock and whiting. This brought them prosperity and pleased everyone (except the 'Herring Board'): it pays for legislation to be flexible.

The overall picture was that the department was simultaneously expanding in many diverse directions—children *and* fisheries; industry *and* prison improvement; hydro-electricity *and* police training; highland policy *and* local government finance; tourism *and* liaison with the Scottish Committee of the Arts Council. The enthusiasm of the department of these years under the leadership of its secretary, Sir Charles Cunningham, was patently obvious. On one point Cunningham was particularly insistent. Small though it was, the Home Department must never have even the slightest hesitation in laying itself alongside the armada of Whitehall. To sail in convoy at the policy planning stage if possible; to engage in close combat if necessary.★

In the late 1940s throughout Britain relief of the poor was altogether taken out of the hands of local government. Both this and old age pensions were brought within the domain of the Ministry of Pensions and National Insurance. This meant that the

★But we lost Sir Charles to the 'armada': in 1957 he became Permanent Under-Secretary of State at the Home Office.

Department of Health, for its part, gave up both the foundation subject of its predecessor, the Poor Law Board of Supervision, and the administration of old age pensions which in 1912 had been devolved to Scotland in anticipation of Asquithian 'Home Rule all round'. Both subjects were surrendered without demur. They were so obviously central to the architecture of the Welfare State which the post-war Government wished to construct in a uniform way throughout Britain. Yet, was there, with hindsight, anything to regret in this cession of responsibility? On balance, obviously not. But it did mean that the Department of Health, now responsible in a general way for the care of the old and the handicapped exercised locally by town and county councils, did not administer social security—and often the old and the handicapped are poor as well. And when, in the 1970s, the Scottish Office found that social decay in the poorer urban communities had become a major concern, some thought that its 'feel' for the complex and interacting problems posed by these 'areas of deprivation' might have been surer had it been involved directly with them as were, say, the local offices of the Great Britain department responsible for social security.

Even with the loss of these responsibilities, by the end of the 1940s the Scottish Office had grown; including the prison staff who were about one-fifth of the total, numbers were now over five thousand. The majority of these were stationed in Edinburgh, but of them less than half were in St Andrew's House itself. For many years to come the business of management was to be bedevilled by the proliferation of smaller offices housing departmental staff in relative isolation, from Carlton Terrace overlooking Holyrood to more hum-drum buildings amidst the council flats of west Edinburgh.

As a new element in the city's life, the Scottish Office was, no doubt, good for Edinburgh. Was Edinburgh good for the Scottish Office? To answer this involves some assessment of the capital's curious personality. Far be it from this author (a west of Scotland man) to pontificate on this, but, happily, there is available the eminently quotable description of Edinburgh in the celebratory volume brought out by the city's illustrious daily newspaper to mark its own one hundred and fiftieth anniversary. This is a touch on the acerbic side.

The anonymous 'Scotsman' staff-member described it as:

'. . . a city cosily ensconced in its own complacency, comfortably superior about its own merits as the capital of Scotland and home of the festival, a city unremarkable for enterprise or originality; a community very much dominated by the genteel society of its upper layers, shrouded in the respectability of its professional classes but occasionally luridly shot through with the extravagance of the Rose Street literati; a city in which it was and is peculiarly easy to overlook the hundreds of thousands of people who lived in the burgeoning housing estates on the perimeter and the slums of the East Side.'

It was—and is—a privilege to spend one's days against the changing backdrop of the Edinburgh seasons; sunlight and sharp shadow on stonework; the bluish haze of a winter dusk. It was—and is—a privilege which Home Counties commuters must envy to spend a Civil Service career with such ease of access to the office. However, in these years of the 'forties and 'fifties, the social geography of Edinburgh still did not quite match the simplicity of its physical layout. 'Auld Reekie' herself was still as in Fergusson's day 'the canty hole/A bield for many a cauldrife soul'. Outwith the old town it was different. Each profession tended to keep to itself; social Edinburgh seemed at times to be a variety of circles which overlapped all too little. Nor was it much in touch with the industrial west. This made it seem a less than ideal milieu for the innovative and lateral thinking about Scotland which has to be an essential purpose of the Scottish Office. Yet it would be churlish to make too much of this; the renowned Edinburgh social formality of pre-war years had already gone by the 1950s, and matters seem to have improved a lot in more recent decades. Certainly, once admission to the magic circles has been accorded, Edinburgh is seen for what it truly is, a city of all the talents.

Joseph Westwood had been succeeded as Secretary of State in 1947 by Arthur Woodburn who had served as Tom Johnston's parliamentary private secretary. Thoughtful, courteous and considerate he would speak with quiet amusement of his earlier acquaintance with the Calton Hill, when he had been imprisoned as a conscientious objector of the First World War. His dynamic successor was Hector McNeil, fresh from the success he had enjoyed as second-in-command to Ernest Bevin at the Foreign Office.★ A striking aspect of McNeil during his short reign was his insistence that the Secretary of State for Scotland must be ready to participate generally in debate round the long Cabinet room table of No 10. He must not confine himself to Scottish issues, still less to what would often appear to others as pettifogging north-of-the-border points. This could put new and unexpected demands on departments and on his private secretaries. The extreme example

★Hector McNeil's rise in the political world was to be cut tragically short by his death in 1955.

of this occurred during the Korean war when Bevin, the Foreign Secretary, was ill. McNeil, until three months before Minister of State at the Foreign Office with special United Nations responsibilities, had a contribution to make on the vexed question of United Nations military intervention. So, for the crucial weeks his private office had the additional task of scrutinising Foreign Office telegrams and sticking pins in a map of South Korea.

For all the increased workload falling on his desk the Secretary of State had still only two junior ministers to assist him. From 1945 one of these was Tom Fraser, like Joseph Westwood a former miner; he was to remain an important figure in several aspects of Scottish administration for the next three decades. From 1950 until the Conservatives were returned at the General Election in the autumn of 1951, his ministerial partner was Miss Margaret Herbison. From the outset her lucid intelligence and patent honesty of purpose gave her an easy command of the areas for which she was responsible; health affairs, home affairs and education.

As controls eased with the warmer economic climate and with recovery from war-time stress well under way, there was now the beginnings of more scope for new ideas and innovation; but, like Lord Rosebery, Hector McNeil 'didn't have time'. A major preoccupation of his eighteen months in office was the rise of the Scottish Covenant movement which now claimed to have enlisted support from over one half of the adult population of Scotland to the establishment of a Scottish Assembly with legislative powers.

In response to this upsurge of feeling, whatever its root causes or ultimate purposes, Arthur Woodburn had reacted angrily at his press conferences. But he also brought about a significant improvement in the handling of Scottish bills at Westminster by taking the effective debate on purely Scottish legislation away from the congestion of business on the floor of the House of Commons to the Scottish Standing Committee and the soporific calm of the high roofed, mock-Gothic committee rooms looking on to the murky Thames. Now in 1950, as the Covenant movement grew in strength, Hector McNeil appointed Lord Catto, a Scots born former governor of the Bank of England, to chair a committee which would examine Scotland's financial relationship with the rest of the United Kingdom and pronounce on the feasibility of showing whether or not Scotland was hard done by. The Catto Committee was also to go beyond this and consider whether it was possible to shew Scotland's share in imports and exports and ascertain the facts of her trade with England. When they appeared, the findings were seen to be inconclusive and did nothing to sustain the high pitch of feeling among the latter day 'covenanters'. But in servicing the enquiry, the Home Department learnt a great deal about the basic facts of the Scottish economy, and acquired the beginnings of its statistical staff; and the Committee's secretary was to become the first Economic Adviser to the Secretary of State.

This sober constitutional debate was interrupted on Christmas Day 1950, when the Stone of Destiny was uplifted from Westminster Abbey, as envisaged in the plot of Compton MacKenzie's 'North Wind of Love', as preceded by an unsuccessful ploy of Hugh McDiarmid and associates in the 1930s who also went to London to appropriate the Stone but failed. (All McDiarmid would say subsequently about this episode was that the problem of its removal was 'leverage'!) Nor was the debate resumed in the succeeding months of rumour and press speculation which culminated—as we learned later—in a meeting hastily, secretly, and appropriately convened by the late Countess of Erroll, Lord High Constable of Scotland, which prevailed on the temporary custodians of the Stone to surrender it to the historic abbey of Arbroath. In all the excitement of 'the Stone' the momentum of the Covenant movement was lost. Then, with the return of a Conservative government in the autumn of 1951 St Andrew's House prepared itself for the close examination of its stewardship by a Royal Commission which the new government's election manifesto had promised.

The Royal Commission of Inquiry was a device of government much used in later Victorian times. As problems, social and economic, rose up before government departments which were both minute in size and swamped with day to day business, it was a means of enlisting the (unpaid) help of members of parliament and other public personages to elicit the facts. We have seen the Royal Commission on the Housing of the Working Classes which Dilke chaired in 1885. In more recent years it has sometimes seemed a matter of chance whether or not a government inquiry is dubbed a Royal Commission. The study of the Civil Service of 1914 which Lord McDonnell chaired was so entitled; Lord Fulton's committee of 1968 was not. The Gilmour Committee of 1937, *accoucheur* to the post-1939 Scottish Office was not; but the inquiry into Scottish administration of 1953 was indeed to be a Royal Commission.

Apart from its power to command evidence and the appearance of witnesses the only obvious difference between the 'Departmental Inquiry' and the 'Royal Commission' is the sonorous declamation of the remit from the sovereign which preambles the Commission's report. But if its wording is a little archaic, like the breeches and silk stockings of Black Rod in the House of Lords it is intended to impress, and so it serves a purpose. Not all departmental committees of inquiry win swift implementation of their recommendations; by and large, the setting up of a Royal Commission means business. And so the Scottish Office welcomed the appointment in 1953 of the Royal Commission on Scottish Affairs,

James Stuart (Secretary of State 1951–57) has mixed
feelings about his portrait?

confident that in the years since 1939 it had proved its worth. That
this Royal Commission's findings would bring about consolida-
tion and advance seemed the more likely since the new government had already strengthened its ministerial team at St Andrew's
House by the appointment of a Minister of State—the Earl of
Home—as deputy to the Secretary of State, and of a third
parliamentary under-secretary. Right away the beneficial effect of
this addition to ministerial complement had been felt, easing the
onerous burden on the Secretary of State and giving him a deputy
who was not subject to the imperatives of House of Commons
attendance and so had more time to move around Scotland, gauge
opinion for himself, and tackle problems as they arose. The
privileged position in which the Scottish Office was now happy to
find itself should also be mentioned, James Stuart the new
Secretary of State having a close friend in Winston Churchill, from
his service as Government Chief Whip in the war-time years.
    The Royal Commission on Scottish Affairs was chaired by the
Earl of Balfour, a Scottish industrialist, nephew to A J Balfour

who had served briefly but so effectively as Secretary for Scotland in 1886. It had a membership from public life in Lowlands and Highlands, from industry and local government, and it also included a distinguished Cambridge economist and a retired Whitehall permanent secretary. The Home Department provided the secretariat. The terms of reference of the Royal Commission as decided by Ministers were refined in successive drafts by the careful hand of Sir David Milne, permanent under-secretary of state since 1946; parliamentary devolution was not within its scope, nor did it extend to the nationalised industries in Scotland. They were simply

> 'to review with reference to the financial, economic, administrative and other considerations involved, the arrangements for exercising the functions of Our Government in relation to Scotland.'

The Royal Commission then got down to a lengthy stint of work involving thirty-four meetings, and the receiving of evidence from all who cared to submit it. There were particularly important sessions of oral evidence from the local authority associations, from the Scottish Council, from heads of government departments in Whitehall, including the head of the Treasury, and from Sir David Milne himself. Northern Ireland was visited to study Ulster's version of devolution, and in particular the encouragement to industrial growth the province was able to offer; not for the first time, Scottish administration was to be influenced by the example of Ireland.

Despite the tightly drawn remit, James Stuart had said in parliament that the Royal Commission was free to receive evidence on parliamentary and political devolution. So the Scottish Covenant Association spoke before the Royal Commission in favour of a Scottish Parliament within the framework of the United Kingdom, and the nationalist bodies advocated complete self-government more in Dominion style. But the Royal Commission's eventual report observed, somewhat disparagingly for the proponents of change, that 'although large numbers signed the Covenant, the issue of Parliamentary separation does not appear to have perceptibly influenced the votes cast at the few elections at which it has been given prominence.'

Nonetheless, at the outset of its Report, the Royal Commission applied itself to 'the deterioration that is widely held to have occurred in recent years in the general relationship between Scotland and England'. It put this down to the extension of government since World War I, exacerbated by wartime and post-war controls for the management of scarcity, and to the consequential fear that Scotland was to be treated as a mere province; also to the allied fear that Scotland's recovery from the economic depression of the inter-war years was lagging far behind that of the rest of Britain. Thus, the commission remarked, government was criticised for doing too much (by way of controls etc) and too little (in directing new industry). This perceptive analysis was to be perhaps the most important aspect of the report, legitimising as it were the barracking to which the Home Department and its ally, the Scottish Council, had subjected the Board of Trade in the latter's exercise of distribution of industry policy.

The report then gave the outcome of its close and careful examination of government administration in Scotland. There were three salient points, two of which were reaffirmation of the status quo. First: industrial development in Scotland must remain primarily the responsibility of the Board of Trade though that department's Scottish presence should be strengthened. Lord Bilsland had been clear in the evidence he gave for the Scottish Council that in his view no good could come of Scotland attempting to go it alone in this field. London control had to be the means of steering industry northwards. Second: the existing division of responsibilities of the St Andrew's House departments should not be disturbed. Third: responsibility for roads and bridges should move from the Ministry of Transport—which, as we have seen, had assumed it after the end of the Great War—to the Scottish Home Department; responsibility for animal health should move from the Ministry of Agriculture in Whitehall to the Department of Agriculture in St Andrew's House; and the Secretary of State should take over from the Lord Chancellor responsibility for Justices of the Peace.

Relative to the whole, these proposed organisational changes seemed modest. Deceptively so. The Forth Road Bridge would not have been the first estuarine road crossing in Britain without the shift of responsibility from the Ministry of Transport. 'The Scotsman' eyeing St Andrew's House critically from its North Bridge windows would have it that the mountains had laboured and a mouse had been born. This was unfair even though, on account of the alarming outbreak of foot and mouth disease in 1955, government was prevailed on not to transfer executive responsibility for animal health to the Department of Agriculture. In the circumstances of the 1950s the Royal Commission achieved as much new administrative devolution as was then attainable. It also legitimised the war-cry of 'Scottish control of Scottish affairs'; witness the ease with which in the later 1950s electricity generation and distribution in the south of Scotland came under the Secretary of State.

The Royal Commission devoted a chapter of their report to the development of the Highlands and Islands, that perennial, if fitful, concern of Scottish administration down the years since Dover House first recognised that sending in the Royal Marines was not enough. It was now clear that with the steeply ascending costs of dam construction and power distribution, the North of Scotland Hydro-Electric Board for all its great and positive contribution could not afford to become quite the multi-purpose development agency for the north (like the much envied Tennessee Valley Authority in the USA) which the commentator of 1945 who had seen the sky 'mackerelled with hope' would have wished it to be. Nor did it now seem at all likely that there would be the abundant cheap electricity to attract large power using industry to the north. In his evidence to the Royal Commission Sir David Milne had conceded that the Board's role was now co-operation with, rather than initiation of, general highland development. However, immediately after the war, the mere fact of the Board's existence had argued against the setting up of a government development board for the highlands and islands; and, instead, Joseph Westwood had appointed an Advisory Panel on the Highlands and Islands with membership of MPs, county council conveners, and others appointed at his own hand, including the enlivening presence of Naomi Mitchison; all working closely indeed with a secretariat and assessors from the department at St Andrew's House. There had been a view that the advisory role should be left to a body outwith government, such as the fledgling Scottish Council, but the opposing view in Agriculture, with that department's longstanding involvement in crofting and the uncertainties of highland farming, was that there should be a more direct commitment by St Andrew's House to highland development. So the outcome which recognised the political necessity of such commitment—and here the permanent under secretary of state made his influence felt—was 'the Highland Panel', an advisory committee with a difference. Now eight years later the Royal Commission endorsed the Panel mechanism which under Lord Cameron's chairmanship was to be of good service to the highlands and the Scottish Office alike over the next ten years, particularly in promoting a consensus of thinking about the highlands and in preparing comprehensive programmes of highland development. That the Commission should have given such a slice of their time to this matter was perhaps implicit recognition on their part that something essential to Scotland's national identity resides in the Highlands and Islands.

One might, however, reflect on the substance of John Buchan's House of Commons speech of over twenty years past with its diagnosis that the Scottish malaise was essentially the fear that national identity was slipping away. The war had stirred Scotland, but this fear of fading identity had not receded. Scots had fought mightily in and over three continents and on the seven seas but (*pace* the 51st Highland Division) not, for the most part, identifiably. There was indeed discontent, ostensibly over the relationship with England; but an upsurge of national unrest—like toothache—does not always in itself indicate clearly where its root cause lies. If fear of loss of national identity was the root cause rather than too much London control of industry, commerce and administration, the Royal Commission might with profit have had its scope widened—might have, say, also had brought within its sights the organisation of broadcasting in Scotland at this the early morning of the television age. But 'national identity' is perhaps too elusive a topic for a Royal Commission.

Lastly, the Royal Commission endorsed the roles of the four departments of the Secretary of State and their separation from each other as this had been ordained in 1939. Here their crystal ball was clouded: within a few years it was to be 'all-change' at St Andrew's House. If there is a criticism of the Royal Commission to be made it is that it did not look far enough ahead.

The Royal Commission's allocation to the Home Department of responsibility for roads was accepted, and this added still further to that department's multiplicity of functions. The new road system to be created in Scotland, and the estuarine crossings proposed would be central to her development; and so it was forcefully argued by the Department of Health that responsibility in St Andrew's House for roads should lie alongside its own responsibility for planning. But the immediate need was to persuade the Treasury to pocket their professed horror at the cost of throwing a road crossing over the Forth; also to beat down the Ministry of Transport's insistence that the project be financed by competitive bids (even though it was clear that only a consortium of bridge builders would be big enough to fulfil the contract); and these were the kind of high level battles in which the Home Department was adept. Another such which the Home Department now gleefully took on was the fight to secure approval for a Clyde tunnel, with the de-congesting influence it would have on Glasgow's cross-river traffic. Nevertheless there was a case for placing roads in the same department within the Scottish Office as planning, particularly now that the Department of Health was well advanced in evolving with the cities, counties and larger burghs the Development Plans which the town and country planning legislation of 1947 had required.

An extension of territory for the Home Department was also opened up by another, albeit indirect, consequence of the Royal Commission's advocacy of Scottish control of Scottish affairs—the creation out of the former British Electricity Authority of a generating and distributing South of Scotland Electricity Board which was sponsored by the Secretary of State for Scotland, not by the Minister of Fuel and Power. The North of Scotland Hydro Electric Board was now into its second decade of vigorous life under the tutelage of the Home Department (though 'tutelage' is hardly the correct word to describe the department's relationship with the Board, still chaired by the redoubtable Tom Johnston). The Hydro-Board was, like the new South of Scotland Electricity Board, a producer and distributor of electricity. The two boards would, clearly, have to work together and could do so best under the one minister. In the climate of the times—thanks to the Royal Commission—that minister had to be the Secretary of State for Scotland, rather than the Minister of Fuel and Power. The integration of coal-fired/nuclear powered generation in the south with hydro-electricity in the north gave great benefits which would improve the setting for Scottish industry. These would later include 'pump storage', that is, the use of off-peak energy to pump water to a high level reservoir in the hills for storage there until required to generate electricity at times of peak demand.

So in 1958 began the crucial debate within the Office on how best to organise its various roles in regard to the development of industrial Scotland. To view the issues we must look more closely at the respective roles of the two departments concerned and reflect briefly on how they had come about.

Staking out with a tape measure and the help of his charming secretary the location of the proposed industrial estate in rain-swept Renfrewshire of pre-war days, Sir Steven Bilsland had been the harbinger of a new area of government activity. By 1939 the Hillington Estate was in business, and by the outbreak of war three more industrial estates were planned in Lanarkshire by Lord Nigel Douglas-Hamilton (later Earl of Selkirk) the Scottish Special Areas Commissioner. As the government minister to whom he looked was the Secretary of State for Scotland it might have seemed that here was a new and permanent widening of the scope of the Scottish Office.

It did not work out like that. In fulfilment of the thinking of the historic Barlow Report of 1940 the Distribution of Industry Act of 1945 established what was intended to be a coherent regional industrial policy. It also placed the creation of industrial estates, like industrial policy generally, with the Board of Trade in London; but this caused no misgivings at St Andrew's House, nor in the Scottish Council (Development and Industry) which with membership from local authorities and trade unions as from industry, commerce and finance had succeeded Tom Johnston's war-time Scottish Council for Industry. Bilsland, the effective head of the Scottish Council, had always been clear in his mind that the purpose of the industrial estates was not so much job-creation itself as the attraction northwards of the new industries of London and the Midlands. 'Come kindly bombs and fall on Slough', wrote the unkindly John Betjeman. More practically minded, Bilsland saw in that starkly modern Thames Valley town the pattern for Scotland's industrial revival. And the corollary to factory provision by government in depressed central Scotland was government control of the location of new factory-building throughout Great Britain in order to force it west of the Severn and north of the Trent. The 1945 Act, and the town and country planning legislation of 1947 with its system of 'i.d.c.' (industrial development certificate) control seemed to do just that.

In this new 'carrot-and-stick' régime the Scottish Home Department saw its role as a seemingly unending series of administrative ploys to persuade the Board of Trade to wield the stick of the 'i.d.c.' to effect, and in all manner of ways to ensure that the carrot of government-assisted Scottish location was well-presented. Just as in war-time the Home Department's Industry division had run a successful double act with the Scottish Council for Industry, so the division's small staff now maintained close and cordial relations with its successor the Scottish Council. There was continuity not only in Sir Steven—shortly to be Lord—Bilsland leading the Scottish Council but also in Christopher Macrae moving outside the Civil Service to become its Secretary at the end of the war.

There were so many battles, great and small, to be fought— from the persuasion of Rolls-Royce to retain their manufacturing of aero-engines at Hillington, to the lobbying of the Ministries of Food and Supply in these years of general shortage to accept the emergence of a new fruit and vegetable processing firm on lower Speyside. Sometimes Scottish Ministers were directly involved. Distinguished ex-patriate Scots also found themselves pressed into service; in this the Scottish Council's London Committee and Bilsland's charm and influence would often swing the day.

Most celebrated of all these exploits to diversify the industrial base of Scotland was the attraction of IBM, the American computer giant, to Greenock in 1950 when Hector McNeil had succeeded Arthur Woodburn in the second Attlee administration. Ronald Johnson was head of the Industry Division at that time and he has left an account of how it was done.

> 'Hector McNeil succeeded Arthur Woodburn as Secretary of State in the spring of 1950, and quickly he persuaded International Business Machines to set up their first plant in the UK on the outskirts of Greenock. Hector had made the acquaintance of Tom Watson, the President of IBM, while he was Minister of State at the United Nations, and had resolved to try to inveigle him to the Caird shipyard, a problem of dereliction which had troubled Greenock and Hector's predecessors as Members since the 1920s. He had hardly been at the Scottish Office long enough to have his plans to do this examined by the Scottish

Home Department or the Board of Trade, when Tom Watson arrived with an entourage, and I was instructed to meet the Secretary of State and him at the Central Hotel, Glasgow, on the morning of Saturday, 29 July 1950.

When he reached the Caird shipyard, Tom Watson refused even to get out of the car to look at this splendid, but secondhand, waterside site. He was only interested in virgins. We fared little better when we went on to the neighbouring torpedo factory which Hector said that the Admiralty were getting out of and would give IBM space in which to get started. Hector did not then know what to do next (as he confessed to us afterwards) but he continued the drive down the Clyde and expatiated on the beauties of the scenery and the sporting opportunities for American executives. It was a lovely summer's day. At Inverkip we turned inland and took a side road when we got to the top of the hill. Here Tom did get out and look around and pointing down the Spango Valley towards Greenock he said—"Here is the valley of opportunity. This is where we shall come."

And so Hector McNeil brought IBM to Britain. From a civil servant's point of view, the choice of the Spango Valley left everything to be argued about from planning permission to development area grants. However, the arguments were successful and the factory opened in the following year.'

Another instance from these years was the attempted attraction to the New Town of East Kilbride of John Deere of Illinois, then, as now, one of the world's leading farm tractor manufacturers. Again, initial contact was made by Hector McNeil, the vice-president of the firm being, by happy chance, a Scot. The rival claims of a Merseyside location advanced by the Board of Trade (who were, of course, the department supposed to be responsible for the wooing) had to be contested; and with such a prize, the battle was hard-fought at all levels with allies quickly enlisted. However, at the end of a frenetic week in London, government ministers agreed to prefer a Scottish location and agreement with John Deere was finalised. Late in the evening one of McNeil's private secretaries was despatched to Grosvenor House in Park Lane to hand over their copy of the agreement to the Americans and toast the new venture with them. But the sequel gave no joy. Later difficulties arose which the Board of Trade did not resolve, and John Deere's European factory was located in Belgium.

If the IBM success-story had seemed to confirm that the Scottish Council—Scottish Office—Board of Trade nexus could succeed in diversifying Scottish industry, the John Deere flop raised doubts. For some it also pointed up another question. The proposed location for the Illinois giant had been the first of the post-war

Scottish New Towns. These as they developed were becoming more and more central to the general strategy of attracting new industry to Scotland, but within the Scottish Office they were the concern of the Planning Division of the Department of Health, not Industries Division of the Home Department. The former now began to feel that the time had come to run the industrial development side of the Scottish Office in double harness with New Towns administration, the whip hand being that of the emerging concept of comprehensive regional development heralded in the Clyde Valley Regional Plan of 1946.

This, however, was not the occasion of immediate debate, and, indeed, the Royal Commission on Scottish Affairs gave its blessing to the existing allocation of functions among departments in regard to this as to all else. But as the 1950s advanced and some parts of the Scottish economy began to flounder, aid to the development of industry began to be seen by press and public as the major purpose of the Scottish Office. John Maclay (now Viscount Muirshiel) who succeeded James Stuart in 1957 recalls that Secretaries of State were now being judged by the performance of the Scottish economy, even though as the Royal Commission's report had made clear it was the Great Britain Board of Trade which still held the reins in its hands. Maclay welcomed this new pressure on the Scottish Office; he wanted it to become the 'lead' Department in Government in regard to the Scottish economy, rather than a terrier, yapping however effectively, at Whitehall. For regional aid to industry was still far too small. Loans given in the decade and a half since the end of the war by the Board of Trade to industry in the Development Areas of Scotland as of Wales and the North of England totalled less than half the *annual* agricultural lime subsidy. Nor did there seem to be enough strategic thinking about the future direction of Scottish industry. The Board of Trade were not fulfilling this role; with foreign competition and the advent of the much more efficient container ship the collapse of shipbuilding on much of the Clyde had now begun; and it had not been foreseen. Nor had the Scottish Office yet succeeded in making good the deficiency: the attempt in 1949 by Arthur Woodburn to develop a consensus within Scotland through the summoning of a 'Scottish Economic Conference' was a failure. Most alarming of all, from the Scottish Office viewpoint, the Board of Trade's commitment of 1945 to the concept of regional industrial development as an integral part of the improvement overall of the economy of the United Kingdom had slackened. As a senior official of the Board informed a Parliamentary Committee at Westminster in the late 1950s regional industrial development was now seen by his department predominantly as 'a social matter'.

Even though from 1960 the Board of Trade (at Harold Macmillan's behest, as Maclay recalls it) made a welcome return to their

former stringency over industrial development outwith the Development Areas, and in their Local Employment Act of 1960 at
last offered realistic grants and loans to the development-minded
industrialist, it seemed to those concerned at St Andrew's House
that the Board were still on the wrong tack in that the criterion for
government assistance to industrial development was now more
emphatically than ever the incidence of local unemployment rather
than capability for new industrial growth. It did not follow that
areas of high unemployment, often caused by the demise of
traditional industry such as coal-mining, were the likeliest habitat
for the growth of new industry. Spurred on by its Secretary of
State the Scottish Office felt that it had an important contribution it
must make to the revision of regional industrial policy. It must
raise its voice. So now the Scottish Council, in conclave with the
Home and Health Departments at St Andrew's House, but also
fully informing the 'Great Britain' departments in Scotland of
Trade, Transport and Labour, set up a committee under the
chairmanship of Mr J N (now Sir John) Toothill of Ferranti. (That
company's Edinburgh factory of 1941 had struck deep roots in the
post-war years). The Committee had a joint Scottish Council—
Scottish Office Secretariat. Its remit was 'to review the present
position and future prospects of the Scottish economy, to define
the forces which control the growth and location of manufacturing
and other employment, to draw conclusions and to make recommendations.'

The Committee's message was the age-old military maxim—
reinforce success. Of its wide-ranging recommendations about the
ways by which faster economic growth could be achieved it gave
prominence to the desirability of the Scottish Office concentrating
expenditure on 'infrastructure'—that is roads, housing, water,
electricity and so on—on those districts which offered the best
promise of industrial growth. 'Regional development measures', it
said, 'should be co-ordinated to enable them to reinforce one
another. The kind of planning this implies should be the responsibility of a new department which should bring together the present
industrial and planning functions of the Scottish departments'.
Within this new department, the report continued, there should be
'an economic unit to advise on the promotion and co-ordination of
economic and industrial policy in Scotland', and it should also, and
right away, consider the need for better economic statistics.

The Toothill Report of 1961 was however only one ingredient
in the vehemently contested debate which now took place within
the Scottish Office about the proposed re-allocation of industry
responsibilities. There was a strong contrary view that the Home
Department for its part had been successful in its endeavours to
strengthen the economic base of Scotland; the steel strip mill at
Ravenscraig and the new car factory at Linwood in Renfrewshire,

John Maclay (now Viscount Muirshiel) (Secretary of
State for Scotland 1957–62); by James Gunn (at Dover
House).

with the hopes of others to follow, would be the foundation of a
re-industrialised Scotland. Nor was it accepted that there was a
vacuum in industrial strategy. The strategic role, it was felt, had
been well filled for many years by the Scottish Council with the
freedom of its independent status. Professor Cairncross's perceptive analysis of the Scottish economy of the early 1950s had been a
Scottish Council initiative, and that had made many of the points
which the Toothill Committee had now taken up in more

receptive times. The words ascribed—perhaps wrongly—to Gaius Petronius '. . . we tend to meet any new situation by reorganising and a wonderful method it can be for creating the illusion of progress while producing confusion, inefficiency and demoralisation'—were recalled.

However, while the success at Ravenscraig and Linwood reflected well on the efforts of the Home Department, winning the arguments at official level as they did, they were also largely due to the personal efforts of John Maclay, the Secretary of State; and the organisation of business in government departments has to proceed in the simple faith that like is best harnessed with like. While Sir William Murrie who had now succeeded Sir David Milne as Permanent Under-Secretary of State had a difficult task in coping with warring opinions, John Maclay had made it clear throughout his years in office that primacy must be accorded to whatever would strengthen the Scottish Office contribution to industrial revival. So, as he approved it, the outcome was much as the Toothill Report, and the proponents of change, had envisaged. The following year saw an end to the Scottish Home Department and the Department of Health. These were succeeded by a Scottish Development Department in which were grouped together responsibilities for local government finance, planning, housing, water and sewerage, roads, electricity, industry and regional development generally; and by a Scottish Home and Health Department in which what might be loosely termed those 'human' aspects of the Secretary of State's activities—health, and law and order—were placed.

Although in its 'union of Solon and Asklepius' the new Scottish Home and Health Department also lacked homogeneity, no longer would there be one department within the Scottish Office with such a variety of functions as the old Scottish Home Department. Its Fisheries Divisions had already gone over to the Department of Agriculture, thus bringing that department, organisationally, more into line with the Ministry of Agriculture and Fisheries in Whitehall. With the Fisheries Divisions had gone the guardians of highlands and islands development policy and the subsidisers of sea transport services to the western and northern isles. The division developing the care of homeless children now went to the Scottish Education Department in this the first widening of that department's range beyond scholastic matters. To some who had been spurred by her strong loyalties and sheer diversity it seemed as if the old Home Department had been dismembered like the body of the great Montrose—'on every airth a limb'.

Regret at the demise of the Home Department was still echoed years later in the memoir Cunningham was to write of his old command. For many a year those who had served with him would, as it were, drink a Jacobite toast to its memory, for the

Home Department had a bottomless well of *esprit de corps*. But the need was now to create a Scottish Office loyalty.

This drama of reorganisation within the Scottish Office should not be allowed to obscure the reality of the day to day within St Andrew's House at the turn of the 1950s. Until the reallocation of responsibilities among the four departments was actually intimated to staff on office notice-boards, relatively few were in the know about the intensity of the debate in the higher reaches of the Office. For most, work had gone on steadily month after month with new challenges to be met. Although the following chapter on the events of the 1960s will frequently refer back to the aspiration of the 1950s there is not scope within this present book—which has perforce to single out what was significant to the growth and development of the Scottish Office—even to attempt an adequate picture of all that the four departments were about in these years.

That would require a book on its own, and, indeed, it was accorded just this in 'The Scottish Office' by Sir David Milne which appeared in 1957. The hand was the hand of the then permanent under-secretary of state, but, as he readily conceded, the voice was that of a host of departmental Jacobs, all neatly marshalled by Ian Robertson whose distinguished career had already included a stint as James Stuart's private secretary. So it must be taken as read that, for example,—and these can only be a handful of examples amongst so many—divisions of the Department of Health still buckled to the task of developing the National Health Service in all its aspects; that great work was done in giving both central and rural Scotland a good supply of water; that in these pre-computer days there were large numbers of women, men, girls and boys, administering the price support, subsidy and capital grants regimes which were the trampolines for farming prosperity; that statisticians in the Education Department peering into the future sought to predict the numbers of teachers required as there rippled through the schools the variations in post-war birth rates; lastly, that far and away the single biggest block of staff in the Scottish Office were those running the prisons.

For much the greater part of their daily round, departments, as always, dealt direct with their public, be they local authorities, hospital boards, Colleges of Education, or individual farmers and their spokesmen of the National Farmers Union of Scotland. There would also be every morning—up to the mid-fifties including Saturdays—trolley-loads of correspondence wheeled downstairs from the Secretary of State's private office in St Andrew's House or brought up by overnight mail-bag★ from his office in

★ Still coming up by the west-coast railway route, as had been required during the war years so that any disaster to the 'Night Scotsman' from King's Cross to Edinburgh Waverley might not obliterate the papers as well as the people!

Dover House. The sheer variety of the ministerial correspondence of these days was neatly caught in the opening paragraph of Milne's book of 1957.

'On a typical day, there will be letters from Members of Parliament and from patients in mental hospitals, from Peers and from prisoners; there will certainly be formally expressed letters from lawyers and local authorities; and there may be informal and even abusive communications, scrawled on a postcard. There will be letters on hand-made paper with embossed letter-headings, and letters written on scraps torn from an old notebook. The subject matter of all these letters will be almost inconceivably diverse. On the same morning, the Secretary of State may be asked to consider appeals against the proposed erection of a large power station in the south of Scotland and of a fish-meal factory in the north; for remission of a sentence imposed by the courts, or against the closing of a rural school. The same post that brings him the considered views of the Convention of Royal Burghs on a Bill may also bring a pathetic letter from someone who wants a house, representations about employment prospects from the local branch of a Trade Union, and a request from a lady in America for a set of bagpipes.'

Today the Private Office post-bag is, perhaps, less entertaining; and with the widening of the Secretary of State's responsibilities formidable items are rather more numerous.

Before we leave the 1950s a backward look and a forward glance at the Department of Health's involvement in the re-housing of Scotland would be timely, for this dominated the political scene rather as the tower blocks would soon dominate the Glasgow skyline.

Each one of the cities, counties and burghs was still its own housing authority, and the Department, working closely with the Secretary of State and Commander Galbraith (later Lord Strath-clyde) the Parliamentary Under-Secretary of State who had been assigned responsibility for this sector, regulated the housing subsidies they received. Legislation of 1952 increased these sub-sidies so that the ambitious housing targets of the incoming government might be met; and there was further legislation to be put through Parliament in 1957 reflecting the policies of St Andrew's House in that it offered higher subsidies for housing to facilitate the movement of workers and their families from over-crowded Glasgow to elsewhere in Scotland. These 'overspill' agreements between Glasgow and the New Towns or with burghs in Ayrshire and elsewhere—even with Haddington in East Lothian—moved workers and their families in close harmony with the movement of industry from Glasgow or elsewhere to new locations; *shortage* of labour was perceived as the main obstacle to industrial growth, as it would continue to be throughout the 1960s.

Housing finance, like any long-standing subsidy regime, had become complicated and more than a little abstruse. Nonetheless in regulating the flow of government money according to Ministers' wishes to finance local authority house building, the Department was in the driving seat. Less easy to influence were the rent levels in council housing. These were often much too low, to the detriment of the town or county council's ability to embark on other services, or on work which should have gone hand in hand with the new housing, as, say, the building of community centres and other amenities. 'Local Authorities are responsible bodies in their own right', a Scottish Office White Paper of 1953 had declared; but the Department now found itself in conflict with some local authorities in a way which had not happened before. Formal investigations into default of duty by Glasgow, Dunbartonshire and Dundee were now carried out by senior members of the Scottish bar between 1957 and 1962 and the doubtful legality of too low rents confirmed. But in this area the Department could not quickly effect the extent of change desired by Ministers. For much of central Scotland rents remained too low for the overall good of the Scottish economy.

Thirdly, the Department now led a determined attempt to preserve the worthier stone-built tenements of the Victorian years which, with age and want of repair and improvement by their owners were going into dilapidation or were far below standard; at the end of the war one third of Scottish housing had lacked its own toilets. Legislation of 1949 had sought by subsidy to encourage the improvement of these older houses, but local authority enthusiasm had been for new houses on 'green-field' sites. Now with the dereliction of the old threatening to keep pace with the building of the new, there were in 1954 generous financial incentives made available to private owners and local authorities to arrest the decay. Then in 1956 the long-standing obstacle of 'owners' rates' was abolished in the comprehensive revision of valuation and rating carried out by the Home Department. This also was long overdue but, despite the frequently and sharply expressed anxiety of the Department of Health about the calamitous consequences of the rating of owners of rent-restricted property, nothing could be done until there was political will for change and a thorough legislative overhaul. Despite all these efforts change came too late for some tenements, particularly in Glasgow. The cry was still for *new* housing.

Lastly there was the Department's seeming control over the design and layout of the new housing. The corps of architectural advisers at St Andrew's House felt unhappy about some of the house design and layout adopted by some local authorities. This did not match the more uniformly good work of the Scottish Special Housing Association. But while the Department argued with local authority housing committees and put out excellent handbooks on better house-design and layout, it was generally deemed unthinkable that the Department should refuse to approve tenders on this account. The sheer intensity of the pressure to get on with house building may be gauged from the *weekly* progress reports which the Department prepared for Ministers. The Department was also inhibited by the continued financial stringency. The subsidy regime was no horn of plenty. Maximum as well as minimum standards had to be enforced; for example in 1952 the Department had had to insist that ceiling heights in new houses be lowered.

All this, coupled with the need to make the best use of building land, particularly in still congested Glasgow, was the background to the Department's initiative in the later 1950s to persuade the bigger local authorities to build upwards rather than outwards. In visits to Scandinavia and to England, small groups of the Department's administrators and architects had seen high rise flats enhancing the city scene and easily accommodating families with children. In an atmosphere of hope and confidence the Department provided that the subsidy arrangements of the 1957 Housing Act should point local authorities towards this sort of high rise construction which for some years the architectural journals had so warmly commended. The outcome of much of the high rise buildings in the 1960s was to be acutely disappointing: as they looked up to the highest housing tower-blocks in Europe some citizens felt that *these* did not 'belong to Glasgow', and subsequent tales of vandalism and discontent deepened their feelings. One aspect which frequently went wrong was the selection of tenants by housing management—and that lay on the edge of the Department's field. To say this is not to minimise the enormity of the problem of managing rehousing; many Glaswegians were not like the amenable Swedes; and the paring of standards by the Department as, say, in regard to lifts and balconies in response to the constant pressure for economy in government spending did not help.

While the physical achievement was vast, too much had to be done too quickly. The consequences were still felt of inaction in the years before 1914, and of the cessation of local authority house-building in the early 1930s (though, as Ronald Cramond has pointed out, these were the years when houses could be built at their cheapest). Even so, the enlightened housing legislation of

Walter Elliot's years might have saved the day. But the coming of Hitler's war was the final misfortune; for Scotland the enforced stop to house-building in the autumn of 1939 had been a national disaster.

VI

THE SWING
OF THE 'SIXTIES

How far short of the new Jerusalem would be the serried ranks of flatted housing rising from green fields was not foreseen at the outset of the 'sixties. And a future seemed to beckon in which the new philosophy of economic development would transform all Scotland.

Within the Scottish Office, the tide of optimism flowed strong and deep. Robert Grieve was soon to become Chief Planner in the new Development Department. His feeling for his native Glasgow matching his dedication to Scotland, Grieve had taken a hand under Abercrombie in fashioning the historic Clyde Valley Regional Plan of 1946. Now, at the opening of the 'sixties Grieve felt that the vision in that Plan was at last to be realised: that the industrial west of Scotland would use all its resources of place and people to heal its wounds. But, as he told the Institute of Town Planning, his hopes now went wider than this: they were for nothing less than 'a new, economically sound and universally pleasant Scotland'. Overcrowded Glasgow would be relieved, and he saw the redistribution of population to the New Towns and by government-backed 'overspill' programmes as the key to the future. Here, he continued, was 'the first foreshadowing of the practicability of redressing our excessively unbalanced population structure . . . the power that lies to our hands in producing new centres of growth in increasingly distant parts of our country.'

Grieve was specific about this. The rationale of 'overspill' programmes was that 'above certain minima of town populations, energy is released and many things become possible that were not possible before'. His concluding remark to fellow planners gathered in the Peebles Hydro was also significant

'I have no doubt in my own mind,' he said, 'that planning is bound to become the most important activity of local government.'

Of central government too: for the Scottish Office, the swing of the 'sixties' was to be the predominance of planning.

'Planning' had two complementary meanings. There was 'physical planning' as in the consideration given to the Development Plans produced separately for each of the cities, counties and large burghs—where the houses should go, where new industry, what major road development there should be, and so on. There was also 'economic planning' as in the vision of the Toothill Report of 1961, which would make physical planning serve the industrial regeneration of Scotland. Both were within the province of the new Scottish Development Department. The two were intertwined; the industrial regeneration of Scotland would not come to pass without an overall improvement in the environment within which the new industries would work. The confident planners at St Andrew's House, most now with university degrees in geography or economics, took an all-embracing view of the responsibilities of their profession.

It had seemed good sense to place economic planning in the Development Department alongside physical planning, local authority matters and finance, housing, New Towns and roads, electricity, industry and tourism, and water and other basic services. However, if the broad equality of the departments within St Andrew's House was to be preserved, the Development Department was too big. There was more to this than simply preserving equality of civil service rank among the four heads of departments who gathered every Monday afternoon round the walnut table in the permanent under-secretary of state's room. Each head of department was—and is—accountable before Parliament as well as to the Secretary of State for all that goes on in his domain. The span of control for each must not become unmanageably wide. So in 1964, when Sir Douglas Haddow, Secretary to the Development Department, succeeded Sir William Murrie in the top post at the Scottish Office he took with him the Regional Development Division and its co-ordinating role in economic planning and development. As Haddow himself recalls, it was also his ardent wish that he should keep himself in the forefront of the new approach to Scotland's economic re-birth. None of his colleagues, aware as they were of his energetic ways, were surprised that he now gave himself what so far had been denied this top post—a mini-department of its own. For the Regional Development Division's boast was that it was 'concerned in the widest sense with the redistribution of economic activity—the whole field'; and that it was the role of this *corps d'élite* 'to give advice to the Secretary of State on the wide range of things that he has to be interested in as Scotland's Minister'. If this is a job description that would have fitted the Scottish Home Department that should be no surprise. In tending the 'penumbral' concerns of his Minister—such as, say, what was happening to air services and airports in Scotland, or Whitehall's tendency to 'disperse' offices to the Home Counties which could just as well be accommodated north of the Border, or a hundred and one other matters—the permanent under-secretary of state would always need the supportive team-work of a staff. As 'PUS of S', Milne had had available to him Cunningham's Home Department. Haddow had now equipped himself with his own praetorian guard.

Throughout the 'sixties the Regional Development Division lived in a frenzy of work. With the Scottish Council, co-sponsors of the Toothill Report, it had enabled Michael Noble, as Secretary of State, to overcome a certain reluctance in Whitehall to embrace the new development philosophy and its implications for enhanced support to industry in the growth areas. The outcome had been the Scottish Office's conversion of the Toothill strategy into coherent development proposals for the new towns and other specific areas of Central Scotland, such as North Lanarkshire and the Vale of Leven in Dunbartonshire. With the coming of a Labour Government in the autumn of 1964, and economic planning still more clearly in the ascendant, the Division had to liaise with the new Department of Economic Affairs in Whitehall as well as survive the flurry of its own secretarial activity. It provided the motor both for the Scottish Economic Planning Council chaired by William Ross, now Secretary of State, and for the Scottish Economic Planning Board of officials, also for the subordinate 'sub-regional' groups such as one for the north-east. And it did much thoughtful work for the meetings in Haddow's room of the 'Economic Consultants to the Secretary of State', that is, four incumbents of economics chairs at the Scottish Universities who provided economic advice at a senior level as an alternative to the recruitment of high-level economic advice 'in house'.

The hope pervading all this activity was that before the end of the 'sixties Scotland's economy would grow by a quarter in accordance with the ambitious National Plan emanating from George Brown's Department of Economic Affairs. While the Secretary of State's Scottish Economic Planning Council included leading industrialists and bankers and promoted a consensus of thinking it was the role of the subordinate Scottish Economic Planning Board to bring together senior officials in St Andrew's House and the representatives in Scotland of Whitehall departments and nationalised industry. It both scanned the horizon and steered among the waves of day to day.

Throughout the long mornings of its meetings in the third-floor conference room looking on to the Calton Hill there would be rapid cross-fire of questioning and argument. Were, say, afforestation and its industrial and social implications discussed, both the immediate problem of finding and housing the work-force needed for the new Lochaber pulp-mill would be considered and the longer vista explored of a Highlands afforested to an extent not seen since the seventeenth century. There would have been a paper tabled giving the views of the economists of the Forestry Commission, of the Agriculture Department and of the Regional Development Division itself on the intricacies of the case for (and against) more forestry; much of sheep farming in the Highland hills might be a loser, but forestry was something of a gamble. The case to Treasury for vastly increased planting would have to be carefully marshalled. From the chair, the Board of Trade's Scottish Controller would be interrogated by James McGuinness, head of the Regional Development Division, about the 'fit' of government grant for the smaller-scale forest industries; and a senior man from British Rail's Scottish Headquarters would be put through the hoops about the uncertain future of the west highland railway line which would carry timber to the new Lochaber mill.

So it would go on, and one could never quite foresee what new prospects would be revealed. With the prospect of great new forests from the Mull of Kintyre to Cape Wrath, the Forestry Commission representatives would be pressed to consider the closer marriage of forestry and holiday-making by building chalets and caravan sites on their vast new estates. And if discussion took this route, the under-secretary from the Development Department would be fortunate if he was not quizzed about the progress of road-building to create a north-south tourist highway along the west highlands. There was a world of difference between all this and the halting efforts of the Scottish Economic Conference of 1949. The paper on afforestation then submitted had sparked off little discussion and no conclusions—to the evident disgust, as is still recalled, of Tom Johnston, then Chairman of the Forestry Commission's Scottish Committee.

Again because their discussions were informal and uninhibited, the 'Economic Consultants to the Secretary of State' gave valuable service in focusing on the distant scene. For example, in the later 'sixties, they would take a searching look at the pros and cons for Scotland of entry to the EEC. By the end of the decade Haddow could well claim that 'Scottish thought and Scottish practice pioneered regional development policies'. In this meshing together of free-thinking university economists, the senior officials of the Planning Board, and the more deliberate counsels of the body chaired by the Secretary of State, there was an integrated and organic concept of Scottish government. John Buchan would have approved.

Inevitably this new mechanism soon brought the condition of local government within its view. The promised land would only be reached if local government was able as well as willing to implement. 'By comparison with sixty years ago', a publication in 1958 of the Home Department had said in praise of the town and county councils of Scotland, 'the structure of local government is simple'. For the task in hand it was now seen to be not simple enough.

But before embarking on a mid-1960's voyage round the rocky coast of local government reform we must first look at what had been happening elsewhere in St Andrew's House, and particularly in the Scottish Education Department and in the Department of Agriculture and Fisheries. There too, the predominance of planning was to be felt.

The Scottish Education Department was now wading through a river of change. Soon it would be altogether different from the edifice Craik and Struthers had built and which Sir John MacKay Thomson had preserved. Previously

'The Secretary of State [meaning the department] was the central repository of almost all power in Scottish education. . . . His inspectors oversaw the work of the schools and his suggestions had the backing of two-thirds of the money on which they ran. He was responsible for the supply of teachers and for supervising their training; his was the right to grant a teacher his certificate and to take it away. He had the last word on salaries. The only national examination was organised and its certificate issued by his officers'.

Even this does not transmit the whole picture. Education authorities provided the schools, but new building was subject to the Secretary of State's approval and its design was much influenced by his architects at St Andrew's House. Nor had there been close collaboration between the teaching profession and the department similar to, say, the partnership between the medical profession and the administrators of St Andrew's House which built the Health Service, or to the easy-going association between the farming community and the Agriculture Department (still known to many of them as 'the Board', whereas to the teaching profession all pronouncements great and small came from 'the Secretary of State').

There was also something of an entrenched attitude in the Scottish Education Department which had to be relinquished. Sir William Murrie had followed Sir John MacKay Thomson in 1952 as Secretary to the Department. Murrie had had some distinguished years in Whitehall after his earlier career in the Department of Health, and this was the first time the department had imported its chief (or anyone else). A significant oddity was that the

department had in the past for too long persisted in addressing the
Secretary of State as 'VP', that is the Vice-President of the defunct
Scottish Education Committee of the Privy Council. In this there
was just a hint that in its relationship with ministers, even in the
1940s, the Scottish Education Department was not quite like the
others; and the department's evidence to the Gilmour Committee
back in 1937 had been singularly unenthusiastic about the benefits
of bringing all together in a closer linkage with the Secretary of
State. Murrie recalls that in 1952 he had detected among some
colleagues 'a lingering feeling that there was a departmental policy
distinct from, and over and above the policies approved by
ministers from time to time to meet current problems'. To the
outsider it might seem that over the years the department had
fallen into the habit of listening too much to itself, and had become
a prisoner to its own distinguished past.

The traditional roles were indeed impeding the department's
ability to meet the new challenges of education. But now began a
process of change. First, the department's role in teacher training
was relaxed; as 'Colleges of Education', the teacher training
colleges were given much more independence and governing
bodies of their own. Then the Inspectorate's elaborate and systematic reporting on schools which the Advisory Council had
deplored as 'a time wasting practice yielding profit to no one' was
curtailed. Most far reaching of all the aspects of this departmental
revolution was the surrender of the time-honoured Higher Leaving Certificate examinations to an independent Scottish Examinations Board. It had been the local authority Directors of Education
who had suggested this profound change (and doubtless it was no
mere coincidence that their views were at one with the enlightened
attitudes of John Brunton who had taken over the leadership of the
Inspectorate in 1955 and William Arbuckle who had become
Secretary of the department two years later). In all this innovation
and change, the department now sought to work as the teaching
profession's collaborator rather than its overlord; each aspect of the
new regime was considered in detail by committees which
brought the department and the profession together. This was
rightly seen as the preferable alternative to advice from an
Advisory Council held at arm's length from the department.

This departmental disburdening continued when Norman Graham succeeded Sir William Arbuckle in 1963. A Consultative
Committee representing a wide range of educational interests took
over supervision of the curriculum of the senior secondary school.
Then, on Labour's return to power, with William Ross the new
Secretary of State and himself once a schoolteacher, the teachers
were given control of their own professional standards by the
setting up of a General Teaching Council for Scotland, independent of the department, paid for by the teachers. The hope was that

William Ross (r.) now Lord Ross of Marnock
(Secretary of State for Scotland 1964–70 and 1974–76)
meets Lord Polwarth and Dr W S Robertson (l.) of the
Scottish Council (Development and Industry).
(Courtesy of *The Glasgow Herald*.)

the new body would enhance professional status; and it signalled
the final passing of the Inspectorate's time-honoured stance as
'dominie' to the 'dominies'.

High time too. The needs of the non-academic majority in the
schools were clamant, would become still louder with the raising
of the school-leaving age to 16. 'For many years after 1945', as the
late James Scotland has written 'further education [that is technological education in all its forms] remained the least interesting and
the worst developed part of the Scottish system'. If the department
had been in part to blame for this, lack of political interest was also
at fault. 'The situation was a strange one', reflected this author of
the comprehensive history of Scottish education, 'for each government was in no doubt that expansion in British industry and trade
depended on improved technical performance'.

However, improvement began in the mid-1950s with a declaration of intent by the department that there should be local technical
colleges available to all. This was followed by an extensive
building programme, with the department in its new freedom

from its past accepting that it must take on the co-ordinating role. In the schools themselves the Inspectorate also set about disseminating the new thinking on the schooling appropriate for the non-academic majority. The Brunton Report of 1963 entitled 'From School to Further Education' with its strong vocational bias is already seen as an historic document in the development of Scottish education.

Standing back, one can see that this jettisoning of the old order and eager adoption of the new had been in the great tradition of Craik and Struthers. The department itself recognised the force of the arguments for a new order of things and with Ministers' concurrence brought it about. With the coming of the Labour Government in 1964 and the introduction of comprehensive education, the department would now have to effect still more sweeping educational change. This was not of its own volition but north of the Border comprehensive education was far from being a novel concept. The closer partnership there now was between Inspectorate and administrators, and between both of these, the teaching profession and the local authorities, meant that the major organisational changes involved could be introduced, and for the most part be working tolerably well, by the end of the 'sixties.

The department had also acquired wider roles calling on a greater range of administrative skill.★ There was that of representation on the University Grants Committee; these were the years when the four Scottish universities became eight in number. From the Scottish Home Department had come responsibilities for the National Galleries of Scotland and for the red sandstone pile of the National Museum of Antiquities. These were now grouped under the department's aegis alongside the Royal Scottish Museum. Liaison with the Scottish Arts Council and the parent Arts Council of Great Britain was likewise now a responsibility of the department. These, however, were modest additions compared with the placing in 1968 of social work alongside education as the department's *raison d'être*.

This also arose out of the transfer to the department of Scottish Home Department business, in this case responsibility for the children's Inspectorate and the probation service. In 1964 a committee on juvenile justice chaired by Lord Kilbrandon had recommended the setting up of social education departments in local authorities to cater for children in trouble; and further back there

★Not until 1939 had the department included a 'generalist' administrator, all senior administrative staff having previously come from the Inspectorate. Until well into the 1950s the rule of thumb from Victorian times which awarded Scottish education a strict eleven-eightieths of what was spent on education south of the Border meant that the department's administrators, unlike their brethren of the other departments in St Andrew's House, were not called on to do battle in Whitehall for more money for distinctive Scottish needs.

had been advice given to the department that inadequate families should not be visited by fragmented services interested only in the different needs of individuals, but should be helped by an integrated service which could take a comprehensive view of the whole family's problems. This led to close consideration by the department of the wider social needs of the community, and it was carried out under the vigorous leadership of Judith Hart, then parliamentary under-secretary of state. By 1966 there was a government commitment to the setting up in Scotland of integrated social work departments in local authorities for all the needful groups in the community, be their problems homelessness, age, or mental or physical handicap; be they children in need of care, adults on probation from the courts, or prisoners released into a difficult and unfriendly world. The interdepartmental unit set up in the Scottish Office to prepare the legislation which would embody this wide-ranging concept of social work, would from 1968 become the Social Work Services Group of the Scottish Education Department. Within it, professional social work advisers would form the Central Advisory Service to work closely with the administrators. This was the biggest single advance in social legislation since the National Health Service; and it was one in which the Scots were proud to take the lead over their colleagues south of the Border.

The end of the decade saw the completion of the process by which the Scottish Education Department was given new purpose. But the delivery of both the education and social work services lay in the hands of local authorities. Like that of the regional economic planners, the department's perception was that the structure of Scottish local government was not simple enough for the tasks ahead, and Sir Norman Graham had said so to Lord Wheatley's Royal Commission on Local Government. But he had also made clear his department's abhorrence of the proposal submitted to the Royal Commission by his colleagues in the Scottish Development Department and the Regional Development Division that all Strathclyde—half the population of Scotland and three-quarters of her problem—should go under one regional authority. The Royal Commission had been impressed by their argument that the imperatives of planning required this, and in their Report of 1969 had given it their blessing. Graham's opposition was as intense as ever, and his department awaited the judgement of ministers with some anxiety.

Since the war, the Department of Agriculture had become an experienced partner to the Ministry in Whitehall Place in all-round support to British farming. At the farm price reviews carried out every year in the damp weeks of a London February the administrators and economists from Edinburgh joined wholeheartedly in the sparring with the farming unions over the appropriate levels of subsidy and support. To raise the level of agricultural production in the interests of the nation's balance of payments as well as of its rural economy was a consistent and bi-partisan objective of government; and farming was now, in return, giving the nation an object lesson in what could be achieved by hard work, abundant state-assisted capital investment, ample scope for legitimate tax-avoidance, no labour troubles, and as much government-funded research, development and advice as the industry could take on board. With everyone kicking the ball in much the same direction, the department's relations with the Ministry were more uniformly easy than those of colleagues elsewhere in St Andrew's House were with, say, the Whitehall departments concerned with distribution of industry policy.

As the years went by, the February drama (and stage-management) at Whitehall Place usually saw the Scottish ball put into the scrum so that it could emerge as agreement to enhanced hill sheep/hill cattle subsidy or whatever the Scottish interest required. Harry Whitby and his henchmen at the successive Price Reviews were all the keener to play their full part in the negotiations because they could see clearly enough as the 'sixties advanced that if accession to the European community ever came down from the clouds they would have to fight for a tempering of the chill wind of EEC doctrine for the 'shorn lambs' of Scottish hill-farming.

Meanwhile the Agriculture Department had taken on wider roles. Just as the educationists at St Andrew's House now looked beyond the schools, so the Agriculture Department now looked beyond farming. With the demise of the old Home Department, the fishing industry had become its responsibility.

The trawler fleets of Aberdeen and Granton which had fished for so many years round Iceland and Faeroe were dwindling fast with age and rust, but the beamy wooden motor vessels of the re-equipped Scottish inshore fishing industry were sailing into prosperity. The two Fisheries Divisions and the officers of the Fisheries Inspectorate took some credit for that, and they were mighty pleased when cogent argument, forcefully presented, for the exclusion of foreign fishing within twelve miles of the coast at last prevailed over traditional attitudes in Whitehall. This twelve mile limit also effectively closed the whole of the Minch to foreign boats, thus assisting the Division's strenuous efforts to bring about the revival of the near defunct fishing industry in the Outer Hebrides.

With fisheries, the patrol ships of the Fishery Protection Service became the department's navy. The maintenance of sea services to the islands was likewise now the department's responsibility. In its last years, the Home Department had ended the thirty year old, tiresome dichotomy of responsibility with the Ministry of Transport for the Western Isles services and taken power to build new ships for these★ and for sea services to Orkney and Shetland. Thanks to this a general and overdue change to vehicle ferry ships was now taking place. The crisis had been how to replace the two aged (and coal-burning) steamers of the North Isles of Orkney Shipping Company, but the legislation was appropriately far-sighted.

The department was also now the acknowledged custodian of Highland policy and it had taken this guiding hand in Highland development on the eve of historic change. To recapitulate briefly, Tom Johnston, when Secretary of State in 1942 had turned his back on the proposals of the pre-war Hilleary Committee for the appointment of a development agency for the Highlands and Islands; the instrument he preferred for the stimulation of development was a hydro-electricity generating and distributing board endowed with a strong social remit. We have also seen that with the leaping costs of dam-building and all else it was soon obvious in the early post-war years that the North of Scotland Hydro-Electric Board would not have the money to make much more of its 'social' remit beyond conferring the boon of electricity, and that in 1947 a Highlands and Islands Advisory Panel rather than a development board was appointed.

However, from the early 1950s the Scottish TUC had kept alive the case for a Highland Development Board, and this was now Labour Party policy. As the General Election of 1964 approached, Sir Matthew Campbell, as Secretary of the Department of Agriculture and Fisheries, recognised that were there to be a change of government there would be a new departure in Highland policy. If there were to be radical change it seemed right that the steering should come from his department. The use of land and sea is at the heart of Highland development, and apart altogether from its buttressing of hill farming and the backing it gave to hill farming research, apart too from its close and friendly linkage with the Forestry Commission, his department already was parent to the Crofters Commission, a body appointed in 1956 to enable the crofting communities to do better, particularly by making more of crofting agriculture.†

★And so the new ships built for that archetypal Glasgow company, David MacBrayne Ltd, carried the Leith registration appropriate to their Edinburgh owner, the Secretary of State.

†This Crofters Commission—the earlier body appointed in 1886 primarily to fix fair rents went out of existence in 1912 when the Board of Agriculture came into being—was appointed after a thorough review of crofting by a Committee of Enquiry which itself was set up at the suggestion of the Highland Panel.

The Highlands and Islands Development Board was duly given legislative birth by the new government in 1965. However it was the possibilities of industrial development in the north which seemed most alluring to some. Robert Grieve, who left the Civil Service and the post of Chief Planning Officer in the Scottish Development Department to become the Board's first Chairman, along with his passionate belief in integrated land use, took with him his vision of a Highlands and Islands partly revitalised by industrial development. Forestry and tourism (but not farming) were for him the future pillars of development. But, continued the Board's first annual report,

> 'manufacturing industry is the third main group and we increasingly regard it as the most urgent of all. . . . Without it, the region will continue to lack any real possibility of a substantial enough rise in numbers to give credibility to Highland regeneration.'

This argued for linkage of the Board with the department at St Andrew's House responsible for planning. On Campbell's retiral in 1968 the liaison role with the Highland Board at St Andrew's House was moved to the Development Department. In the same year the Board took note of a major industrial development—the location of a huge new aluminium smelter at Invergordon on the shores of the Cromarty Firth.

Were the Highlands indeed to have a future of greater industrialisation than happened—another pulp mill, perhaps, as well as an aluminium smelter, and a mix of light industry where the value of the product was high in relation to the transport costs involved in Highland manufacture—this move could not be faulted. Furthermore, with the liaison role with the Board there was transferred to the Development Department the new involvement in ship ownership in regard to the island services. This too seemed to make sense because a consequence of the Transport Act of 1968 had been that the Secretary of State would be actively involved with passenger transport services throughout Scotland. Lastly, tourism, which in the Board's eyes was one of the three major props of the Highland economy, lay within the province of the Development Department, as did the Scottish Tourist Board. However, as industrial prospects slipped somewhat, land use, agriculture and fisheries took on rather greater importance in the Board's portfolio of roles. Furthermore, with the Crofters Commission and the Board looking to different departments in the Scottish Office, any *rapprochement* between the crofting communities and the more modern aspects of the Highland economy would now be more difficult to achieve. There was also some inevitable duplication of function. For the crofting communities, the Crofters Commission had a general developmental remit (albeit one unbacked by government money) which was not much different from the general developmental remit entrusted to the Highland Board for the whole of its area. These however, are difficulties for level-headed administrators to resolve; and the ease with which the Board at Inverness were to work with the Department of Agriculture and Fisheries at Edinburgh in the early 1980s in making something of the largely Brussels financed 'Integrated Development Programme for the Western Isles' showed that resolution is possible.

What does stand out in retrospect is how much a Highlands and Islands Development Board was needed. Forestry was to disappoint the high hopes that by itself it would re-people the glens; the mechanisation of afforestation from the planting of the infant sitka spruce to extraction of mature timber would see to that. Tourism would not quite live up to the great expectations of the 'sixties that there would be a torrent of motorised townsfolk exploring the Highlands from early spring to late autumn every year. It is likewise clear that as the hard times of the 'seventies set in, tender regard for Highland difficulties by all manner of national and nationalised bodies would become increasingly at risk, as would the ability of an advisory Highland Panel to coax them into line. Nothing less than a Development Board armed with wide powers, generously financed and backed by political commitment would do; and the close study of rural development in Norway which Lord Cameron and his Panel colleagues had carried out in the early 1960s was already bringing them too round to this belief. So they too welcomed the new Board, but with a tinge of regret that its coming would end the Panel's unique ability to bring about a consensus of thinking among members of parliament, county councils, other leaders in the community, and Scottish Office officials about the development of the north and west.

Was something beyond development also receding from sight? Some, including the hard-headed first Chairman of the Crofters Commission had looked to the Highlands for the rebirth of a way of life which would not conform to urban values. So had Naomi Mitchison; in one of her trilogy of 'Poems for the Highland Panel' her verdict was to be

'I looked for a thing and I could not find it.'

VII

ALARMS AND EXCURSIONS

THE NINETEEN-SEVENTIES were to be the most momentous decade yet in the hundred years of the Scottish Office. In themselves the United Kingdom's accession to the European Communities and the finding of undreamt-of riches of North Sea oil would have been enough for that. But these were the years in which the Secretary of State also won the high ground which made him indeed the industrial minister for Scotland, and in which the Scottish Office set to the comprehensive reorganisation of local government. In 1975 a new Scottish Office headquarters began its domination of the Edinburgh skyline. Then in the second half of the decade the Devolution drama made us, like John Milton's lady-love 'the cynosure of neighbouring eyes'.

The high hopes that went with 'joining Europe' stand out in memory. (Were these opening years of the 'seventies to be optimism's last fling?) Scottish industry in general welcomed the prospect of open access to the markets of western Europe; so did the Scottish Council which had done so much to attract the electronics industry in particular to central Scotland. As to agriculture, most of lowland farming stood to gain from accession to the protected agricultural regime of the European Community; and misgivings about the future of the hill farming subsidies were assuaged when appropriate leverage by Scottish ministers and the Department, followed by some adroit negotiation at Brussels, ensured their survival as assistance to the 'less-favoured areas' of all countries which could persuade the EEC Commission that they had them.*

Euphoria was dampened when our future partners on the eve of the entry negotiations cobbled together the rudiments of a Com-

---

* 'Less-favoured areas' was a clumsy translation of the French *'régions défavorisées'*; it proved more difficult to translate into Brussels French the word 'croft'—*'exploitation minuscule'* was the linguists' solution.

A view from the roof of New St Andrew's House.

mon Fisheries Policy which sought to give equal rights of access to all inshore waters of the enlarged Community—this to the delight of fishermen from Brest to Hamburg, and to the dismay of our own. It was to prove a difficult task to secure even a ten-year derogation from such unrestricted access to British waters, a breathing space during which a less harmful Common Fisheries Policy could be negotiated.

In seeking both to safeguard Scottish interests and to keep the Secretary of State 'in the picture' about the complicated entry negotiations as they proceeded, those involved in the Scottish Office had to get to grips with the unfamiliar ways of European governments; and they were helped in this, in a way which their Whitehall colleagues might well have envied, by an initiative of Edinburgh University. There, the late Professor John Mitchell of the Chair of European Community Studies convened from the late

1960s a succession of informal and confidential discussions with leading European personalities to which Scottish Office attendance was invited. The ease of these evening discussions beneath the Raeburns of the University's handsome Senate Room assisted understanding. Goodwill even survived the *gaffe* of one Eurocrat who assured his audience that while Scottish hill-farmers might have their problems within the EEC, 'wheat-growers in the Highlands would do very well!' Within two weeks of the signing of the Accession Treaty, the large and impressive presence of Dr Mansholt, President of the EEC Commission, came to Scotland to spread reassurance and his faith in United Europe in which the rationalisation of backward continental agriculture would fuel prosperity and thus provide no end of new jobs and opportunities for industry and commerce. 'Bliss was it in that dawn to be alive'—or so it seemed.

Dawn seemed the more blissful because the first big finds of oil under the North Sea were now being made. From the late 1960s outlandish looking craft for the towing of oil rigs had begun to appear in the Forth, but it was not until 1971 and the proving of what was to be British Petroleum's Forties Field, a hundred and twenty miles off Aberdeen, that the gold-rush began. In successive licensing rounds, with scant regard to the on-shore implications, and, at first, without Scottish Office involvement the waters of the North Sea were now licensed for exploration and oil extraction all the way up to the basin off Shetland. With the flare-up of war in the Middle East there was both an abrupt increase in world oil prices and recognition of the uncertainty of traditional supply. Speed of development of North Sea oil became an imperative of government. Suddenly there were giant production platforms to be built, and supply bases to be created on the east coast and in Shetland. Suddenly Aberdeen became an oil capital.

The Scottish Office was now totally involved and its response had to be swift. There were crash programmes for house and road building to be drawn up with the burghs and county councils along the shores of the Moray Firth under the surveillance of the St Andrew's House-chaired 'Moray Firth Working Party'. (Aberdonians required no such help.) It also fell to the Scottish Office to assist school building and the provision of health services for the new population. Aberdeen airport would soon become the third busiest in the United Kingdom; Inverness's Dalcross, once the best farmland in the county, also had to be rebuilt, and so had Shetland's Sumburgh that it might take larger aircraft with less chance of diversion. The heaviest burden fell on the planners of the Development Department who had the task of recommending how best the massive on-shore requirements of the oil industry itself could best be accommodated. The outcome was their publication of an impressive Coastal Survey and of planning guidelines for the new developments. One aspect of all this was the identification of sites round the coast, in east coast firth and western sea-loch alike, for sites in which to build huge concrete platforms which—said the energy experts—would all be wanted in the North Sea in a hurry. (In the event, the industry's preference swung towards steel platforms and the sites were not needed, but by then there was an expensive hole in the ground by the shores of Loch Fyne.) Also to be taken into account was the other side of the coin, the fears of the fishing industry that some of its North Sea and Shetland grounds would be lost to it.

In 1973, Edward Heath as Prime Minister had announced that Lord Polwarth, in a new Minister of State post at the Scottish Office, would co-ordinate all aspects of North Sea oil development affecting Scotland. Lord Polwarth now chaired the Oil Development Council which brought together both the industry at senior levels of management, finance and environmental interests. Other co-ordinating bodies of officials under Scottish Office chairmanship were also brought into being. Within the Scottish Office there was a certain *cachet* in being engaged in oil activity.

'Just imagine', Willie Ballantine would say back in the 1950s as we pondered the intractable problem of the development of a Scotland seemingly on the periphery of all progress as well as of all Europe, 'just think what it would be like—if oil was struck in the North Sea!' We would shuffle our feet and wait for Willie's fantasy to pass. A pity he did not live to see it become reality; and indeed, how difficult it is now to think back to these days when Aberdeen had a stagnant economy and there seemed little hope of reversing Shetland's downward drift.

Gordon Campbell had succeeded William Ross on the change of government in 1970, and he now authorised the creation of a new department in the Scottish Office. The new department was named the 'Scottish Economic Planning Department'. As well as oil activities, it took under its wing the Regional Development Division; on Sir Douglas Haddow's retiral in 1973 he had been succeeded by Sir Nicholas Morrison whose range of Whitehall experience was outwith industrial development, and so the arrangement by which the Regional Development Division came directly under the head of the Scottish Office was no longer appropriate. The new department also became the sponsor for the Highlands and Islands Development Board and the Scottish Tourist Board, for the New Town Development Corporations, by now five in number, and for the two electricity boards responsible respectively for the north and south of Scotland. However, the division between this new department and the Scottish Development Department could not but be somewhat

Uncompromising modernism: a detail of New St
Andrew's House.

arbitrary; the creation of infrastructure ashore for oil development
remained within the ambit of the Development Department; on
the other hand, the New Towns had still much to do with
housing. So the creation of this new department accentuated rather
than lessened the need for co-operation across departmental
boundaries within the Scottish Office.

From the creation of the Economic Planning Department it was
a short but important step for William Ross, Secretary of State
once again in the Labour government which took office in 1974 to
become, in effect, the industry minister for Scotland. Two years
before had seen the introduction of selective—that is discretionary—financial assistance to industry in the regions needing help. In
a significant new departure in practice, to achieve which Ross's
predecessor had lent his weight, the Department of Trade and

Industry delegated to their regional headquarters in Glasgow the responsibility for administering this assistance rather than having the work done in London. Relations between that department's Scottish Controller and St Andrew's House were good, but with a Scottish Economic Planning Department now established within the Scottish Office it was a natural development that the administration of these grants should come under it, and so they did in 1975. In retrospect it was a 'famous victory': forty years had passed since the first tentative steps had been taken by the Scottish Office to promote industrial development in central Scotland. It also gave the Scottish Office what it had lacked, a major office in Glasgow.

A complementary achievement of 1975 giving still more substance to the new Economic Planning Department was the creation of the Scottish Development Agency. Much had been done since the war in attracting American industry to Scotland, but for some time it had been felt that the stronger promotion of 'home-grown' industry was just as necessary. In the 'West Central Scotland Plan' it inspired, the Regional Development Division at St Andrew's House had also pointed to the need for a development corporation in Scotland, funded by government but less pre-occupied than government departments have to be with the day to day running of parliamentary or ministerial business. But here too, the realisation of the concept, the setting up of the Scottish Development Agency by Act of Parliament in 1975, was a major achievement.

The Agency took over from the Scottish Council responsibility for the attraction of 'inward investment' ie of industrialists from abroad. It would now run the Scottish factory estates which government had built; it would provide investment finance for industry by equity or by loan; and under other aspects of the legislation of 1972 it would make an eminently practical contribution to the improvement of the environment for industry in taking over from St Andrew's House administration of the rehabilitation of the derelict land which still blotted too much of the landscape of central Scotland. Together the Department and the Agency could now attempt a different industrial strategy for Scotland, all the more readily since their two Glasgow offices were cheek by jowl. A new strategy would indeed be needed. By the mid-1970s it was already coming clear that the strategy of the 'sixties, built as it had been round the introduction of major new heavy industry to Scotland, was under threat. Lord Ross (as he now is) has paid generous tribute to the round-the-clock work of the Scottish Economic Planning Department which in late 1975 helped him stave off the first of these threats—to the great car-factory which government money had assisted in Renfrewshire in the early 1960s. Relief would not be lasting.

These middle 'seventies also saw the reorganisation of Scottish local government. Six years had passed since the Royal Commission under Lord Wheatley's chairmanship had, in their report, accepted the Development Department's prediction that there would be extensive future movements of population as, say, from Clydeside to Tayside, and that 'existing towns will have to be drastically reshaped to deal with new levels of traffic and new patterns of social and commercial activity.' Lord Wheatley and his colleagues had been made well aware of the eight regional development studies under way or intended by McGuinness's Regional Development Division in association with the St Andrew's House planners and outside consultants. This profoundly influenced their thinking about future structure of Scottish local government. 'National Plans will have to be devised' said the Royal Commission. 'They set the frame within which a plan for Scotland has to be worked out. These in turn set the frame for area plans within Scotland.' Area planning, the report continued, was a task for local government suitably reorganised in a regional structure within which all Strathclyde and the whole of the east of Scotland from the middle of Fife to the English border would each be seamless garments. Education and social work, like housing, should all go to the new regions, though the Royal Commission recognised the strong objections to this from those directly concerned at St Andrew's House with the first two of these services. But in the climate of the times Wheatley and his colleagues felt that the planning requirement must predominate.

That was 1969. Now in the early 1970s planning on a national scale was no longer in the ascendant. The prospect of an eruption of big new industry with very large consequential movements of population was receding fast. There was an uneasy feeling that the very success of the New Towns was contributing to Glasgow's plight, as they leached away some of the more able and ambitious of the city's people. Indeed, plans for another New Town—at Stonehouse in Lanarkshire—would soon be given up, and the assembled planning and architectural teams switched to the new Scottish Development Agency for the rebuilding of eastern Glasgow. This retreat from macro-planning* was accompanied by acceptance of the strong representations from the Borders and from the Kingdom of Fife that they should be regions on their own. The Royal Commission's views on the need for regional supremacy were likewise put aside, in that housing was made a responsibility of the new District Councils. However, the Wheatley proposal that there should be one and only one region for the industrial west was accepted; and indeed this region would be made greater still by the addition of all Argyll from the Mull of Kintyre to the island of Coll. The essential unity for planning of

---

*Significantly, Gordon Campbell had the Scottish Economic Planning Council renamed the Scottish Economic Council.

Clydeside, as in the Clyde Valley Region Plan of nearly thirty years before, was seen as an inescapable fact. To this extent planning still predominated, however inconvenient for other aspects of the Scottish Office might be the imbalance in size between Strathclyde and the other regions. Strathclyde Region would now be responsible for the major local government roles in regard to half the population of Scotland. It would also have on its plate three-quarters of 'the Scottish problem' however that is defined.

In the flurry of legislative work in the Scottish Office leading up to the actual reorganisation of local government in 1975 there was little time to reflect how far reaching must be the impact of the new local government regime on the Scottish Office. Moreover, with the coming of the Labour government in 1974 the great devolution debate had begun, and with it was the prospect of change infinitely greater.

Meanwhile the Scottish Office had a new home.

Edinburgh had long found it possible to ignore the squalor of St James' Square, only a bottle's throw as it was from the east end of Princes Street. As the new Scottish Office rose from the clearance of the sleazy old square, it was only too obvious that this hollow hexagon, in concrete, six—in part eight—storeys high, could not so easily be ignored.

The need for the new building was not in doubt. St Andrew's House held less than a thousand of the five thousand staff in offices throughout Edinburgh. The new St Andrew's House would only bring together some of these, but it would provide a bigger headquarters for the Secretary of State and his ministerial col-leagues. It would also house most senior staff of all departments except those in Agriculture and Fisheries; they, with that entire department, had already moved to Chesser House, a large, unexciting, rented office block in West Edinburgh.

As it became plain that New St Andrew's House*—as the new building was to be named—would be no easier on the eye than Chesser House, and a great deal more conspicuous, overtowering as it does Robert Adam's masterpiece at the east end of Princes

---

* As GK Chesterton pointed out, 'Dr Jekyll and Mr Hyde', though ostensibly set in London, is an Edinburgh novel. Within Victorian Edinburgh, only St James' Square answered to Stevenson's description of the surroundings to Jekyll's house, 'a square of ancient, handsome houses, now for the most part decayed from their high estate and let in flats and chambers to all sorts and conditions of men'; a square which backed on to a small disreputable street (Clyde Street that was), and which was approached by a short steep street (Elder Street that is). From his troubled youth Stevenson had evil memories of St James' Square.

Ancient Monument—the Stones of Callanish, Isle of
Lewis. (Scottish Development Department.)

Street, the Royal Fine Arts Commission for Scotland added their
voice to the chorus of disapproval from the citizenry. The massive
uniformity of appearance, they said, was unappealing. The city
planners had indeed overcrowded this, surely one of the finest city
sites in Europe, giving it a congested appearance. (Would that the
'Scotsman' reporters had been able to repeat their City Chambers
coup of 1929!)

The unwisdom of so detracting from Edinburgh's architectural
heritage seemed all the greater when contrasted with the elegant
official residence which adroit negotiation ten years before had
secured for the Secretary of State. Three houses in the middle of
the world famous north side of Charlotte Square ('the finest thing

that Robert Adam ever did') had been conveyed to the National
Trust for Scotland by the Marquess of Bute in part satisfaction of
family death duties. Number 6 became the Edinburgh residence
for the Secretary of State where distinguished visitors could be
entertained, an independent trust being formed to meet the cost
of the initial redecoration and furnishing. So at last the Scottish
Secretary had an Edinburgh home. 'At last', because King George
VI had expressed his kindly concern at the lack. Walter Elliot had
tried to get something done about it; and in the intervening years
many Edinburgh possibilities had been considered from the Abbey
Strand near Holyrood (but it was a tea-shop and not quite the
thing) to an apartment in Edinburgh Castle itself (but the unfor-
tunate minister would be either imprisoned in or excluded from
the Castle on every night of the Festival Tattoo). To bring Bute
House, as it came to be known, into the kind of prestigious use for
which it was so well suited showed how the Scottish Office could
help enhance the Edinburgh scene. But the same could not be said
for New St Andrew's House.

However one July day in 1975 the Queen graciously opened the
new building, visited the efficient layout of the various floors with
their views from Ben Ledi to the Bass Rock, and she met members
of staff in the smart conference suite. The building got off to a
good start.

A Scottish Office headquarters building in which all staff—and
all Edinburgh—might take pride would have been much to be
desired as a means of promoting *esprit de corps*. For the old, intense
departmental loyalties which had taken a 'dunt' with the reorganisation of the early 1960s had been still further infringed by
necessary change. From 1965 there had been a Scottish Office
computer service established in west Edinburgh which would
progressively take over more and more clerical work from the
departments; ten years later this employed over 400 systems
analysts, programmers and supporting staff as well as impressive
IBM hardware. This was followed by the pooling of the divisions
for personnel and staffing so that much more emphasis might be
put on management and organisation. Clerical officer to head of
department, all were now 'Scottish Office' staff; transfer and
promotion from one department to another would now be the
norm. Next, with the increasing significance of financial management, the Finance Officers and their staffs in each department were
amalgamated under a Principal Finance Officer into a Scottish
Office Finance Division which also took over responsibilities for
local government finance. This amalgam of computer, personnel
and finance staff was joined to all manner of office services
including several hundreds of typists and secretaries, to the
expanded Scottish Information Office and to the Solicitor's Office,
itself a large legal department all under the uninspiring title of

'Central Services' though it far outnumbered even the largest of the five departments. These departments were themselves no longer freestanding. With their old identities still further blurred by the dispersion of staff throughout Edinburgh, small wonder that the forging of a stronger Scottish Office loyalty was wanted.

The Devolution drama enacted on the political stage in the second half of the 1970s has been analysed elsewhere; only some fairly brief comment on how it appeared from within the Scottish Office would be appropriate here.

Like the biennial encounters of these years at Murrayfield or Hampden Park, Devolution was an aspect of Scotland's relationship with England on which each Scot had his own views. Scottish Office staff were no exception to this, the more so since they had spent all their working lives making the most of undevolved government. From their experience they were sharply aware of what it could achieve and where it creaked. But, throughout, the staff were never in any doubt that their personal views must not obtrude. The Civil Service exists to carry out to the very best of its ability the wishes of the electorate as transmitted through Ministers: that is the source of its pride. Nor in issues of political debate does it seek to present coherent views of its own to the public at large; as, say, the Law Society of Scotland or the British Medical Association are able to do.

Devolution having by now dropped so far astern, a reminder of the sequence of events would be timely. In 1968, the then Conservative leader's 'Declaration of Perth' pointed towards Devolution, and a committee which his party then set up under Sir Alec Douglas-Home proposed a directly elected Scottish Assembly. In 1969, at the instance of James Callaghan, then Home Secretary, a Royal Commission was appointed but on the diffuse and disparate matters of Parliament and Government 'in relation to the several countries, nations and regions of the United Kingdom', and with a 'Scottish membership' of only two out of its twenty. Latterly, one of these, Lord Kilbrandon from the Scottish bench was the Royal Commission's Chairman. The 'Kilbrandon Report' was published in 1973. A strong majority recommended a measure of political devolution (but no revenue raising powers) to Scottish and to Welsh Assemblies. A minority report applying principles of constitutional logic rather than political reality sought by extending devolution to a proposed English pentarchy to solve the perennial problem—which the majority had recognised but avoided—of reconciling devolution to only two parts of the United Kingdom with their continuing representation at Westminster. This problem was to feature greatly in the subsequent parliamentary debates, and as this was the very dilemma which had caused the Secretary for Scotland and Joseph Chamberlain to quit Gladstone's Cabinet in 1886 it would seem that the constitutional debate had not advanced so very much in 90 years.

Publication of the report caused no immediate stir, and there was little support from the regions of England for the minority's views. Nor did publication hold up the reorganisation of Scottish local government which would give a fair measure of administrative devolution to the proposed local authority regions. With the General Elections in 1974 there came a substantial increase in Scottish National Party representation at Westminster. The new Labour Government committed itself to devolution to Scotland and Wales on Kilbrandon lines, and complex legislation embodying Ministers' wishes was prepared by a Cabinet Office Constitution Unit to which Scottish Office officials were seconded and with which other parts of the Scottish Office worked closely. The implementing Bill ran into trouble at the Committee Stage and failed. Its successor, the Scotland Bill of 1978, was amended in the House of Commons so that more than 40 per cent of the Scottish electorate would have to indicate their support in a Devolution referendum before this new Act with its modest reversal of 1707 could take effect. The outcome of the referendum on St David's Day 1979 did not meet this requirement; and so 'Home Rule' brought down James Callaghan's government just as it toppled Gladstone's ninety-three years before. The referendum also showed less enthusiasm for devolution away from the Central Belt with Shetland the extreme example (but Shetlanders have always been just a little ambivalent in their feelings towards Scotland south of Fair Isle). After the General Election, the incoming Conservative administration took the Scotland Act off the Statute Book.

What had to be uppermost in Scottish Office minds as the referendum approached was the massive change in the offing, reflected in the general upheaval of preparation. Also the speed with which Devolution would have to be implemented if the requisite 40 per cent approval was given. Scottish Office staff, while remaining United Kingdom civil servants, would have to become within months servants either of the new Scottish Executive or of the continuing Secretary of State for Scotland. An Assembly debating chamber would have to be equipped and ready by the summer. After a close look at a number of possibles among Edinburgh buildings in which the old uses were failing, the choice fell on the classical elegance of the former Royal High School buildings on the side of the Calton Hill, their entrance just across the road from old St Andrew's House. But the Assembly would also need offices of its own—old St Andrew's House was the obvious choice for that—and the Secretary of State with a much diminished Scottish Office would have to quit New St Andrew's House for new quarters at the other end of town.

Ancient Monument—the old Corn-mill, New
Abbey, Dumfriesshire. (Scottish Development
Department.)

   Like most jigsaw puzzles there was nothing in this that application could not solve. Given that Ministers, agreeing with the
Report of the Royal Commission, had decided that the Scottish
Assembly should not have independently raised revenues of its
own it was less easy to envisage how the Assembly would
function. (Indeed, some of our new acquaintances from the
supremely confident French Civil Service were adamant that
devolution was an impossible concept, because their language had
no precise word for it!) How the diminished Scottish Office under
its post-Devolution Secretary of State would work also called for
crystal gazing; so did the relation to each other of Assembly and
Secretary of State over the wide range of business which would be
the joint concern of these two political foci. Overall from 1975 to
1978 hundreds of meeting hours were spent in the Scottish Office,
some integrated with Whitehall discussions, in devising arrangements which might work. Three considerations kept recurring.
How would reorganised local government work with the Assembly? Over a wide range the Scottish Office was already having to
pull back from its previous close involvement with local government, now that its reorganisation into bigger and, hopefully, more
efficient units had taken place. What would be the Assembly's

role? Housing, planning, education and social work, roads and other infrastructure would be the Assembly's main concern; but these were the direct responsibility of reorganised local government. Bluntly, would the Assembly have enough to do?

Secondly, those working on the economic side of the Scottish Office hexagon—that is those working on economic planning, industry and agriculture and fisheries, were concerned that the new order of things should not weaken the influence in Whitehall of the cut-down Scottish Office which—not the Scottish Assembly—would be mostly responsible for these vital sectors. Influence in Whitehall depends so much on knowing it all and being known there; and that depends on a wide-ranging and continuous involvement in the Whitehall scene (and at Westminster and Downing Street, for the same point no doubt holds good in regard to Scottish ministers attending Cabinet or Cabinet committees). Where as so often negotiation is about the adaptation of measures which do not *quite* suit Scottish conditions, the importance of being a 'kent face' is constant. Lastly, and although the Assembly's main responsibilities were in those areas where the Scottish Office was already sovereign, and so the transfer of power could be relatively easy, there were at the margin quite a number of areas where the division of responsibilities between the Assembly and the post-Devolution Secretary of State could not but be untidy; and this had to be done without the 'Department of the Scottish Assembly' or the 'Department of the Secretary of State' spending excessive amounts of time watching what each other was doing. Even though the staffs of both would be of the one Civil Service there seemed the risk of a new, unhappy element of divisiveness.

To the best of our ability, by the 1st of March 1979 arrangements were ready for floating off the new order of things. Then on the 2nd, the referendum count at New St Andrew's House was the main news story of the day for the world's press.

A week later or so the National Museum of Antiquities, which the previous winter had equipped the entrance hall in New St Andrew's House with a showcase, took out of it the mediaeval wooden carving of St Andrew cheerfully shouldering his cross, and replaced it with a broken sword from Flodden. Some professed to see this as symbolic: Flodden, the national catastrophe of the later middle ages 'where shiver'd was fair Scotland's spear/and broken was her shield' and they argued that an opportunity for great new beginnings had been lost; and that in time the Assembly's relationship with local government would have settled down. Some simply observed that it might have been better if King James IV had never set out for Flodden!

The Devolution drama was enacted while another new pressure was bearing on the Scottish Office. For 1976 was the watershed

year, the year of the International Monetary Fund's intervention at
Britain's request and the consequential cuts in government spend-
ing. Now began that process of reduction in the size of the Civil
Service which has continued ever since.

Throughout the 1960s and the first half of the 1970s Scottish
Office numbers had grown steadily in line with the general
increase in Civil Service numbers and in response to the accumula-
tion of new initiatives which ministerial policies and continuing
administrative devolution required. By 1976, including the prison
service, the Scottish Office total was approaching the eleven
thousand mark. But the cuts in staffing now beginning caused real
difficulty for the Scottish Office, made up as it is—the prison
service apart, and no reductions could be made there—of so very
many disparate, usually quite small groupings with their concentration of 'policy-formulating' rather than 'executant' staff. As the
cuts went deeper, a determined attempt was made to lighten the
workload in keeping with the reductions in staff numbers, but this
met only partial success. The workload had built up over the years
in response to ministers' policies and 'the fell clutch of circum-
stance.' By and large policies were not changed; nor would
circumstances ease its grip.

However, it is never enough merely to recite this complaint. In
any large organisation, in good times as well as bad an enforced
weeding out of less necessary work is essential. Crises come, and
to cope with them a new grouping of staff is brought into being,
an administrative division is strengthened or a cadre of professional
advisers raised. Crises go, but as often as not rather slowly: it is
rarely possible to say 'problem solved' and snap the book shut.
The extrication of the additional staff becomes a matter of heat and
contention and so is delayed. Or again, increases in staffing take
place imperceptibly but steadily like the growth of a coral reef (and
like the coral reef are as hard to break down). This in Scottish
Office experience is usually because of the simple truths that the
nation's social and eonomic problems are vast and the possibilities
of improvement detected by intelligent men and women are
limitless.

But with the approach of the 1980s reduction in numbers there
had to be. It was well that centralised staffing control had begun
some years before, for both Sir Nicholas Morrison and his
successor of 1978, Sir William Fraser, as permanent under-
secretaries of state were to find the agenda of their Monday
morning meetings with heads of departments often clogged with
this topic; as the cuts continued it was essential to attempt a
Scottish Office view of priorities. Sometimes the exasperated
manpower controllers of Central Services, in the face of persistent
pleading from departments for their 'special' cases, felt that only
the brutality of uniform percentage reductions all round would

serve. But the true lesson was that management in all departments, and indeed at all levels, had to be made to feel by their superiors that the husbanding of staff resources was *their* problem and *their* priority. Every line manager had to become his own game-keeper. There was no place for poachers; but the habits of a life-time were sometimes not easily set aside.

So to the Scottish Office of the present day. The point already made has to be repeated. Concerned as it is primarily with the changing shape of the Scottish Office down the years this book cannot easily convey a sense of the diversity of all it does; from the transformation the engineers and administrators of the Development Department have wrought in the trunk roads of Scotland, to the fishery cruisers—smaller than Royal Navy frigates—now patrolling two hundred miles into the Atlantic; from social work advisers confronting the consequences of urban decay, to the large agricultural inspectorate stationed around Scotland to serve the thriving agricultural industry. To cite these few examples, is incidentally, to be reminded of the important fact that from the middle to the upper reaches of the Scottish Office the professionals outnumber the administrators by two to one.

Even where the individual role may not seem to have changed with the passing years, the workload it contains usually has. Take, for example, the 'law and order' sectors. There has been change, notably in the reorganisation of the courts in 1972 under a Scottish Courts Administration which is responsible to the Lord Advocate. But there continues to be a Police Division within the Scottish Office as there has been since Dover House days. Yet the police service of today, so greatly increased in numbers, trained at the Scottish Police College at Tulliallan, reorganised from thirty-three separate forces into eight, and given all manner of new equipment, electronic and otherwise, has changed greatly—and so has the work of the Police Division which has been intimately involved with all this change. The prison service likewise came within the ambit of the Duke of Richmond and Gordon a hundred years ago. But over the past thirty years alone the number of prisoners has doubled, and with this the staff of the prison service has now grown to be nearly three thousand strong, and is today the biggest single unit in the Scottish Office.

For the Prisons Directorate this has also meant the building of new prisons and the enhancement of security generally in collaboration with the Scottish Office Buildings Directorate. Over the years the mentally sick, the young and the more obviously reclaimable have been taken out of the mainstream to the State Hospital at Carstairs, to institutions for young offenders, and to the open prison created out of a country house in quiet Galloway.

Fishery Cruiser—the *Westra*—on patrol. (Department
of Agriculture and Fisheries for Scotland.)

Prison workshops have been established and new prisons built.
But there has still to be reliance on Barlinnie and Peterhead (both
older than the Scottish Office itself); and it may be that in the
words of Sir Charles Cunningham, for some 'perhaps all society
can do is to mark its displeasure in ways not inhumane and keep
the more dangerous out of circulation'. Neither in Cunningham's
day, nor now, has this deterred the quest for progress.

Or look more closely at that sector of the Home and Health
Department which with so much else is responsible for liquor
licensing law. In organisation for this the department has not
changed greatly since the war, but during these years it has put
through two sizeable pieces of modernising legislation dealing
with the sale and consumption of John Barleycorn & Co, both
being preceded by departmental Committees of Inquiry. The

second of these might be thought to be an example of the 'lateral' thinking about Scotland which the Scottish Office exists to promote in that it was chaired by a distinguished medical; to the liberalisation of the liquor laws which it recommended may be ascribed some lessening of Scotland's drink problem in recent years. The department had, incidentally, long enjoyed some practical experience of the liquor trade in running the 'state pubs', those curious anachronisms of state monopoly of the sale of drink around Invergordon (which had not seen much of the Home Fleet since its 'mutiny' of 1931) and around Gretna (where the munition factories had closed in 1919). Running the State Management Districts had long been a cherished enclave of the Scottish Office, but it could not withstand the logic of privatisation, to use a word not then current.

A common theme throughout the Scottish Office of recent years, has been deliberate withdrawal from involvement in the everyday running of services to a new stance from where strategy may be better guided. The sea-change in the Education Department in the 1950s and 1960s, already described, had this consequence; without it, the strategic reshaping of much of secondary and further education now going ahead in the 1980s would not have been possible. But it can be hard going. When the National Health Service was reorganised in 1972—this, incidentally a major matter, with each of the fifteen new Health Boards providing a comprehensive health service, and one in which Scotland went her own way—the opportunity was taken to excise from the Home and Health Department a range of health functions, research and intelligence, health education, the large Supplies Division, and so on, placing them with a Common Services Agency under joint management by the Department and the reorganised health service. 'It must have seemed a tidy idea', Mary Macdonald observes in her succinct narrative of the recent Scottish Office. 'The Department would be left free to concentrate on its policy functions while various other *ad hoc* management devices, such as the provision of ambulance services by contract with the St Andrew's Ambulance Association, would be rendered unnecessary by bringing all these units within one agency. But the result was an unwieldy body which soon developed management problems.' In parallel with this a Scottish Health Service Planning Council with a large number of specialist groups was set up together with a planning group within the Department. But here was the reverse of 'disengagement'. The Department's medical professionals were now to be involved directly with the running of the health service; previously theirs had been mainly an advisory role. Consequently, more of them were needed at a time when the Department was beginning to come under the general pressure to reduce numbers quite severely.

Disengagement, by the later 1970s, was the order of the day all along the Scottish Office interface with local government, as the upheavals of its reorganisation into regions and districts began to subside. Detailed consideration of tenders for local authority housing had already been abandoned. The Development Department henceforth would apply itself to five-year housing plans from the new district councils. These would plan according to their own concepts of housing need and of the balance between the renovation of the old and the building of the new; but the capital expenditure programme overall would be subject to the Secretary of State's approval. Similarly, in physical planning the department's main effort would now be consideration of local authorities' periodic strategic plans. In the same way the new regional councils would be required to submit to the department programmes rather than projects for improvement of roads and public transport within their areas. Most important of all was the outcome of the joint working party of the Scottish Office and the Convention of Scottish Local Authorities which devised a financial planning system for all local authority capital expenditure. This, too, involved the submission of proposals for five years ahead and freedom to the local authorities to determine priorities between their various services. It seemed a far cry to the days of specific government grants for specific county or burgh council services— but these, in fact, were less than thirty years past.

'Local authorities are responsible bodies in their own right', the Scottish Office publication of 1953 had said when the persistence of war-time controls threatened their traditional measure of independence. With the responsibilities of choice it gave the new regional and district councils, disengagement in the later 1970s was intended to impart to local government a new sense of freedom; and so, it was hoped, a new vitality. Since then, the overriding necessity has been that local authorities should curtail their annual spending, current as well as capital, as levels of rate support grant from the Scottish Office fall in compliance with central government's cuts in its own expenditure. This has brought the Scottish Office into conflict, sometimes sharp conflict, with some local authorities.

Disengagement of a kind also went ahead at Chesser House. Enabling crofters to buy their land on easy terms, as it did, the crofters legislation of the mid-seventies renounced past intentions to coax crofting townships towards comprehensive reorganisation into smaller numbers of holdings; and in the lowlands a parallel process began of selling off the thousand or more 'department' holdings to their sitting tenants (and is now near completion). On the other hand, the Department's new role on behalf of Scottish agriculture and fisheries at Brussels intensified, with an EEC regime for lamb (in officialese, 'sheepmeat') and an elusive

Common Fisheries Policy the objectives. This last put a heavy burden on the fisheries administrators, for with the collapse of distant water fishing from Hull and Grimsby, Scotland now had two-thirds of the fishing effort.

From the early days of the Scottish Office, as successive new areas of government activity opened up, it was the practice to create new bodies outwith itself. What began as expediency—Dover House of 1886 could not itself fix fair rents for highland crofters, so there had to be a Crofters Commission for this—continued as a conscious attempt to involve in Scottish administration a great many Scots outwith the government service even after the long overdue transformation of the Edinburgh boards into Scottish Office departments. So today there are expert advisory committees and consultative councils. There are bodies like the fifteen Health Boards with executive power in the name of the Secretary of State. Operating almost wholly on government money are the Trustees of the National Galleries of Scotland and the Boards of Governors of many specialist education establishments; that is, Colleges of Art, the three great Colleges of Agriculture which in Scotland also provide the advisory service to farmers, the Colleges of Education and a number of institutions for technological education. There are the Governing Bodies of the seven institutes of the Agricultural Research Service which have a special concern for the agriculture of the northern half of Great Britain. There are the marketing boards for agriculture and fisheries and the post-war extensions of government activity into the economic or environmental field *via* the New Town Development Corporations, the Highlands and Islands Development Board as well as the Scottish Development Agency, the Countryside Commission for Scotland and the Scottish Tourist Board. The list is indeed formidable, as is the task descending on all departments of identifying possible candidates who might be willing to take on some of the membership of the host of bodies which make up this essential, indeed majority, aspect of Scottish administration. But there is a world of difference between these Grand Duchies and Counties Palatine of the present day in their dealings with the Scottish Office, and the Edwardian Boards in relation to Dover House. For the strategies of the present day bodies are the continuing and intimate concern of the Secretary of State and his departments.

In the early 1980s, the French company which had taken over the big motor-car factory in Renfrewshire from Chrysler was obliged to close it in the face of world-wide over-production. Then British Aluminium in dire financial difficulties closed their plant at Invergordon in Easter Ross, likewise pointing to a world

Fisheries Research Vessel—the *Scotia:* also in the
Scottish Office 'navy'.

market over-supplied and in decline. The price of aluminium had
dropped to one-half of what it had been, and the company's hopes
of cheap nuclear-produced electricity had not sufficiently material-
ised. At the southern end of the Great Glen, the mill built with
government grant in the 1960s to pulp the torrent of thinnings out
of the new forests from Argyll to Sutherland was likewise closed.
The industrial process its owners had installed had proved uneco-
nomic and unsuitable; this difficulty might have been surmounted
with new owners and the government help which was available
but for fears that the Lochaber mill could not compete with North
American imports while the pound stayed strong in relation to the
dollar. This was a relationship which the financial pundits said *must*
last as long as there was oil in the North Sea. Within a year the
pound was sliding fast. Despite the most strenuous efforts it was
not possible to find a new investor, and the great mill looking
across the loch to Ben Nevis remained closed. Then in 1983 the
impending closure of British Leyland's truck factory at Bathgate
was announced, the company's view being that the fall in the
world market for trucks left them with no alternative.

    These were bitter blows, salt being rubbed into the wound by
dismissive comment from some quarters about the regional
development policy in Scotland of the 1960s of which Linwood
and Bathgate, Invergordon and the Lochaber mill, along with the
steel strip mill at Ravenscraig in Lanarkshire, had been the
corner-stones. In his revealing account of his years with British
Leyland—years in which the Bathgate plant was coming under
constant review—Sir Michael Edwardes has made plain his dislike
of 'the legacy of the geographical dispersal policies of the past'

which put British Leyland's Scottish factory 'far from the centre of the company's commercial vehicle activity' in Lancashire. But he also dwells on the difficulties caused for Bathgate by the bad name the company had earned for itself from the immense labour problems in its Midland car factories and from certain failures of management and of the unions throughout its operations. The only common factor to the quartet of Scottish industrial reverses of the early eighties catalogued above was the world recession.

The Scottish Office took part in the agonised grappling by government with each of these setbacks. It may be imagined what were the feelings at New St Andrew's House as the cherished strategy of reviving the Scottish economy by the introduction of large scale industry was seen to be so low in the water. Even so, there remained 100,000 new jobs which regional development policy had helped create over the years. And with the wider powers gained in 1975, the response of the Economic Planning Department to the new situation was to make new arrangements with the Scottish Development Agency, situated as it is close to the Department's industrial development division in Glasgow, for the stronger attraction of industrial investment from abroad. This integrated operation was given the jaunty title of 'Locate in Scotland'. Some previous Secretaries of State had visited North America in search of such 'inward investment' for the Scottish economy. George Younger who had succeeded Bruce Millan when the Conservatives returned to power in 1979, travelled to Japan on this quest. Particularly in the electronics industry there has been a measure of heartwarming success for these efforts, especially from the United States but also from Japan. Central Scotland is now close to the goal of self-generating growth in this industry of the future. Those concerned would also point to the necessity of Scotland being within the European Economic Community; none of the new industry would have located in Scotland if this had not been so.

There were other new responsibilities. In 1976 the Secretary of State was given joint sponsorship, with the Secretaries of State for Employment and for Wales, of the Manpower Services Commission. The obvious relationship between the industrial training schemes which are the province of the Commission and the vocational emphasis increasingly being given to much of Scottish education made this a natural development. A Director of Manpower Services for Scotland had been appointed as was a Scottish Manpower Services Committee to both of whom the Scottish Office—and other Scottish interests—could more easily relate. Joint sponsorship is sometimes awkward and frustrating but it is an administrative arrangement which sometimes has to be accepted. However as a consequence of the spring-cleaning that accompanied preparation for Devolution it was found quite possi-

Dover House and the Whitehall view today.

ble to bring the care of Scottish ancient monuments, previously
shared with the 'Great Britain' Department of the Environment,
into the Development Department where it could lie comfortably
with existing responsibilities for historic buildings. Ten years
before, this had, surprisingly, been thought too difficult to bring
about.

So 'Scottish control of Scottish affairs' is now very much wider
than it was when the Royal Commission of thirty years ago
surveyed the scene. With the transfer from the Department of
Industry at the end of 1984 of the administration of 'fixed rate'
grants to manufacturing industry to be run, along with the scheme
of discretionary financial assistance, by the Industrial Department
for Scotland (for so the Scottish Economic Planning Department
has at last been renamed), the scope of the Scottish Office is now
nearly as wide as could be wished. The five Departments have,
perhaps, now approached a plateau of stability. However, this
widening of Scottish Office territory has not eliminated the
'penumbra', the rim of matters with which the Secretary to
Scotland though not strictly his Ministerial responsibility. These
are many and diverse—airport policy to whisky taxation; they are
often unpredictable; and all Departments of the Scottish Office

stand ready to support him as need arises whatever the field of battle. 'Penumbra' is an outlandish word which used to appeal to Sir David Milne. Perhaps it should be matched with another, meaning 'the Keeper of the Castle'. You might say that it is the privilege of the Secretary of State to be *castéllan* of Scotland. With society's values in such flux as they are, and with existing employment ever more eroded by technological change, this is an awesome as well as a proud duty. There will be still greater challenges to confront.

There will in any event continue to be a stream of new responsibilities to be accepted. For example, recreation, leisure and the arts will inevitably take on ever more importance. But the Scottish Sports Council looks to the Education Department for sponsorship, as do the national museums and art galleries; and the Department's linkage is strong with the Scottish Arts Council, the Arts Council for Great Britain and the Whitehall Department for the arts. Conservation of nature will be another 'growth area', to use the management jargon. But here there is an anomaly. The Secretary of State for Scotland is both the planning minister and the minister for Scottish agriculture and fisheries, and in Great Britain as a whole the leading forestry minister. The Countryside Commission for Scotland looks to him as do that triumvirate of 'land-use' agencies in Inverness, the Highlands and Islands Development Board, the Crofters Commission and the Red Deer Commission. But the Nature Conservancy and its Scottish Committee look to the Secretary of State for the Environment in Whitehall, though as nature conservation becomes ever more important, there is the inevitability of some land-use conflict. But there are possibilities of informal co-ordination of policy which are, perhaps, easier in Edinburgh than in London if we make full use of them. For example, the senior individuals in the Scottish Office and in other bodies concerned with land use in all its aspects have met regularly (but informally) since HRH The Duke of Edinburgh's 'Countryside in 1970' conference.

However the feeling persists that to ensure a truly comprehensive approach to land-use it may soon become necessary to bind more closely together these various rural interests of government. In the 1960s regional industrial development in Scotland was influenced by innovative French thinking: maybe there is something more to be learned from France in their grouping together of government concern for rural land use. Argyll and the hilly Auvergne have much in common.

Two other aspects stand out in this last glance at the departments of the Scottish Office. There is the growing importance of 'Central Services'. One of its senior people has ruefully likened it to Wordsworth's Lucy 'A maid whom there were none to praise/ And very few to love'. But it is Central Services' unsung Finance

Bute House, official residence in Edinburgh of the
Secretary of State for Scotland.

Divisions which are in the front line of the contentious and
long-running debate over local government finance. The 'finan-
ciers' are also at the heart of things in that most of the Scottish
Office spending programmes are now lumped together for Treasury purposes as a single block with some scope for the switching of
expenditure from one area to another without further reference to
Whitehall. Secondly, with the coming of these 'block vote'
arrangements—incidentally a by-product of the spring-cleaning
which went on during the Devolution debate—and the fact that
Scottish Office staffing is unified, the permanent under-secretary

of state's management group now has a crucial role in the running of the Scottish Office such as its predecessor in Milne's day thirty years ago never knew.

Throughout all departments there is a splendid ease of personal relationships. There always has been. The Scottish Office is pleasant company. Yet, have Scottish Office people fears for the future? The answer to this is that there are such apprehensions, some small, some less so.

First of all, there is a certain apprehension that with all the slimming down, the hiving-off to outside bodies and the disengagement from local government, future generations of Scottish Office administrators may have some difficulty in learning their trade. As Sir Ronald Johnson observes in his memoir of his years as Secretary to the Home and Health Department: 'If you don't see the run-of-the-mill, how can you understand the difficulties'. However, careful career management coupled no doubt with some cross-postings to the outside bodies can see to this. The Scottish Office civil servant must also expect several times in the course of his or her career to be spirited away to very different kind of work: five years of, say, negotiating the small print of the Common Fisheries Policy in Brussels, Copenhagen, Paris, the Hague as well as London may be followed by a quinquennium of health service administration. Here again there is an intricate task of careers management to be done. And there is the perennial problem that with so much more frequently to be gained from the cultivation of good relations in Whitehall than from confrontation we often cannot afford to crow about our successes—and so the Scottish public is left in the dark! Like his eighteenth century predecessor in the management of Scottish affairs a present day Secretary of State has to 'love power too much to hazard it with ostentation'. But the Earl of Ilay did not have to carry the public with him.

What else? Scottish Office people have to be as expert in whatever specialised area they are working as their Whitehall counterparts *and* to be knowledgeable about the broad sweep of Scottish administration; in short, they must also know Scotland. The first leg of this dual requirement is made the more difficult by the likelihood that the Edinburgh individual's scope of responsibility will generally correspond to that of a good half-dozen London counterparts—though if this confers width of view on the Scots it can be a help in Whitehall bargaining.

Then there is the abiding problem that the Scottish Office works within a Great Britain which thinks of itself as in the main organised by function. Furthermore the Scottish Office is no longer a unique anomaly. Its people resent the rather insensitive Whitehall practice of lumping together the Scottish Office with the Welsh Office created in 1964 and the Northern Ireland Office created by the early 1970s as 'the territorial departments'. This is an

The Secretary of State's room at Dover House.
[George Younger at his desk.]

odd label to apply to the administration of component parts of the
United Kingdom. (Are not the Department of the Environment in
its Westminster skyscrapers and the Ministry of Agriculture and
Fisheries at Whitehall Place equally 'territorial departments'?) This
is more than Scotch prickliness, as has already been remarked,
status is of the first importance in Whitehall.

Scottish Office people see the need for a Scottish Office *esprit de
corps*. The fierce loyalties felt for the individual departments, which
saw them through the stresses of war-time and lasted until its
reorganisation of the early 1960s and the subsequent creation of
common establishment, finance and office services, have not yet
been fully replaced by a strong Scottish Office loyalty. 'In the old
days', one hears it said, 'the head of Division would not address
you by your christian name as he probably does today, but there

was a greater feeling of belonging to the highly individual departments of home, health, education or agriculture with which you could identify'. This fading of identity matters, because recent years have been something of a bumpy ride. The previously undreamt of, indeed unthinkable, phenomenon of industrial action in 1979 and 1981 caused new kinds of tension. The progressive reduction in numbers since 1976 by about one fifth has likewise caused strains. The disciplines, however necessary, of the new cost-consciousness reaching to all divisions and groupings can be exasperating. All this carries with it the risk of some slow erosion of morale, and this can only be counteracted by the office's self-esteem. How that is to be done is the challenge of today—and tomorrow.

These are matters within the competence of the Scottish Office to resolve. There are, however, two crucial considerations outwith its power which will determine its future. The first of these is that there should be a continuing commitment by the government machine down the years to 'Scottish control of Scottish affairs' as the attainable ideal, despite the pull of London and the possibility (usually the illusion) of making some small saving in Civil Service numbers overall by putting Lands End to Muckle Flugga all in the one administrative packing case. The second is that the future of the Scottish Office depends more on the vitality of Scotland's distinctive self-expression than on her civil servants. Ultimately, you might say, it all depends on the poets, not the politicians, though this is not to detract from the contribution which politicians and civil servants can make to the maintenance of a national culture; particularly in Scotland, where there is so deep a fracture between the culture of Gaeldom and that of the rest.

Much of this book has been written within sight of Rosebery's Dalmeny, the same arc of vision taking in the super-tankers loading North Sea oil at the Firth of Forth terminal. This has been a constant reminder of the need to view in perspective the Office's hundred years of history. Surprisingly, what stands out is more the newness of so much of the Secretary of State's domain, rather than its antiquity; that the Scottish Office did not really get going until close to its first half-century, when those outmoded bodies, the Edinburgh boards, were transformed into departments of the Secretary of State; and that down the years the acquisition of power and responsibility has been piecemeal, and in some important respects, recent. At the same time the historical perspective brings out the durability of the Scottish Office. Eighteenth century management of Scotland by the House of Argyll died with the 3rd Duke; Dundas rule could not outlive the 2nd Viscount Melville; the nineteenth century predominance of the Lord Advocate was extinguished, not before time, in 1885. But the Scottish Office has shown an ability to adapt and a capacity for change which has enabled it to grow and strengthen. It has, perhaps, yet to show all its paces.

The last word must be one of hope. That elusive concept, the national identity of Scotland, has also shown a remarkable capacity for survival and renewal. 'King Jamie the Saxt' was wrong; Scotland did not become an appendage to the north of England. Lord Chancellor Seafield of 1707 was wrong; it was not 'the end of an auld sang'. Crusty old Cockburn was wrong: Scottish individuality was not on the point of dissolution. For there is something about place and people within our rectangle of latitude and longitude north of the border which eternally renews the individuality of Scotland. That individuality must continue to be given scope to express itself. For if the strength of Scotland lies in diversity, so does the strength of Britain. The United Kingdom would forget this at her peril.

✳

SOURCES

M Y MAIN 'source' for the 18th and 19th centuries was discussion with the historians, but mention has to be made of Dr William Ferguson *Scotland; 1689 to the Present;* Oliver and Boyd, 1968. I also relied heavily on *The Union of 1707: its Impact on Scotland* ed. T I Rae; Blackie, 1974 and Dr John Shaw *The Management of Scottish Society;* John Donald, 1983. The Scottish Record Office has an historical *Memorandum on the Secretaryship for Scotland* written for the Scottish Office in 1920 by Professor Sir Thomas Rait (SRO HH 1/888).

For the past hundred years of the Scottish Office there are notably:

Professor H J Hanham; *The Creation of the Scottish Office 1881–87;* the Juridicial Review, 1965.

Professor H J Hanham; 'The Development of the Scottish Office' in *Government and Nationalism in Scotland* ed J N Wolfe; Edinburgh University Press, 1969.

Sir David Milne; *The Scottish Office;* Allen and Unwin, 1957.

W G Pottinger; *The Secretaries of State for Scotland 1926–76;* Scottish Academic Press; Edinburgh, 1979.

Mary Macdonald and Adam Redpath; 'The Scottish Office 1954 to 1979' in *The Scottish Government Year Book 1980* ed H M Drucker; Edinburgh; Paul Harris, 1979.

And for a very human view of the Scottish Office of twenty years ago there is a distinguished novel: James Allan Ford; *A Statue for a Public Place;* Hodder and Stoughton, 1965.

For the earlier years of Scottish Office involvement with the highlands and islands there is J P Day; *Public Administration in the*

Highlands and Islands of Scotland; University of London Press Ltd,
1918. For the growth of regional policy there is Gavin McCrone;
Regional Policy in Britain; Allen and Unwin, 1969. The Scottish
Record Office has reviews of achievement by certain administra-
tions but these are not particularly revealing. Much more informa-
tive are the oral history tapes by Sir Charles Cunningham on *The
Scottish Home Department 1939 to 1957* and by Sir Ronald Johnson
on his Scottish Office career from the 'thirties to the 'seventies,
both in *Scotland's Record;* National Library of Scotland; Acc 7330.

I made general use of the successive Annual Reports of Boards
and Departments but, for the past fifty years, my main source has
been the recollections of colleagues.

For the most part I limit myself to the identification of quota-
tions and of out of the way sources, but Scottish Office files from
the Scottish Record Office are logged. (The papers of the Queen's/
King's and Lord Treasurer's Remembrancer—that acrid critic of
the Edinburgh boards—are also in the Scottish Record Office.)

Page 1	Salisbury-Richmond	Hanham, as above (ie *The Creation of the Scottish Office 1881–87,* 229–30).
	The following day's *Scotsman*	For 19 November 1885.
Page 3	John Buchan	*Hansard, House of Commons,* 24 November 1932; Vol 272, Col 267.
Page 4	Godolphin's views	Robert Wodrow *Analecta* III 308; Edinburgh 1842–43.
Page 5	Defoe's views	Letters of Daniel Defoe ed G H Healey; Oxford, 1955; 336–37.
Page 7	The Earl of Ilay's love of power	'Memoires of the Last Ten Years of the Reign of George the Second' by Horace Walpole; London, 1822.
	Duncan Forbes' view	'More Culloden Papers', ed D Warrand, II 332.
Page 8	Sir John Clerk's view	Quoted in 'Administration and Law' in Rae as above.
	The Forfeited Estates	Annette Smith *Jacobite Estates of the 'Forty-Five;* John Donald; Edinburgh, 1982.
	Milton and appointments	Rait, as above.

Page 9	Brodie of Brodie	John S Gibson *Deacon Brodie;* Paul Harris, 1977; 115.
	The Lord Advocate should be a tall man	G W T Omand *The Lord Advocates of Scotland* Vol II, Edinburgh, 1883; 179.
Page 10	Boswell dines with Dundas	*Boswell: The Applause of the Jury,* 1782–85; Heinemann, 1981; 145.
	Melville 'a Minister of State for Scotland'	Sir Walter Scott's *Journal* March 10, 1826.
Page 11	A 'Scotch Secretaryship'	Cockburn's *Journal* Vol I; Edinburgh 1874; 26.
	Reaction of *The Times*	Quoted in Sir Reginald Coupland *Welsh and Scottish Nationalism;* Collins, 1954; 287.
Page 12	Views of the 'older, querulous Cockburn'	Cockburn, Vol II, as above, 294–95.
	Lord Elcho's memoir	Pages 260–266 of *Memoirs* Vol I (unpublished). Kindly made available by the Earl of Wemyss and March.
Page 14	Views of Medical Officers of Health	Professor Thomas Ferguson *Scottish Social Welfare 1864–1914;* Livingstone, Edinburgh; 1958; 165.
	The 1872 legislation	'The beginnings of State Education in Scotland 1872–85' by Bruce Lenman and John Stocks; in *Scottish Educational Studies Vol 4, No 2, November 1972.*
	Debate of 1864	*Hansard, House of Commons* 3 June 1864.
	Debate of 1867	*Hansard, House of Commons* 22 March 1867.
Page 15	Report of the Scottish Office Inquiry Commission	*Report of the Commissioners appointed by the Lords Commissioners of Her Majesty's Treasury to inquire into certain Civil Departments in Scotland;* Edinburgh; HMSO, 1870.

Page 16   Footnote   Day, as above.

Page 19   Debate on 'neglect of   *Hansard, House of Commons*
           Scotch business'   23 February 1877.

Page 20   Robert Rhodes James   R R James *Rosebery: a
                                          biography of Archibald Philip,
                                          fifth Earl of Rosebery;*
                                          Weidenfield and Nicolson,
                                          1963.

           Professor Hanham   'The Creation of the
                                          Scottish Office 1881–87', as
                                          above.

           Charles Cooper   Charles A Cooper *An
                                          Editor's Retrospect;*
                                          Macmillan and Co, 1896.

           Debate of June 1881   *Hansard, House of Lords* 13
                                          June 1881.

           Rosebery to Harcourt in   Photocopies of this and
           1881   other Rosebery papers of
                                          the 1880's on 'Scotch
                                          Business in the Home
                                          Office' are held in the
                                          Scottish Office Library,
                                          New St Andrew's House,
                                          Edinburgh.

Page 24   The January 1884 meeting   *The Scotsman* for 17
                                          January 1884.

           The educationists and the   *Hansard, House of
           Bill   Commons* August 3 1885.

Page 26   Trevelyan quits   J Enoch Powell *Joseph
                                          Chamberlain;* Thames and
                                          Hudson, 1977; 8.

           Balfour in the Cabinet   S H Zebel *Balfour: a
                                          political biography;*
                                          Cambridge University
                                          Press, 1973; 75.

           Balfour calls out the   SRO HH 1/3.
           Marines
           Balfour seeks information   SRO HH 1/842.

Page 27   Gladstone at Dalmeny   Cooper, as above; 392.

Page 29   Dr Pellew's study   Jill Pellew *The Home Office
                                          1848–1914;* Heinemann
                                          Educational Books, 1982.

Page 30   Boy typists preferred   Treasury minute of 17
                                          March 1894. Scottish
                                          Office Library.

Page 31 Home Secretary's tussle   SRO HH 1/816.

Page 32 Convention of Royal   SRO HH 1/881.
         Burghs
         Dunbar's memorandum   SRO HH 1/816.
         The Secretary for Scotland   SRO HH 1/877.
         Act, 1887

         For a contemporary (and rather over-enthusiastic) view
         of the 1885 Act there is *The Secretary for Scotland Act, 1885*
         by W C Smith.

Page 33 Ponsonby's letter   SRO HH 1/878.
         Queen Victoria on capital   SRO HH 1/879.
         cases

Page 34 The shoemakers of   SRO HH 1/944.
         Linlithgowshire
         William McGonagall   SRO HH 1/1109.

Page 37 Trevelyan preferred to   John Wilson *A Life of Sir*
         Bryce   *Henry*
                                      Campbell-Bannerman;
                                      Constable, 1973; 234.

Page 38 Lord Lothian and the   SRO Lothian Muniments
         crofting problem   (also papers in the Scottish
                                      Office library, New St
                                      Andrew's House,
                                      Edinburgh).
         The Royal Commission   The Royal Commission
                                      (Highlands and Islands)
                                      1892.

Page 39 Balfour of Burleigh's   Lady Frances Balfour *A*
         biographer   *memoir of Lord Balfour of*
                                      Burleigh; Hodder and
                                      Stoughton, 1924.
         Trevelyan and the General   Lady Frances Balfour, as
         Assembly   above.
         Campbell-Bannerman at   Wilson, as above.
         the Royal Albert Hall

         For Captain Sinclair/Lord Pentland there is Lady
         Pentland *The Right Honourable John Sinclair, Lord*
         Pentland GCSI; Methuen & Co, 1928.

Page 40 Rosebery's views   *Hansard, House of Lords,*
                                      2nd Reading of the Small
                                      Landholders (Scotland)
                                      Bill, August 13 1907.

Page 42	Lovat's views	Sir Francis Lindley *Lord Lovat;* Hutchinson, 1935.
	Asquith on Pentland	E David *Inside Asquith's Cabinet* (An edition of Sir Charles Hobhouse's diaries), 1977. [Asquith's words were 'the brains of a rabbit'.]
Page 43	Sir George MacDonald's view	Quoted in Lady Pentland, as above.
	'Open'd their pack . . .'	George Lockhart of Carnwath *Memoirs concerning the Affairs of Scotland;* 1714 edition, 205.
Page 45	Dover House for the PM	Carlingford Journal for 12 March 1985 quoted in Kenneth Rose *King George the Fifth;* Macmillan, 1983; 99.

Page 46 Sir John Struthers' and Sir George McCrae's evidence are in the Minutes of Evidence to the Royal Commission on the Civil Service of 1914.

Page 50	The Dilke Report	Second report of Her Majesty's Commissioners for inquiring into the Housing of the Working Classes—Scotland HMSO, 1885 (c.4409).
Page 52	Burrell's views	Richard Marks *Burrell;* Richard Drew Publishing, Glasgow, 1983; 53
Page 53	The origins of the Royal Commission	See Lady Pentland p.107 as above; also paras 6–10 of the *Report of the Royal Commission on Housing in Scotland* (cd 8731).
Page 55	Balfour of Burleigh's views	Lady Frances Balfour, as above, page 179.
Page 58	Haldane's views	*Report of the Machinery of Government Committee;* HMSO 1918; CD 921/30.

Enid Gauldie *Cruel Habitations: a History of Working Class Housing 1780–1918* Allen and Unwin, 1974, illuminates the pre-1914 housing problem.

Page 60	Munro's view	Robert Munro (Lord Alness) *Looking Back;* Nelson; 258–283.
	Johnston's views	Thomas Johnston *Memories;* Collins, 1952, 40.
Page 63	Nigel Nicolson	Nigel Nicolson *Lord of the Isles;* Weidenfield and Nicolson, 1960.
Page 65	The Calton Jail site	SRO HH 57/6.
	Lord Addison's memoirs	Rt Hon Christopher Addison *Four and a Half Years Vol 1 1914–16;* August 4 1916.
	The 'Bolshevist Rising'	PRO CAB 23/9.
	Oscar Slater	William Roughhead *Knaves Looking Glass;* Cassell, 1935.
	Secretary for Scotland and the War Cabinet	Munro as above.
Page 66	Birkenhead in the Lords	*Hansard, House of Lords;* June 7 1921.
Page 68	Portraits	SRO HH 1/893.
Page 70	Baldwin's visit to Glasgow	*The Walter Elliot papers;* National Library of Scotland; Acc 6721.
	Chamberlain on Elliot	*The Chamberlain Papers* (at Birmingham University) 18/1/509; letter of 14 November 1925.
Page 73	Oscar Slater	Roughhead, as above.
	Adamson's peerage	Johnston, as above.
	The Debate on the Address	*Hansard, House of Commons* 24 November 1932; Vol 272, Cols 235–360.
	Compton MacKenzie	*The Glorious Privilege: the History of the Scotsman:* Nelson 1967; 102
Page 76	There are informative Annual Reports of the Special Areas Commissioner for Scotland up to 1939.	
Page 78	Chamberlain and the Cunarder	Keith Feiling *The Life of Neville Chamberlain;* Macmillan; 1947.

Page 80   The Hilleary Committee   E L Hilleary (Scottish
                                      Development Council
                                      Economic Committee)
                                      *The Highlands and Islands
                                      of Scotland,* Glasgow,
                                      1938.

Page 81   Baldwin refuses   SRO HH 1/896.

Page 82   The Gilmour Committee   *Report of the Committee on
          Report   Scottish Administration;*
                                      HMSO; 1937.

          Health Services   *Report of the Scottish Health
                                      Services Committee,* 1936
                                      (Cmd 5204).

Page 83   The Edinburgh Office   SRO HH 1/2550.

Page 86   Problems of Scottish   T R Bone *School Inspection
          Education   in Scotland 1940–1966;*
                                      Scottish Council for
                                      Research in Education.
                                      University of London
                                      Press.

Page 87   Elliot's paper   SRO HH 1/581.

Page 88   The implementing   SRO HH 45/34.
          legislation

Page 91   *The Scotsman:* journalistic   *The Glorious Privilege,* as
          enterprise   above; 114–120.

Page 94   Air Raid on the Forth   SRO HH 50/5.

Page 98   Air Raids   SRO HH 50/1–4, 97, 100,
                                      101, 103.

Page 102 Johnston and Churchill   Johnston, as above, 148.
          The Council on Post-war   SRO HH 50/166 to HH
          Problems   50/204.

Page 107 Johnston and the S.E.D.   Johnston, as above, 153.

Page 108 Scottish Information   A view is in Alastair
          Office   Dunnett *Among Friends; an
                                      autobiography;* Century
                                      Publishing; London 1984.

Page 109 Fishery protection cruisers G Somner *Scottish Fishery
                                      Protection* The World Ship
                                      Society, 1983.

Page 111 Lord Novar's   SRO; Sir John Gilmour
          non-reappointment   Papers, GD 383/17.

Page 112 Attlee on Johnston   C R Attlee *As It Happened;*
                                      Heinemann 1974, 125.

Page 114 The Clyde Valley Plan   Abercrombie and
                                         Matthew *The Clyde Valley
                                         Regional Plan,* 1946;
                                         HMSO, Edinburgh 1949.

Page 119 Edinburgh and the   *The Glorious Privilege,* as
         Scotsman   above; 154.

Page 129 Hector McNeil and IBM   From Johnson, *Scotland's
                                         Record,* as above.

Page 132 The Toothill Report   *Inquiry into the Scottish
                                         Economy 1960–1; Report of
                                         a Committee appointed by
                                         the Scottish Council
                                         (Development and Industry)
                                         under the Chairmanship of
                                         J N Toothill CBE.*

Page 138 Ronald Cramond's views   R D Cramond *Housing
                                         Policy in Scotland
                                         1919–1964;* University of
                                         Glasgow Social and
                                         Economic Studies;
                                         Research Papers No 1,
                                         Oliver and Boyd.

Page 145 1958 publication on Local   *Local Government in
         Government   Scotland;* HMSO,
                                         Edinburgh, 1958.

         S.E.D. as it was   James Scotland *The
                                         History of Scottish Education*
                                         Vol 2; University of
                                         London Press, 1969.

Page 147 Further education   Scotland, as above.

Page 151 Footnote   Report of the
                                         Commission of Enquiry
                                         into Crofting Conditions,
                                         1954, Cmd 9091.

Page 172 Mary Macdonald   Macdonald and Redpath,
                                         as above.

Page 174 Lord Ross and Linwood   'Approaching the
                                         Archangelic' by the Rt
                                         Hon W Ross MP in *The
                                         Scottish Government Year
                                         Book* 1978; Paul Harris,
                                         1977.

| Expert advisory Committee and Consultative Councils etc | 'Appointed and *ad hoc* Agencies in the field of the Scottish Office' by Sir Douglas Haddow in *The Scottish Government Year Book* 1979; Paul Harris, 1978. |
| Page 175 Sir Michael Edwardes' view | Edwardes *Back from the Brink;* Collins, 1983, 169–170. |

INDEX

Printed in Scotland for HMSO
by McCorquodale (Scotland) Ltd.
Dd 762073   HS 4371   5/85   C30.